The "F" Word, No not that one... FAITH, Why it matters!

The F-Words: Forgiveness, Faith, Fear... Book 2

Doug Giesler

Praise for
'Faith'

"I'm absolutely blown away by "The 'F' Word—Faith" and I can't wait to share why this book is a game-changer in the personal development world. What sets this book apart is its raw, unfiltered approach to understanding our internal landscape.

The author has crafted something truly special—a roadmap that goes beyond traditional self-help rhetoric. This isn't about positive thinking; it's about deep, transformative awareness. By introducing concepts like the "Over-seer" and exploring the mechanics of our internal "selves", the book provides a revolutionary framework for personal growth.

What I love most is how the book challenges readers to become the "mechanic" of their own consciousness. It's not just about reading—it's about actively rewiring how we experience life. The insights into faith, presence, and self-awareness are profound yet practical.

If you're tired of surface-level personal development advice and want a genuine tool for transformation, this book is your ultimate guide. It's like having a GPS for your inner world—showing you exactly how to navigate your thoughts, emotions, and potential.

Trust me, this isn't just another book. It's a life-changing experience that will shift how you understand yourself and your capabilities. Grab a copy, buckle up, and get ready for an incredible journey of self-discovery!"

Garry Johnson
Infinite Mastery Consultant, Retired Master Hypnotherapist

DOUG GIESLER

"You need this book! Doug's 'Game Changer" strategies in working through your limiting beliefs, fear, and GROWING in your understanding of how you can truly be your best self! Doug takes you through a deep dive and journey to discovering the roadblocks and obstacles that are holding you back from your greatest potential."

Heather Glass

"Doug Giesler's writing style is conversational and engaging; it feels like you're having a chat with a wise friend over coffee. He shares personal anecdotes and uses clever metaphors (the "faith bus" is a standout!), making the concepts easy to grasp and apply. He doesn't shy away from the complexities of the human mind, but he breaks them down into digestible chunks.

The core message—that faith is a skill that can be developed and honed—was particularly refreshing. Instead of simply telling you to have faith, he lays out a clear roadmap for how to cultivate it, emphasizing presence, awareness, and the importance of dealing with the "ego selves" (the parts of your mind that hold you back).

If you're looking for a practical guide to cultivating faith and breaking free from self-limiting beliefs, this book is highly recommended. It's insightful, engaging, and leaves you feeling empowered to take action and create the life you want. I'll be looking forward to the next book in the series!"

Robin Nemesszeghy
Author, Relationship Intelligence Coach

Contents

TERMS

In order to really grasp some of the concepts in this book, it is important to understand a few general terms & ideas:

1. Higher "SELF" is capitalized and referring to the highest "SELF" we are capable of being in any given moment at this stage in our evolutionary consciousness.

2. Lower "selves" or "self" is referring to our lower nature, lower "ego" selves or our programmed / habitual nature.

3. These carry through when referring to "YOU" as higher "YOU" or "you" as lower you.

4. These also carry through as "I" and should be referenced and interpreted as the higher "SELF" within "YOU".

5. I capitalize words for emphasis so that this can be seen / heard within the writing.

6. Lastly, references to "man" are a generalization for human, and not specifically the male form. This is meant for ALL of us! The same is true for "him", "he", or "she", etc. Please understand these to be generalized references to the human form, and not gender specific.

This is fairly easy to grasp within the context of this book, but worth mentioning to be sure that this is noted because these ideas are not explained in every instance, but they are seen quite often throughout this book.

INTRODUCTION

FAITH: What Is Faith?

F AITH IS ANOTHER ONE of those words that has deep spiritual connotations. It is typically associated with religion, or spirituality, one way or another, and can be thought of as reserved for the "high and mighty" so to speak. This book is about taking the stigma away and making it understandable, usable, and extremely POWERFUL as a methodology geared towards MAXING OUT the moment. Being one's BEST SELF, with PRESENCE, NOW with TRUST and massive confidence. NO FEAR! In order for that to happen, first we must get through some challenges because the word can throw up some roadblocks for a lot of people.

THE PROBLEM: It begins with the word itself. "FAITH" has many meanings and can be interpreted differently and / or cause confusion, hesitation, and even resistance. This can result in an inability to effectively implement it and to make it useful as a strategy / skill. It is easily misunderstood, can be mis-directed, mis-guided, and even not explained very well in some cases. Sometimes, it is not explained at all or just not understood the way that it was intended to be "used" which throws it into the "unknown" and the unknown is typically avoided. What exactly does the word mean anyway? It seems to change, depending on our upbringing and other factors. Lot's of really GOOD people spend their whole lifetime trying to explain it. That's the point, we all define words in our own ways and by defining them, we LIMIT ourselves in the ways that we use them in our minds and lives. Let's take those limits away and truly understand the power and might behind this philosophical word. That is what this book will do; Clear the air & pave the way to a comprehensive understanding of FAITH and show us how to use it to BREAK FREE from our limitations NOW! You deserve a BREAKTHROUGH! So, let's talk about the initial challenges and then progress through to an experiential understanding of what faith is and how to use it consistently vs haphazardly. Faith is not a vague philosophy; it is a SKILL to be mastered and enabled to take advantage of its power. In fact, it is used, every moment, the question is: How are YOU using it? The people that know how to implement it have a tremendous advantage. Being in the dark is no place to be when it comes to a resource like this. Faith can be used to UN-limit our limits, among other benefits, once understood and implemented. So, let's get through the initial challenges!

THE CHALLENGES: Vague perception, fragmentary interpretation, and an obscure understanding relative to faith doesn't get it done when speed & skills matter. Faith is a skill, and it requires precision timing and implementation on the cutting-edge of time. Once understood, internalized and mastered as a core competency faith can be a reliable tool. However, faith is difficult to define in a concise way and do it QUICKLY, so that it is able to be internalized on a moment's notice. If it isn't effectively switched "ON" then it can't be made immediately useful at a core level, nor can it be managed & directed as a mental / behavioral capacity. People want SPEED, this is a word that is not interpreted as something that is speedy or provides instantaneous results. In fact, patience is often recommended right along with faith which almost makes us question the validity of the word itself. Anything that takes too much time in today's world is probably "OUT" as a strategy. That's problematic because it seems that no one has any time. I am here to tell you that faith, the way that I explain it here, is going to make this TOOL one of the most effective and <u>fastest</u> SKILLS you know how to use. In fact, it is so good, and so fast that there will never be a moment when you don't use it. So, you will be dialed in on it, and making sure that you are using it in the best, most efficient & productive way possible. Worthy? NO DOUBT!!

THE ROADBLOCKS: Generally speaking, and in an effort to break past the initial challenges, let's try to define the potential perception & interpretation issues, so that we can determine if any of them might stand in our way. What does it mean for us individually to "have faith"? Let's throw out some possibilities and REALLY think about it, from our own and other people's perspectives as well. This is not intended to be a comprehensive list, but it is to be used as a prompt to nudge your imagination and put it into consideration mode. Opening the mind to DIG a little bit into our own mental processes will help us to see any potential limits this word may impose on us and other people alike. By all means, please do make this personal and try to get past any of these possible stopping points with an open mind, in an effort to UN-LIMIT the "self" that might want to draw a line in the sand, so to speak.

First and foremost, It's PERSONAL! When the word is spoken or thought of to start with; certain expectations / interpretations & mental imagery might come into our minds as a result of hearing it. As a result, our face, and / or body may also react. Pay attention to this no matter how minor it may seem or feel. There might be an internal acceptance or resistance to the word itself. We may be drawn to it, want more information, or have an aversion to it. To one degree or another, what we need to observe is whether we are meeting the word in the mind with a level of acceptance or resistance, or completely dismiss it / avoid it as an internal strategy all together. This is a beginning point. This just shows us where we are starting FROM! Due to all these intricacies, we may hesitate to say or use the word at all because we don't want to open up a can of worms, when faith is EXACTLY what is needed.

So, having said all that, here are some things that might arrive in the mindscape relative to the word. The perception that "I" must go to Church, believe in GOD, or join a "believer" type organization of some kind. I must hold myself to a higher standard of living. Certainly, there are obligations to be met before one can expect to use—incorporate faith as a part of any philosophy or belief system. I suspect that is why it is "PooPood," and often gets a good old eye roll, whether that is internal, or externally demonstrated. We resist change. The ideas that people can self-generate as a result of hearing this word are many and varied for sure. It might mean that we must show up at a particular place, wear some fancy, or weird clothes, act a certain way, donate money, eat some unknown "treat" or drink out of some secret cup, and of course, be good right? Good is defined how? Exactly! Being good is a judgement call in and of itself, which can be problematic or subject to interpretation / defined in many personalized ways. It can also be measured in degrees as we individualize our good-gauges, so that is just scratching the surface and brings up even more questions. This also might include specific behaviors such as kneeling, or bowing, speaking, or chanting with special words, praying in a particular manner or sequence, which might be different on particular days, or times. Many ideas have the potential to roll around the mindscape as a result of hearing this word. I am not condemning or judging any of these behaviors or traditions, it is just a lot of stuff to consider. The array of thoughts generated by this word can throw the mind into a type of defense mode in some cases, because it doesn't know what is expected, or even what to make of it. It is hard to define to begin with and people describe it in a myriad of ways, which can be quite complex. Complicated means DIFFICULT / SLOW and we tend to shun stuff like that. We very much prefer FAST and EASY.

As far as an individual response to the word, how might that go as an "ego" relates to things? Resistance or avoidance seem like a good option because it resists what it does not know. (the unknown) Faith is not "known", is it? It is one of those things that is to be believed in before it is seen, felt, or known. Add that to the fact that the ego does not have time to consider all of these unknown variables before it needs to decide. Ambiguous is not a recipe for a speedy & conclusive response and it certainly doesn't want to be bogged down. It just wants an answer, and it needs some help right now, not later. So, the mind starts to consider... "*Well, how long is that going to take?*" There could be a notion that without a certain amount of study, considerable contemplation, or some other unknown requirement, such as an element of sacrifice, it can't truly grasp what that word really requires before it can be relied on. That might mean time, a certain amount of "good deeds" to make up for bad ones, etc. So, what would that mean relative to trustworthiness? Is it even worth it? That's what the ego asks, and rightly so if it has never been explained in a useful way. It tries to assess cost / benefit relative to time & effort required as it relates to the idealized outcomes we want. Oh, and the ego loves to WANT to control outcomes, it may feel as if it NEEDS to be in "control", doesn't it? Would faith fit into that box?

Relative to understanding though, quite honestly, even the most devout folks might not know what the word means or how to use it with any degree of certainty / trust. I mean, seriously, how often are prayers actually answered? Like, can anyone give me a true and accurate percentage? Even that would generate an array of probabilities. I guess that's why we get the resistance to it, people just say "whatever", so that they can move on quickly, without having to consider all the unknown ramifications. From a mental / "ego" standpoint, that might mean, run don't walk, away from whomever or whatever mentioned the word. Shut the door, turn off the video, and hurry up about it. I don't want to have to deal with that right now. C'mon, let's go... Let's not waste time here. I mean, what will be will be. Oh, and there is that thought like "what if I do have faith and I FAIL?" What then? That might equal PAIN or embarrassment, among other less than desirable unknowns. I'll look like an IDIOT!

SAD, but true. We don't want to waste time or risk being wrong, so we offload the responsibility onto chance or luck, or fate, or whatever else. That's unfortunate, knowing this word and living it is REALLY incredible! Faith is a truly a WORTHY alternative to the same old same old.

So, to say the least, there are a lot of expectations & unknowns surrounding this crazy and misunderstood word. People are busy and they lack the time / energy to consider all the various modalities that faith, as a word, could mean. There are implications and expectations and unknowns that immediately transform into images and scenes in the mindscape, relative to what is required of me...IF "I" am required to have faith! Oh boy, back to school...Noooooh!

So, after all that as an intro, what does this mean when this F-word pops out? FAITH, or Have Faith is spoken or recommended as a strategy. What happens next internally for you and others? I suggest considering it both ways as it may be helpful to see it from multiple angles.

1. Is it possible that you or other people don't completely understand the recommendation, or don't have a firm grip on what the word faith means? Is it still a question mark as to how to interpret or implement "faith" as a methodology? Is it completely understood, like 100%... or is it only marginally understood as a vague philosophy? Certainly, a superficial application of faith is not going to prep the internal system well enough to use it immediately or effectively. So, if that's the case, then can it be implemented properly on a moment's notice, like NOW? Dismissing it, or brushing it off doesn't change the fact that people use it constantly, all day long every day.

2. Some people were not taught anything at all relative to faith. They may not know what to make of the word, or they just don't believe in it. Is that true for you? That could be from having limited exposure to it, or after spending many years studying it, the result is still questionable. It could be that you or they have given up on it as a strategy all together and found a different belief system. Limited belief, NO belief, belief in something else...all possibilities. Not understanding faith does NOT change the fact that it is being used essentially every moment of every day.

Based on the above, when someone else says the word, we need to interpret what they might have meant. That could leave us a little bewildered, or even baffled as to what to make of it. Minimum, it is guesswork and / or assumptions need to be made and when we get bogged down in interpretation mode when decisions need to be made, that can be problematic.

I guess that's why when people are told to have "faith", it's like a virtual wall goes up, in some cases. In others, it just goes in one ear and out the other. That's unfortunate, because it is an extremely powerful word. If understood, this word can have MASSIVE implications. It can change lives, for sure...but the "ego" can't get past the word. That is an ego specialty, avoidance. "It" doesn't have time and fails to consider a lot of vantage points that are truly empowering and beneficial.

In this case it means a new vision, a new way to step forward in life. Too bad, missed opportunity...another ego specialty!

Let me put this in plain terms. Let's say that I am carrying around a GIANT magnet, but I don't know that I am carrying the magnet around. Nor do I know what that magnet DOES! I am completely "unaware" of it, or how it works. If that magnet has a negative charge, what happens? Negative "stuff" would tend to pull towards me, but I don't know WHY!?! Now, change the scenario. Unbeknownst to me, the magnetic "pull" is changed to positive vs negative, what happens? All of a sudden, positive "stuff" starts flowing in my direction. If we are unaware of this magnet and what is providing the charge, then we have no control over what we are magnetizing. We start attracting all kinds of positive stuff, good is coming towards us but again, we have no idea WHY! What if we were taught and shown where from, how, how much and when the magnet is magnetized? We learn the intricacies of the magnet and gain the ability to CONTROL the magnet. That's where FAITH comes in. Faith works in a similar way with some caveats, so let's break it down so that we can BUILD IT UP!

Conceptually. If faith is to be used as a magnet and we could CHOOSE what it magnetized, what would that look like as a mental landscape? How would we control the "settings"? Let's say we wanted to change our internal magnetism to silver vs gold, or "GOOD" vs "BAD". Maybe, as a hypothetical, you might like MORE vs less of something. FAITH CAN DO THIS! It can also do the opposite, such as if you want LESS of something and MORE of the alternative. It goes both ways, but the focus is different, and it can be managed flawlessly!

Faith can neutralize the extreme negatives and provide BALANCE. It can neutralize extreme positives and provide balance! You might say, well I don't want to neutralize the positives!?! What will ultimately be seen though is that with an overarching awareness, we can experience these extremes with poise and presence. Experiencing life in this way allows us to truly enjoy the presence, so by "neutralizing" a positive it is not really taking it out, per se, it is fully experiencing it but in a balanced way! Balanced meaning with a level of neutrality, not one sided and BLIND!! This way, every element is still taken in. With no blind spots, we are OPEN, receptive, wide awake and aware. We are so dialed in to everything that we don't MISS anything. It's like an integrated performance management system whereby the RPMs are monitored, and the engine is cooled, lubricated, and responsive, like "sport mode" in a high-end vehicle. Faith is essentially the energetic "governor" in this situation because it is teamed up with awareness and used to maintain presence. Our meters don't overload, max out, sputter, or stall. The engine is firing on all cylinders, yet we don't blow a gasket or "BLINK"! We can also take it to the max, turn, and shift gears more easily. So, we are NOT taken out of the moment, NOT blindsided by some elemental distraction or energetically sent into overheating mode. That lack of presence would equate to another letdown because we were momentarily blinded by excitement or emotionalized. So, presence has a way of keeping us centered, even keeled, and much more stable as a moderator / stabilizer that provides a high-level oversight of the energy internals and guides with sovereignty. Life doesn't feel like a roller coaster where the highs and lows perpetually barrage us with these peaks only to be followed by the inevitable let down and another extreme valley. That equates to pain and suffering when we hit these extreme lows, and they seem to come out of nowhere. NO MORE! It isn't that we don't experience letdowns, it's just that there isn't any suffering as a result. (Not mentally anyway.) We may have some bumps and bruises along the way, but this commanding presence is masterfully executed when faith is implemented as a skill. Life is GOOD! When we hit the valleys we simply downshift and hit the gas. Faith is an amazing tool; it has incredible dexterity and can transform / transmute energetic charges with SPEED and grace.

THE SOLUTION: Understand FAITH! With the previous few pages as a preview, please don't put a wall up. Try to open your mind and put it into creative, expansive thinking mode, and / or prepare it to think outside the box. I encourage you to really dissect this book, page by page, topic by topic so that each is truly grasped at a detailed level, and you are able to implement it in your life. I will explain the word in such detail that not only is it understood, but it is also internalized and experiential to the extent that it is able to be LIVED and conveyed to others as well in a meaningful way. Together, we will really dig into and explore this enlightening word as more of a philosophy of MIND. This will give it new meaning, and value, worthy of its use, no doubt. In doing so, in the few pages that follow, we will set the stage for a new "knowing", and a state of empowerment / integration. Making a foundational "knowing" experiential, for you and me, opens us up to true insight & abilities that enhance our skills and create NEW opportunities, formerly unavailable in previous moments. We enable growth out of limited mind "sets" that had formerly made growth inaccessible. NOW, with this key enabled, developed and assimilated as a skill, rather than just a lame word, we will unlock the door to a new level of FREEDOM for ourselves that was unattainable otherwise. Let's get started UN-LIMITING our "selves". That begins with understanding how, why, where, with whom, and very specifically WHEN we are drawing LIMITS to begin with and how we can use faith to break through these limits. This F-word works. HOW?

I want to begin by reviewing the concept of forgiveness because if we are looking at time sequentially, that leads us into the moment, from the past. In other words, in order for FAITH to be an option, we have to arrive to the moment to use it. Being locked up in the past, or any degree of unconsciousness would mute it out, so getting in the zone, being in the NOW, and PRESENCE are truly essential. This has an empowering effect for the tool as freedom is realized. In fact, there are endless opportunities to be a positive force in the world. Having FAITH is truly a strategy worthy of consideration. Using this tool effectively often requires letting go of the past, which is sometimes more difficult than others. If we are locked in the past, mentally speaking, how is that even an option? It's NOT, so let's go through forgiveness and some basic methodologies that help us RELEASE the past and LET GO so that we can arrive in the moment, FREE to HAVE FAITH! Freedom is key.

OK then, forgiveness...

1

FORGIVENESS

MANY LITTLE THINGS GO wrong every day. We adjust, self-correct, and don't think much about these little speed bumps and proceed as if nothing happened. Small inconveniences & mistakes are brushed off, a lesson is learned quite quickly, and we move on. We learn, grow, and let it go...especially when we are energetic and happy. What if we could do that for the BIG STUFF too? Since our state is absolutely critical, relative to our availability & presence, we need to ensure that we are releasing the past for the small trivial stuff as well as the BIG, more moving experiences that don't go so well. Forgiveness is one of the most powerful tools available to help us accomplish this. It is a skill we need to develop for the times that maybe the past didn't go as well as we would have liked, whether that be a moment ago, or a week, month or year in the past. Once mastered, it can be done in a fraction of a second too. That's the good news, it works SUPER fast. You might argue that in some cases, forgiveness takes a lot longer. My argument would be that any decision, once made with CONVICTION (no wavering), is DONE the moment the choice is made. No second guessing, no looking back. As far as the speed goes, it can be done in an instant. So, let's talk about forgiveness, the implications and internals around it, as well as when it can be considered DONE!

I know that forgiveness is covered in the first F-Word Series book, however, I wanted to touch on it again here because it is relevant in very powerful ways. It enhances faith when used in combination with it. They are actually used in similar ways and essentially act as team members. It is almost as if the moment / time is a relay race, these two tools basically hand the baton off inside the moment from the past to the future. In doing so, they maintain their position on their respective side of NOW! Conceptually, they are bridging the gap between the past and the future with a manner of protection. There is a point in time where the baton MUST be let go to release the past. At that exact moment, the past is then shielded and protected by forgiveness and in doing so, 100% PRESENCE is attained. With awareness and oversight, presence is maintained with vigilance and focus as it is guarded by the use of faith. So, conceptually the baton called "PRESENCE" is bridging the gap between the past and future. I am using this as an example in an attempt to identify and isolate that time slot called NOW! Once seen, implemented and understood as a strategy, these two very powerful tools are enabled and empowered with awareness and SKILL which allows us to stay present inside the moment. So, for the purpose of context and as a general reminder, let me point out that this "F" series is the TRINITY and named that for a reason. They combine to make a TEAM of "F's".

Forgiveness

+

Faith

=

Freedom!

It is important to understand that these skills are essentially our GUARDIANS! They protect us in a type of armor from the past and future mindset wise. Forgiveness is geared towards shielding us from the past, and faith is protecting us from the "unknown" future, relative to the time slot of "NOW" and PRESENCE. Now please try to visualize these components from a mindset perspective, conceptually. If we are to maintain our presence in the moment, these are the tools that allow us to attain and maintain that FREEDOM in the moment, empowered on the razors edge of time called NOW! By using these effectively, as we master this skillset, our presence in the NOW becomes more consistent & stable. You might even say unwavering at some point. That is the power of NOW but first we have to get there. We need to be FREE in the moment to make effective decisions. What does that mean? As an ideal, I would suggest the following:

FREEDOM = An unrestricted & balanced foundational state characterized by: Independence, peace of mind, focus and massive awareness anchored unwaveringly in the moment of NOW, optimized and MAXIMIZED! Another way to look at it might be to say we are not "bound" or enslaved by "needs" / LIMITS of any kind, by anything, or anyone. We are released from our virtual shackles, completely 100% liberated. FREE from the past, and FREE from the future: PRESENT NOW!

When all the various skills come together for us and "click" so to speak, "in the zone", this talent is masterful. With a foundational steadfastness like this, it can become unwavering at this super drilled down point of focus in the moment. As a result, we are completely FREE and "Becoming" NEW with NO "self" imposed LIMITS all the time in a state of constant creation. We are able to live a life that is much more effective and peaceful as a result. In very simple terms, if we are not free from the past, well then, we don't even get the opportunity to use the faith tool, so freedom is not an option anyway. As a progression, assuming we are on a timeline, we never get there if we are "stuck" in the past. Keep this in mind as a conceptual guide towards accessing the moment. If the goal is presence in order to maximize the power of the now moment, we will consistently use these tools situationally, mentally, and need to know them experientially in order to arrive to the moment, as well as maintain that presence in the moment in an optimal state. FREE!

As a general attitude, people say that they forgive others, but do they really let go 100% and RELEASE THE BATON (the past)? More importantly, do you? That's not what I see in general. We tend to let it go partially and then hold on to a small percentage of it, which prevents us from completely moving forward because we are somewhat tethered to it, one way or another. It is kind of sort of, but not really let go, maybe temporarily, marginally, or only in degrees. Of course, this is dependent on the extent to which we have let it go...or NOT let it go. I am not being critical, but sometimes we don't let it go at all, do we? Trust me, I get it. I am just as guilty when I am not present, if I am overtired, over hungry, or just not 100%. We hold on for various reasons, and even reach back to complain about things, or rebel / lash out in frustration. We exhibit other negative emotions as well, like regret, loss, embarrassment and guilt among others. This is effectively holding onto the baton which keeps us from presence and freedom.

Human ≠ perfect

We try though, and often times we try really HARD, but the past can "haunt us", we know this all too well. I am bringing it up for a reason though, not as an accusation, or to make anyone feel bad, but to show the lesson in it... which is often missed. This is another one of those "out there" vs "in here" scenarios. We tend to package up the past and carry it with us internally in both cases...that's why I call it baggage. The problem is that we don't see ourselves do it. The moment it is done is passed through in a manner of unconsciousness. Go back to the first sentence in the last paragraph, the remainer of that 100% was not released. That's the part of the BAGGAGE that we carry forward and in that moment, it is quickly placed in the unconscious, right along with all its shadowy friends. Not only did we not let go, but we also added MORE BAGGAGE to the hefty load we are already carrying. That's how it becomes unconscious, we stick it there by stamping it with some manner of DIS-approval. (Regret, remorse, anger, frustration, disappointment, etc.) Usually this is done with a level of emotional emphasis vs. acceptance and a lesson learned. This is also how we set ourselves up for failure because sooner or later this "baggage" will come out of the shadows and haunt us. (triggers) Why? Because we put it in there pretty forcefully. We packaged it up and delivered it personally into our own unconscious storage to begin with when we failed to let it go, so it is still with us. To further this dilemma, we bury it deeper in the unconscious as we add more baggage on top of it UNTIL we consciously decide to let it go. In fact, the more it hurts the deeper we try to bury it, which means that later it takes more "digging" and concentrated effort to flush it out. Mindset wise, as we peel back these unconscious layers of the mind, we "empty our cup" of our personalized baggage. We need to let it go layer by layer, which reveals more IN-sights. They sometimes refer to this as "peeling back the onion". Each layer reveals yet another one to be discovered and by using the forgiveness tool, we can release layer after layer of unconscious "STUFF". Once we LET GO completely, we are FREE! That process ultimately releases the baton that had us hinged to the past and allows us to move forward, and that means 100%! That is done "in here" (WITHIN) as well as "out there" externally. Letting go is POWERFUL!

In order to know whether this was done effectively or not, we can use another tool. This is one that my Mom taught me that is really cool. It's a simple way to assess things, like as in, whether or not someone "means it" or not. She said, and repeated this all the time:

"<u>Actions</u> speak louder than words!"[1]

It is an indicator. It tells a lot sometimes and it is pretty darn accurate too. Of course, as a kid, I didn't understand it, or how powerful the lesson was. In fact, I got tired of hearing it...and resisted it. What I heard was blah blah blah. I should have listened better. LOL. I hadn't had enough pain yet. First, we have to see it in our "selves", as it relates to our own actions and reactions, and then we will see it in others as well. This is relative to pretty much everything, but in this case,

I am focusing on forgiveness and forgiving. It may be a surface level "let it be" attitude, or a "let it go" and karma will get them. What we tend to do though, is carry that with us by internalizing it, or by offloading it right away, in a negative way. One way or another, it eats at us. It eats at us because we just stuck it inside our unconscious where it doesn't belong. We didn't let it go, so we either feel bad, or sometimes we actually offload it partially and then swallow the rest of that bad feeling, for a lifetime. Ever heard of a grudge? A lot of people just can't ever really let it go if they let it go at all. Again, I am not being critical, I am being HONEST, there is a difference. Our ego can get in the way. It is difficult, I agree, and our actions indicate whether or not we are forgiving and / or letting go. When someone "wrongs you", or makes you feel bad, it is sometimes extremely difficult to just let it go, straight away. Bad things happen, I don't disagree for a second. Depending of course on the severity of the "offense", or "intent". What is needed, is the level of forgiveness that we will ultimately give ourselves now for making errors over and over again, WHY? Because NOW, with this new understanding, we GET IT! It is a REQUIREMENT to move forward. We understand, and deliberately choose to process and LET IT GO 100%!

By seeing this with awareness we can observe that it is instant. This means that not only is it done, 100%, we accomplished 2 very major things:

1. We did not internalize ANYTHING, so we did not add to our baggage (Unconscious shadow "selves", or Karma).

2. By learning the lesson, we eliminated some OLD baggage and removed some weight we were carrying with us. Instead of offloading onto our "self" or someone else, we UNDERSTOOD something within, and it simply dissipated. It ended with us and the negativity did not reflect out into the world.

3. We RELEASED the baton...the past, allowing us entrance into the PRESENT: NOW!

Letting go = FREEDOM: That's the power of forgiveness! It's huge. It releases us from the past and offers us a new level of FREEDOM! It also grants us access to the moment Anything less would be uncivilized, quite foolish, if we are consciously progressing & evolving. Let it go with forgiveness, don't be a FOOL!

"The fool doth think he is wise, but the wise man knows himself to be a fool"
-William Shakespeare[2]

We just need to catch our lower "selves" in the act of doing this...being foolish. Living this philosophy makes "moving on" more seamless, EASY! We don't bog down with negative emotions. Even the BIG stuff seems like little stuff, or at a minimum, it seems smaller. Smaller bites are easier to chew and digest. We all make some blunders; some are just more noticeable. We see it all the time, WITHIN! This is why I refer to these fools as the little lower "selves" within us. They are fools, and when they take us over, they make mistakes. We just need to understand this and be alert to their stupidity! So, understanding the human situation within our "selves", and that we are all human, doesn't that make it a little more understandable as we look inside and "out there"? In other words, as we look out, externally, we could see it the same way as we would internally. In doing so, and by practicing this positive action, we can more easily forgive and move on in both cases. We can forgive our "selves" and others.

As examples:

If a spouse, or child, mother or father or someone we really LOVE a lot says or does something that disturbs us, is it easier to forgive and forget? Do we immediately throw it back in their face and try to make them feel guilty or berate them for the way we feel because of their "action" or "word"? Do we internalize it so that we can throw it in their face later? How about if someone outside the family, or someone we don't love or care about does the same thing? Is it different? Are they any less or more human, "innocent", or are they not deserving of our forgiveness? Do they get a little forgiveness or maybe a lot, or do we complete the transaction with unconditional LOVE and total forgiveness 100%? Just understand that this is a serious matter, and this is one of those all or nothing things...we either did it or we didn't. Actions speak louder than words. If we didn't let it go, it will show up again because a part of that made an impression on us. There is a possibility that it caused an internal "bruise". The reaction may be muted and internalized, or we push it outwardly and externalize it. We can do these things unconsciously, semi-consciously, or we can become aware of them and let them go.

Without awareness, whether we internalize it, or offload it onto someone we love, or someone / something else... we don't get the lesson. We will get it again. We need to pay attention to our own actions and words, particularly when they are not aligned. It is easy to see this in others, what we need to do is reverse the vision, and instead of looking OUT, LOOK IN. Now, as situations happen and we are the "guilty" one and made a mistake, maybe offended someone, or maybe we even deceived ourselves and / or failed at something. We can get the lesson and let it go with forgiveness and "make it right" with our "self" and / or them. Maybe an apology is necessary. Either way, and emphatically: FORGIVE! That means the "selves" internally, and others externally, as well as situational dynamics. Let it go...just don't keep doing that same thing expecting a different result. JUST LEARN!!

The reason I bring this up in this way is because the tendency seems to be that if we don't let OTHER people off the hook, we are JUST AS CRITICAL of ourselves. If we don't forgive our "self" we are holding onto it and carrying that baggage forward. Where does it go? We have to put it somewhere, so we basically internalize it one way or another, and kind of "save it for later" as we emotionalize it into the unconsciousness, OURS! That is BAD! Internalizing things translates to PAIN, either now or later. It is usually measured. To the extent that we let others off the hook, we do the same for ourselves. Or we don't, and that's really important to SEE and understand. It goes both ways, and we'll get the lesson BOTH ways until we "get it"! The longer we go without "getting it" the more "stuff" we accumulate in our storage container. That storage container is our unconscious mind. In "TIME" that storage container becomes extremely FULL, stuff is stacked upon other stuff and that is why we must peel back the onion. We need to uncover what lies beneath each layer. That personalized baggage is held in somewhat of a "TIME-lock" JUST FOR US...it's typically called the PAST, and because it is ours, they call it our "karma". That's our baggage and we must let it go. In order to let it go 100%, we must be conscious enough moment by moment to see when it comes up to be let go.

How do we know if we let it go? Being watchful with awareness. Actions speak louder than words, and we can show our "selves" by watching our own reactions on life's stage. So, to start with, that means we need to ask ourselves some pointed questions in order to see the answers. If we don't let anyone else off the hook, do we also beat ourselves up when we make an error? If so, why, where, with whom, when, how, and for how long? The point is, whether measured or not, it's not a contest, either way we don't get the lesson. The energy is not released, and the past is not "LET GO", it is carried forward in one way or another internally. This is very important to see. If paying attention, we can literally FEEL that weight being carried forward, NOT GOOD! That's the reaction speaking louder than words. We need to see it, hear it, or feel it as it weighs on us. We want the lesson, so we can let it go and move on, whether it is shown to us "in here" or "out there", we have to get the lesson. That is the key that unlocks the handcuffs to the past. 100% forgiveness is a requirement. To be FREE from it, and the PAST, we must use the key and LET IT GO! If we don't want freedom, then by all means, point the finger...and hold on tight, the lesson is going to circle right back around. Brace yourself, because that "tether" is like a sling shot and it snaps that rubber band back with some force. That's being "attached" to the past. That's NOT free. Free your "self"... NOW! LET IT GO!

In order to let it go, first we must be awake and aware enough to either see, hear or feel the result as it is transpiring to determine whether we tried to do something, or we actually did it. 98% in this case is not going to get it done. There is no state of trying. Actions speak louder than words. Either we did it, or we didn't. This is very relevant to forgiveness, so we need to pay attention to our actions and the words being used relative to the selves, situations, and the other people involved as well as what stories are being told in the mind. FORGIVE 100%! Our FREEDOM is at stake!

We the people, in general, are unconscious of certain things that blind us, and again, we are all different, ME included. I am not putting myself on a pedestal, I get blinded too from time to time, particularly when I am tired or hungry...or both. While we "try" to do the best we can, we are not present 100% of the time. That's just the reality of it. We are human, and we make mistakes when we are not present. So, anyway, having said that, we get blinded in different areas, situations, with certain people, and by different things, and that is based on our biases and programming. We see that within, when we are looking "in here". The compliment to that is that when we are looking "out there" so to speak, it would be THEIR biases and THEIR programming...so they cannot see, or let's just say that they see the world a little bit differently than we do, and so they are also failing forward, making mistakes. We can see how that might happen and relate to it. We truly do understand, deeply.

When we are unconscious, or not in the moment, we make mistakes. Others make mistakes too. Our humanness gets in the way some "times", no one is perfect right? We are all at various levels of consciousness, or UN-consciousness, which varies moment by moment for all of us. So, that is a very good reason why we can justify using this very powerful tool to excuse our "selves" and others. We know and understand the challenges in this human realm. Remember that these lower "selves" are the "fools" WITHIN us. This is what happens when we let them choose / react for us.

As **Jesus** said:

"Forgive them, for they know not what they do"[3]

Now we have a thorough understanding of why this is true, and needed, and why he said that! It's not just a good idea, or a noble goal, it is a requirement to move forward with our lives, free from the past! When we are not awake, aware, and present, we literally do not know what we are doing, the "selves" choose. We are unconscious! We do it, they do it...and **ALL** must be forgiven to move forward. Let's be honest here, sometimes we can't see something within ourselves, we are just too close to it. What happens then? The universe, or the powers that BE so to speak, whatever you want to refer to it as, it tries to show it to us through someone else, or in another way, LOUDER! Seriously, that's what happens...and it keeps getting louder, which should make it more obvious, but for many reasons we just keep right on missing it, until we don't miss it, we finally get the lesson. Once we do, we kind of wonder, how did I miss that for so long? What the heck, how was I so blind, or deaf, unfeeling or uncaring / unaware?

KARMA, if you really want to break it down to the essence of what it is in my opinion, is AUTOMATIC, just like this. It is the result of NOT being free from the past. In some cases, this is the result of NON-forgiveness. This is the natural process of US bringing our "selves" back to the growth opportunities / obstacles, by our own magnetism, needing certain LESSONS. So, we get brought back to them, or them to us... over and over and over again UNTIL WE GET THE LESSON! If we get the lesson, its done, gone, it doesn't have to come back unless it is only maybe marginally forgiven, let's say, less than 100%. We get the lesson 100% when we have finally had enough pain to FULLY let it go and we realize the power in doing so. It is our UNCONSCIOUS, under the surface of our minds "MAGNETS" bringing us situations and people so that we can learn and grow and LET IT GO! That stuff we internalize sort of bubbles up and arises within for us to become conscious of it. Once it is consciously addressed, learned, handled, understood, processed and let go...well then, it isn't SUB-conscious anymore. Karma = unconsciousness in the form of MAGNETISM that we bring our "selves" to, or that "bubbles up" from within for our attention. Presence and awareness observe these via conscious mindful attention in order for us to process and learn key lessons. This requires focus, and SKILL...the skill that is needed is LETTING GO, forgiveness enables and empowers the skill.

Actions—technically RE-actions speak louder than words so that we can:

Learn and grow, and let it go!

Emerson calls our reactions our "Angels" because they teach us. I'll explain that in detail later in this book. Getting lessons, in some cases, is so that we can help others learn and grow too...it is a give and take. One way or another, we are going to get the lesson well enough at some point to LET IT GO 100%...eventually, why not NOW?! Once we get the lesson, we can pay it forward. Obviously, it's just like what my mom tried to teach me when I was young, but I didn't get the lesson for a lot of years. We can't force it on people...they'll get it eventually, but we can lovingly, with empathy and kindness give them a nudge, a kind word, maybe even some guidance if they are open to it and willing to listen. My mom told me that one lesson (Actions speak louder than words) when I was a kid, but it took me 30 years or so to get the lesson. Actions do speak louder than words. We just need to heighten our intuitive capabilities so that we can be more aware of our RE-actions. Very insightful, looking IN and OUT.

If we catch our "selves" from a mindset perspective getting caught up in the past, reliving it for whatever reason in the theatre of the mind, we need to regain our presence. The screen play could be negative or positive, the point is that we are NOT present. The same applies to the future, if we are attached to outcomes and a future "NEED" as an example then the future will draw the mind there and it will be glued to that imagery. The wants and NEEDS of the ego are the culprits. If we are to maintain our presence in the moment and use the power of NOW, then both the past and future need to be released. Forgiveness is geared towards the past, and faith is geared towards the future, and that is why I call them the guardians of the gates on the opposite sides of NOW. As a progression, forgiveness comes first to get us to the moment, faith comes second to get us THROUGH the moment. Combine the two and that leaves us firmly planted in the NOW to take action. FREE! For a more in depth analysis of forgiveness, see book one of the series "The F-word, no not that one, Forgiveness, why it matters".

Now that we have arrived in the moment, let's talk about how to maximize it. That can be limited by these internal "selves" and their associated BELIEFS. Please remember that these internal selves can be foolish, so we need to be mindful of what these jokers believe. After all, sometimes that joker is ME! That means that I need to know what my beliefs are, and how they affect me. So, let's talk about that.

2

BELIEFS AND BELIEF SYSTEMS

A T A CORE LEVEL, deep seated faith is more of a belief system, or philosophy, not just a surface level tool. It actually changes the way we see things and BE in the world. It's a stance, like a platform / foundation, and a certain way of being in or arriving to and staying present IN the moment, available and READY! It's presenting the highest "SELF" we can in a state of preparedness, an amped up and empowered vantage point, highly attuned, receptive and available in the moment in a malleable and adaptive state of presence. The dutiful part of faith relative to presence is that it gets and keeps us untethered to the future, IN THE MOMENT! That's my take, anyway, a little more powerful than just an attitude that "I CAN", although that's a good start. I can do or BE whatever is required of me in this upcoming moment, and the "I" that does enter this moment is entering it with not only an expectation that something good is going to happen, but a full on KNOWING that it will. It is that "knowing" that allows us to TRUST and LET GO to **BE PRESENT and STAY PRESENT!**

While we hear that recommendation repeatedly…to "have faith"? That's not exactly what we hear, is it? If it were, maybe we would be more receptive, and interested in trying it out. Fact is, "have faith" is used somewhat generically. As a matter of fact, it is passed along by almost everyone, somewhat unenthusiastically. It's a good word, and it truly is a positively spirited idea. It is MUCH MORE worthy though, once it is truly understood, than a run of the mill catch phrase. From a more detailed MIND perspective, it is a highly advanced switch within the gearing of the mind. Once it is enabled, it is like a huge power boost. Having faith, the way I see it, and will explain it, is certainly different than having a generally positive attitude or an expectation of something good to come down the road. While faith and positivity do typically go together, and a positive attitude is good, as well as productive, that is not what I am talking about. We hear that and we are like, yeah- yeah, whatever. I have heard that 1000 times before, right? "Think positive" or "have faith" …does that really accomplish anything? You can almost feel the response without even looking, an internal shaking of one's head, with little to no beneficial uplifting effect, certainly not as effective as it was intended. What I am talking about is like firing up the twin turbo or supercharger, instantly…ON COMMAND!

HAVE FAITH!

So, having said all of that, please consider what faith means to you as far as a word, "belief" or set of beliefs goes. Don't glaze over this. Beliefs matter, I am sure of that! If you have firm opinions about a belief, in this case, what "faith" means, it may be a barrier of sorts, and form a layer of resistance, small or large. Just keep that in the back of your head as I explain it. I am not asking you to join a group, change your religion or anything like that, or even take what I am saying at face value. In fact, I encourage you to challenge ideas for yourself, as far as how you define and use them. As with other knowledge, it is probably a good idea to "test" thoughts that throw up walls. Definite, always, and never perspectives might do that. Confronting these roadblocks is often a good way to challenge, sort of push on it in various ways, and "TEST" a "limit" on one's "self". This will open up opportunities for growth. Knowledge is LIMITED, faith, as a word is UNLIMITED! I'll show you the difference.

As discussed in the previous book on forgiveness, we use words to define "stuff" and the ego tends to be a labeling machine. By using labels, the ego defines things and US, as the "selves". A definition creates ever changing LIMITS based on how we define things in our minds. Faith as a word, to me, is explained in paragraph one of this section. It is more of a belief system that enhances our way of being in the world and establishes a new foundational platform from which we can be of service, to our "selves" and others in a boundless fashion RIGHT NOW, in this moment.

Spoken as words though "have faith" is almost like the universal response to everything, and it loses its oomph, true power and meaning when delivered or heard that way. People don't hear those words as un-limit the lower "self", it will completely change your life. They hear something else that is rarely defined, maybe even burdensome, confusing, or thought to be laborious, at best. Honestly, I think a lot of people don't know what to make of that statement at all.

They hear it and internally go, "uh, ok what does that mean?" (Confused, at best.) Like if it was a cartoon, and that thought was written out in one of those speech bubbles coming out of the characters head, it would just be a couple of big question marks "???" or "HUH?" or even WTF.

I like to substitute the F-word with either Forgiveness or Faith. This is as if to question, what I am letting go of, and why? Or What I am having faith in, and why? It is a purposeful pause / strategy session within me in order to optimize my state for the next moment. While faith is most definitely worthy of consideration and a powerful strategy / skill, this directive when used as a suggestion is kind of hazy or obscure with unclear directives. There are no precepts, like a specific set of rules, instructions, or requirements that are aligned with this statement / word. As a result, people tend to just blow it off and don't think it is worth the effort to even say it or hear it when it is used in a hollow, more superficial manner like that. Seriously, that is how it can be perceived. We can see that in the faces, tones, and demeanors that receive the message, regardless of the many different routine ways in which it is delivered. One dimensional flat delivery and limited absorption of the true meaning of "have faith" is not going to get it done internally or externally.

So, let's look at both sides of that statement, how it can be said, received, perceived, and "taken", whether it is absorbed, and useful, and / or when it is falling on deaf ears, "out there", as well as "in here" within. In doing so, it will help us to understand faith more deeply as we see it operate internally over time. We will arrive at a more useful way to look at it, see it, hear it, and potentially, as a result, it will help us use it to help our "selves" as well as deliver that message in ways that are truly uplifting and beneficial to others as well. With practice & understanding and using the tool ourselves over time, it does sink in more as we internalize it as a mind strategy / SKILL. By using it repeatedly in our lives with consistency & awareness, we can grasp the concepts more intimately, experientially, maybe even masterfully. This is the level of understanding we need in order to enlighten those around us as to how they too can use this skill more productively as well. It is no longer just a word; it is a knowing that is being delivered and shared. It is invigorating, energizing, and quite a blessing to be able and willing to help people in this way, particularly the folks that are close to us. These tend to be the people we would like to help the most, right?! As a result, when the word or phrase is spoken, we and they have deep KNOWING that it is useful, and beneficial, and the true meaning behind it. Everyone wins!

Understanding our beliefs action plan:

To start with, say the words out loud. "Have faith". State it boldly, as if you were instructing someone to do this with 100% confidence that it was the best advice you could ever give someone. Don't get all funny about it, this isn't a test. Just say it out loud as if it is a directive, even if you are using it to sort of command yourself to do this "have faith" thing.

Notice how this statement makes you feel, any emotions, or thoughts this generates. This is a clue to the beliefs that surround that statement, or the actual word for you. In other words, is it possible that there is a little bit of a stigma around it? You may have a hesitancy to use it at all, or even while stating the words, it feels uncomfortable. You might be a little unsure of yourself simply because you don't understand the word, and what it truly means. So, take a few minutes and do this several times. Each time, try to notice any feelings or thoughts that pop up within. This might give you an insight into whether you are personally understanding the command and / or believe that it is useful. No need to go any deeper at this point, but you may want to come back to that later, and test that vocal a time or two after reading this book and see if it is any different. The idea is that if this statement has no meaning to you, internally, then it is essentially useless. What we want to experience is something truly uplifting, and useful, something that unequivocally enhances our state of being. In other words, the body physiology changes, and the mindset improves in a definite way. Overall "tone" and PRESENCE is something we carry into the moment. FAITH, in that sense is a TONE, and it can certainly be BOLD, once understood. This can have a MAJOR impact on how that moment goes for us and those around us, so let's get into the mechanics of it.

The mechanics start with changing the way we look at things. WTF turns into "What the faith", as depicted in the diagram below. That means being extremely diligent in paying attention to what I am having faith in, moment to moment, with focus and an unwavering broad-based awareness that is completely dialed in to the state of the mind. That is what the rest of this book is about.

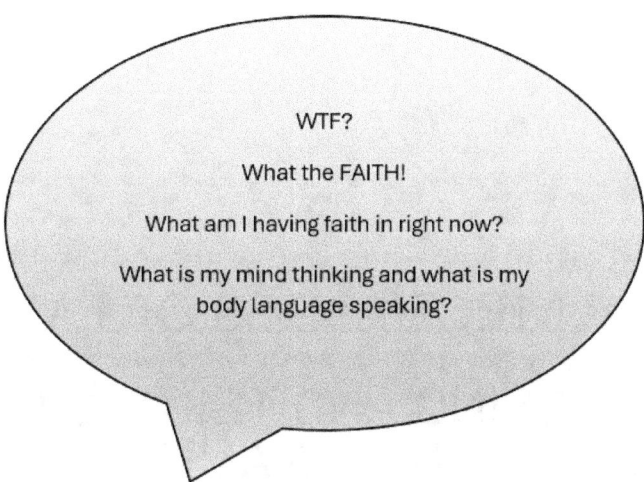

This is interrogating internally as our higher "SELF" as the watcher of the mind / body with an intricate detailed focus. So, as you may have surmised, this is a test. It isn't to judge though; it is to establish a starting point in order to understand our own mechanics. They matter A LOT! So, let's talk about these internal mechanics in detail.

3

THE MECHANICS OF FAITH

ASSESSING AND TESTING OUR "INTERNALS"

LIFE HAPPENS FOR US, not TO us...so HAVE FAITH! This is complicated and will require some diligence, patience, and exploration internally. Please consider taking a moment here and there to contemplate these concepts, rather than breezing through this material...it will be much more impactful. In fact, as we learn these concepts, we can implement them internally and as we do, we must then exercise the internal muscles so that these inner gears get stronger, more fluid, like greasing the linkages. That means TAKING ACTION, using them, testing and seeing where they FEEL the pressure and maybe even break from time to time. Using these skills in our lives, in all kinds of situations and many varied weather scenarios, some of which may be inclement... makes the internal gears stronger so that they don't break when we experience higher-pressure situations. Pressure introduces us to our "selves" and that is where, when, and how we can see the tension building on these internals. They show up as: stress, worry, fear, anxiety, etc. By watching our own internal mechanistic behaviors and responses we see how much we are weighing things, or how much they are weighing on US. It also shows us where and when we break, why, and what failed...internally, the exact mechanism or linkage. Lots of things to consider WITHIN our own mechanics.

The mechanics. What exactly does that mean? Our internals, basically. Before this stuff can be understood at this deeper level and used in a consistent way, we obviously have some challenges to get through. This is a very complex topic with lots to examine. The fact is, we use faith ALL THE TIME. The unfortunate part of that realization is that often times we use it in unproductive ways, or backwards. This is obviously a self-defeating behavior, so why would we knowingly do this? We don't do it "knowingly", we do it unconsciously as a pattern of thought that we have not yet unlearned. The understanding of our own internals and how they affect our lives is yet undiscovered to the level of "self" currently running the show in our MIND! This is where the higher "SELF" must be engaged to essentially STUDY the lower selves to "Know thyself" and understand. This is truly a necessity in order to teach the lower "selves" a lesson or two, and guide them in an appropriate manner. In order to do so, we must KNOW the "selves" INSIDE and OUT! We do that by watching them diligently.

In an effort to learn where these patterns and behaviors affect us, let's take a minute to explore some conceptual vantage points and how they relate to one another:

1. The little "selves", lower "self"

2. The higher "SELF"

3. Other people (externally)

4. Situations

5. Awareness of how, when, why, and how much these elements weigh on our INTERNALS!

Adopting and enabling methodologies to decipher these elements above as to their weight in the moment, seeing who or what is "weighing" on US and KNOWING how that is affecting us is imperative! All of that obviously affects our internals, and the weight / magnitude of it affects our ability to regulate these internals and our overall mind & body. Higher "SELF" control is at stake, particularly when we introduce pressure. After all, if we are really trying to assess faith, as a strategy or component, as well as understand what we may or may not be having faith in, we need to be able to oversee these internals within regardless of what life may bring to our doorstep, the one called NOW! As we achieve this milestone with some manner of consistency and awareness, THEN we can know whether the faith we are having is geared towards something that is good or bad as it relates to what we like and want vs what we don't like and don't want. To begin with though, we need to know from moment to moment who is in control of the mind, from an operative standpoint, what that level of self is relating to and the intensity of that attachment (weight).

Yikes, that's a lot of "selves" and things to consider. Haha. Yes indeed, but we really need to understand this quite literally backwards and forwards in order to make it useful. You may want to re-read that last paragraph a few times to really digest the implications. Sounds hard, but it's really not with awareness. Once we work through the logistics which is quite an eye opener, it will make perfect sense. We use faith all the time, we just need to open our eyes to see HOW we are using it. This is KEY! In fact, it is a requirement in many situations, as well as mind type scenarios, and so it is going to take a new level of awareness, and some time to explore / see this in more detail. Situationally, we need to be conscious of how we are using it, and of course WHEN as well so that we can modify the internals surrounding the habits. This will grow new and stronger internal muscles as we learn new behaviors and develop more powerful and productive mindsets. That equates to core stability. This might only require a very minor tweak to turn us from a negative to a positive stance, and it is quite miraculous in terms of how that affects our results.

Whether we actually use the word faith or not is irrelevant. With awareness, we can see that it is being used all the time WITHIN our gearing or mechanics, internally. Recognizing this and seeing it experientially as a life pattern is certainly powerful. What is even more powerful is the realization and IN-sight that we aren't always using it in a positive way. That, of course, goes both ways, internally and externally. When we believe in our "selves" or demonstrate a lack of trust in our own abilities or capabilities, as an example, internally that has consequences externally in our results! Same goes for applying that principle towards someone else. It is true, without a doubt that life moves fast, and we don't always see the signs of this in others, nor do we see it in our "selves" when we are, or they are unconscious / producing a mindset that is doomed to fail. In moments of stress, or distress, we create mindsets very quickly that have very little chance of producing anything positive. This is about creating a level of awareness that's sees this and immediately changes our state of mind. As a result, in a flash, we are optimized and mobilized for a much better conclusion. Need I say it again, faith is not just a word. It is most definitely a SKILL! We need to become more masterful at using it in ways that benefit us and our world.

When spoken silently to one's "self" internally or externally / vocally to someone else as an instruction or motto, "Have faith" must be delivered in a way that it can be understood, integrated, and used which often requires more empathy & consideration. Typically, that means a more personal involvement, and "digging" in order to truly understand the context and internal dynamics that are going on. This is very much the same as what would be required relative to the various "selves" that we often have to "coach" within. The good news is that when we are using our own internal dialogue, at least we know who we are dealing with. In that regard, we can proceed with a level of understanding not necessarily known otherwise because we kind of know our "selves" and the various demeanors that we tend to demonstrate...our reactive mind. Talk about a mechanism, holey moley, ha-ha. That's why we need to dissect it, it's always changing. Our internals are constantly in a state of flux, that's why we need the flux capacitor. Haha, just kidding. In all seriousness though, we do need an overarching awareness of our state. This is paramount. It is incredibly empowering, because then we can manage the state we are in moment to moment.

With investigation, we can see that the lessons we need in order to coach with the F-word are underneath the face values or surface emotions internally which can make them a bit of a mystery sometimes. That means we need to pry the meaning out of our "selves" in a manner of speaking to understand a vantage point or "attachment" as it may relate to "the lesson" required. It's like we must take a little time out to understand the "self" that we just were a moment ago in order to gain a new understanding / perspective. Else the lesson isn't always available, applicable or usable situationally because we don't see the context. Context matters! In order to discover context, awareness matters. It's a MACHINE! In order to discover the element, or quirk, that just quirked internally we need a mechanic to watch the engine run, listening with an intent ear and watching how the machine is "running". We are constantly and alertly doing an overall diagnostic check frame by frame. This can be related to ME and mine, or them and theirs. The considerations and implications are mind boggling, the key in this oversight mode is the constant alert presence overseeing the mechanics going on internally. Pause here to really digest this before moving on, this is super important. How to be the overseer of the mind / body relative to the little selves / ego: that is our challenge. The answer is by being the watcher, the mechanic...with a heightened level of awareness, listening, seeing, feeling and intuiting at a whole new level. LOOK WITHIN!

As life happens, does the fool rush in? Or are we able to maintain our presence watching the lower selves along with observing the attitudes and beliefs that are activated and energized WITHIN them in the moment? The basic and more pointed question is this:

When the little ego selves get involved...
Do they have faith? If so, IN WHAT?
BE WATCHFUL!

The same applies externally, with others, however, digging for context is not always possible, or wanted, when dealing with someone "out there", particularly if it is someone that we don't know all that well. Certainly, with a heightened focus, a lot of energy, and awareness we can see our own internal gearing and drivers pretty clearly most of the time. That is obviously impacting our own results, however, with someone "out there" we would not even know where to begin. Fact is, we do not know how they see, hear, and interpret incoming data because we all do it differently. Context for them is different than context for us. In addition, when numb, or resistant from having been beaten up by life, or the "selves" within, the words "have faith" can often fall on deaf ears, or eyes that cannot see, for example. We know that applies internally, and so externally we understand that this could be true for them as well. At this very specific juncture, in this state, they do not have the power or understanding that is needed to provide that lift to guide as it is intended to and should. That could very well change with a new moment, or a different state, so let's remember that this is an applied science, the recipe for success can change and often needs to, based on context and energy among other things.

Faith, or "have faith", when used as just a rigid word, or forced as advice in some ways can often have a certain "tone" to it. Whether it be condescending, or otherwise, perception wise it can hit in ways that are less than useful. The reception can be that it is just BS, as an example, when people just don't believe in it. Alternatively, they may have lost it momentarily as a result of some chaos in their lives. That may mean temporarily, it is muted to one degree or another, or they have completely lost it. It can be perceived in other ways too, like that it is being used as a catch phrase, as a way to offload responsibility, or even to avoid being too involved, to keep one's distance, safety. There are a lot of less than productive ways that this statement or word can be perceived that are less than optimal from the receiving end. What does that mean on the giving end? The delicate effort to help, but not "pry" into another person's business can be difficult, and there can be a tendency to want to avoid it because of these intricacies. Attitudes and EGO's get involved. Human nature, right? Often times that means we try to avoid confrontation, or just speak the words and get out of dodge, so to speak. It's not that the intent is not genuine, people often do want to help. The point is that there is "risk" in getting involved, in more ways than you might imagine. We live in a complex world; some folk's lives are much more complicated than others. It's not just our delicate feelings that may be affected, but it requires time, effort, energy, and much more sometimes. Let's be honest, the thought will occur at many times, in different ways, to let it go and leave it alone. I need my time and energy for my own "stuff". I have my own issues to deal with, or something to that effect.

Certainly, in the wrong situation, or with the wrong tone, even an innocent "look" on someone's face can be perceived as malicious. The attempt to "advise", or help can be violently rejected in some cases, where EGO's get involved, and in heated situations. It is often ill advised to try to interject in this environment, certain situations are just better left alone until the stigma is gone, so to speak. Even though we may have a deep understanding and be able to explain an amazing vantage point that would help instantly the way we understand it, it just won't be heard, no less absorbed. Pick your battles, right? Good advice, we would think. In less dramatic fashion, it may simply be that "have faith" advice, or attempt to help is not digested, understood and "available" to the person that is advised to "have the faith" so it is considered a waste of time and energy. That might even mean that the effort just isn't made, which is sad. Fact is, we don't know if there will be another opportunity like this, particularly like this soon...so as always, presence is imperative. It's always a "game time decision", and the clock is ticking!

We must always be ready for what the moment NEEDS vs. what we want out of it. A casual nonchalant verbal "have faith" statement is often just not enough. Not saying it or anything at all isn't good either...so where does that leave us? I mean, either way it feels like we gave up on the other person involved, for whatever reason. That may arguably be a very valid reason too. Bottom line, giving up on someone because they just can't hear or understand doesn't feel good at all, because in essence that means they will continue to suffer, or struggle, and we know it... whether that be now, or later. Have you ever given up on your "self"? How does that feel? A lot of times, because these people are close to us, we need to watch it happen too which is equally painful, maybe more so. We could have provided a solution, but we held it in, because the last time we got our head chopped off, so to speak. Not good, that's not LOVE, nor is it an understanding of the word, faith. I find that these situations can often be revisited very quickly, before the thought is lost, and yet after the tensions have cooled slightly. It is very similar to revisiting a situational thing with a version of "self" within, that needed to learn a lesson, but may have missed it. In fact, it is very much the same. Having faith is very powerful, we know it, and we see it everywhere. Remember these strategies are to be used internally AND externally. Internally, relative to helping the little ego "selves" grow and externally to help our loved ones and others.

To expand on that concept a little, we are not here to be enablers, internally or "out there". That doesn't mean we have to interject ourselves into everything out there or every situation either. That is one example where the confrontational aspect of it may turn us in the moment, and we just avoid it all together. It's tough, yes, I get it. Sometimes, it is possible, and warranted… others, not so much. How does that work within though, to choose avoidance and not get a lesson? How does it work to choose by default to have faith in the negative vs the positive? Not so good, right? My take is that when we truly see something, we see it for a reason. Take that however you wish. It is either for us, or them…maybe both. I believe that we are all here to help one another, as well as our "selves". The best way to learn is to teach our "selves", and then of course, we can share an experiential KNOWING. Keep in mind that this doesn't mean to JUDGE, it is intended to help when situationally, it makes sense. This can put us into very delicate situations though. It's one thing to give our ego "selves" some tough love to whip ourselves into shape, but knowing just what to say to help others can be a tall task and situationally, more of a challenge.

Everyone has a lower version of "self" right? That could mean a lot of things. It could be bad habits, or bad mental thought patterns. We understand now that it truly affects everything. That could mean within, or "out there". Either way, they ultimately hurt the individual and bringing it into the light of day may hurt us. It certainly will if it is within and we do not acknowledge it, right? Seems to me that once we understand something, it is the wish of the universe, or the powers that be for us to share that insight. Assuming the intent is genuinely aimed to help, and the delivery is with empathy and love, we would think it would be received with appreciation. However, that isn't always the case. Mind your own business is one of the attitudes that will inevitably come back at us. Unfortunate, but true…what is that? Resistance.

Just remember the way our EGO, and our "selves" respond in similar situations, and that sometimes these lessons don't really hit home until well after the dust settles. If someone doesn't truly understand what it means, when receiving this type of advice, "Have faith" might sound like blah blah blah…and it could almost be annoying. Right? Can you see this? In the wrong frame of mind, or in a situation where it is truly not understood in a way that is useful, it would be like putting salt in a wound, especially while tensions are high. First, unless highly diluted, salt crystals have very sharp edges…such as approaching things without empathy, or tough love for instance. It might even sting a little because it re-opens the wound, increasing the pain vs what was intended to be helpful. That's when we get the more confrontational re-actions, like get out of my face, get off my back, leave me alone, or a worse response…regardless of how genuinely we want to help, the wall goes up. This can be true for the people really close to us as well. These experiences can set us back a little bit from time to time when the advice is not wanted, resisted, or even avoided…if not thrown back in our faces in an attempt to hurt, because they can't stand the pain of the truth or the emotions get involved, or both. This understanding allows us to absorb it, and not reflect it back out into the world, it ends at us, period end of sentence. It's GONE at that point. This goes back to understanding and forgiveness.

We have to revert back to empathy, and love. Understanding cannot be forced. What can be done though is having the presence of mind to call that person shortly thereafter, maybe an hour or two later, and sort of check in. At that point we can evaluate whether it might be the right time to discuss it in more detail. That is often the time when we get an apology, which opens the door to make a suggestion. "Oh, you know, _____ I meant to say earlier..." That opportunity may or may not be available, you will know. Just offering up some ideas and methodologies that work. We all need a positive uplifting spirited boost from time to time, be willing to be that person. We can't do that though if we were "offended" or holding a grudge. We can't let our egoic emotions get in the way. These situations are opportunities to step up and make the world a better place because it is ever so slightly a little brighter for someone else. We have given them a boost, just when they needed it most! Not that we are doing it for ourselves, but that LOVE will come back to us in spades. What we put out into our universe comes back in multiples. We do it for THEM though, that is the only way to understand the situation so completely that a valid loving response is generated. That comes from WITHIN us, with PRESENCE! The reality of it is that the better we become at seeing and managing our own internal state, the more capable we will be to provide a platform for foundational faith WITHIN! As we grow into this as a regulated internal environment, optimizing it and using it experientially to take that next step in life, we enable a self-help feature / skillset within ourselves that is more easily conveyed to others externally as well.

I remember times when I was the receiver of such a gift, and they are always memorable. These typically come in a time of NEED and are very impactful to our lives. I am grateful to have been blessed with special people who have stepped up in a personal time of need for me. Family members, friends, coaches, clients, and even some people I did not know have had amazing affects on me. That is another impactful reason that makes me want to do it for others going forward because I know what it feels like to be in that state. I expect that we are all there from time to time, life certainly has its ups and downs. Understanding the nature of faith though is the key to delivering a heartfelt and genuine message that is powerful, inspirational and usable, internally and externally. It doesn't even have to be the words, "have faith", either. It can be as simple as a look and embrace in someone's eyes that really shows a deep understanding, almost like a virtual hug and nod, when a true hug is not necessary, appropriate, or possible. It could be an action, or even just a true genuine hug of reassurance, and an offer of availability. It might be just an internal "wink" that says, "YOU GOT THIS!" have faith! That instantly changes our internal tone. There are always opportunities. In my life people have demonstrated this capacity in ways that I have really appreciated because they transported me, changed me, in a moment and brightened my world. A few of these are explained in the book "Be the Instrument", so I am not going to re-write them here. The point is that we have a capacity to understand and explain FAITH in more ways than just by using the word. Faith changes us. Sometimes, as in my examples, it fills a void within our hearts with love and kindness. People can be amazing, BE AMAZING for someone else, it'll make them, and YOU feel better, if not GREAT! Remember to do it for your lower "selves" internally though as well.

Be mindful and maintain a balanced perspective, to the best of your ability. Presence offers opportunities to use faith in order to help the "selves" internally, as well as others...and remember the funny stuff. It is helpful. The thing is, with keen reflection, like a parallel relativity, we see this same stuff within, in our "selves" as well, right? We observe things like kickback, resistance, avoidance, and even some animosity from time to time as we get lessons we may not want to hear. Do we give up on our "selves"? NO, we persist, sometimes begrudgingly! A different angle, tone, or situational reference may explain the insight in a way that is more productive. "Tough love" is almost always a last resort, as it is rarely as useful as it seems it should be, and often feels needed. Sometimes that means a 3rd party reference might be beneficial, an example from someone else's life that has worked. This makes it less personal because otherwise it might seem accusation oriented, and / or "pointed", which can mean people can't see it because there are feelings involved and / or they are too emotionally close to it. It has already overwhelmed their system. Reframing it can offload the tone, or pressure, situationally so they can see it from a different perspective more easily and then it becomes useful in their life as it relates to their situation.

A "sales" objection handling methodology I learned when I was very young in my sales career is a wonderful tool. It is called **"Feel, felt, found"** and it goes like this. The empathetic side of us says, I often feel that way, or I understand how you FEEL, which is the ice breaker. It shows empathy, and care. Then, with their approval, or an implied NOD of yes, we proceed with explaining it in a way that has affected someone else we know, and you show them and explain the way that they FELT. This shows them that they are not alone in feeling this way. It also establishes trust that we actually know what we are talking about, having been there, and that leads us into providing the solution. Lastly, as a way of explaining the understanding, since they are now listening, you convey what you have FOUND. The mental strategy employed to get through the situation, in this case, a deep understanding of how faith is useful and beneficial. That is conveyed by saying, I have found that in this situation, the following has proven beneficial: FEEL, FELT, FOUND. Use it, internally and externally.

Another way to truly change the direction of the sinking ship, so to speak, is to lighten the load, with humor. I find myself in uncomfortable situations like this quite often, where the tension amongst people is palpable, so I understand how you might feel, I feel a little anxious myself in these situations. As a result, I use this methodology a lot, mainly because I have felt that it is wildly successful and FUN. You see, I have used this in many situations, and I have found that _____ Do you get it? I just did it again. So, what have I found, as an example you can use? Here's one:

I like to think of it this way, which makes me laugh, and the laugh helps all by itself, it's like an instant attitude adjustment. A whole internal or even external room ambiance change can occur in an instant using this technique, but there is a risk, it might feel and even be extremely awkward. You have to be quick, and almost literally BLURT IT OUT, kind of loud....so you will know rather quickly if it worked. Imagine you are hearing this through a loudspeaker system, on a plane, with a little static. Use your imagination here and keep in mind that this could be big ME talking to little me, the selves, or me talking to my best friend, wife, family member, or anyone else for that matter. It's actually quite fun, and that's the way it is intended to be delivered. It goes like this, with a somewhat amplified and deeper tone of voice, hands cupped and curled in a "O" shape near your mouth one in front of the other as if blowing a trumpet, or speaking through a megaphone, say:

"This is your pilot speaking, we are experiencing some turbulence here, please buckle your seat belt, the next few miles are going to be a little ROUGH while we are searching for some more stable air"

Ha-ha. Look around for the response. It's like a breath of fresh air...I can't help but laugh, I think it's hilarious. Tension can be relieved with humor, and then logic prevails, more often than not. Level heads are certainly more coachable, in my experience. That applies internally and externally. LAUGH! It's a healthy release knowing not to take things so seriously all the TIME! LET GO a little here and there.

It is actually very funny how a lesson can hit us and really be meaningful, seconds, hours, days and even weeks or years later. Have you flown recently? Keep this example in your back pocket for the next time tensions are climbing. You may like it as it acts as a pressure release. If nothing else, use it internally, or for a nice little chuckle. Either way it opens the door to be the mediator, which makes you a true leader, from this point forward, as higher "SELF" overseeing within, or a leader amongst your peers "out there". Interjecting a laugh or smile, with fun sort of playful mockery, a joke, or a weird funny facial expression can often have amazing effects. My dad used to do this to my sister when we were younger, and it would almost unfailingly make her laugh and get her instantly out of a foul state. We could literally see her holding back the laughter, face all red and all, even though she wanted to "pout". Then we would all just bust out cracking up. Pressure relieved, OK, let's move on. Good job Dadaroo! The heated moments are most definitely not as much fun right, I mean, for heaven's sake, we are truly just trying to help, only to get our hand slapped, or ego bruised, if we let it. It is wonderful to have a GO TO in order to snap us out of a poor state.

We can just as easily get fired up within as we can dealing with stuff and people externally. Obviously, when we are the receiver in that foul state, whether we attempt to help ourselves, or someone else tries to help us, we are not seeing or getting ANY lesson in a less than stellar state of mind as long as we stay there. If we, or one of the "selves" is stuck in one of those rotten moods, for example, we might even say to ourselves under our breath, "Yeah right, shut the heck up", or the other F*** word, while licking our wounds. Not good right? That could be directed at our "selves" amongst the selves internally, or the little selves directed towards the higher "SELF" as an example, or some other "Authority". Some dissention, resistance, even though it is seen and understood as we progress...sometimes that means the dust has to settle for a minute, or longer before we are receptive to a more productive line of thinking and an attitude adjustment. We almost have to slap our own wrist, or use one of these other playful ideas, if only to wake us out of our temporary slumber and spark a bit of energy to climb ever so slightly up that proverbial ladder, where the air might be a little less turbulent. Inspiring a laugh or changing the tone / tune can do this. Forcing a smile in a situation where it takes digging deep to grab one can turn that frown upside down a little easier and faster. From here, the message can be heard, felt, or seen from a more elevated, aware perspective. Instantly, more receptive. We typically know what works for our "selves", and possibly the people that are close to us as well, so we can be super ridiculously persistent, and maybe even push a little to ensure that the message is heard or seen sooner than later. That doesn't necessarily work all that well when the advice is pushed on someone else though, "out there"...so we do need to be sensible, and present.

When "have faith" is being directed towards someone else "out there", even gently, with love, it is not universally accepted nor is it absorbed and understood. Be prepared and alert too because the reactions can be at the extreme ends of the spectrum. The quieter version of that is that in some cases it can be very subtle, almost imperceptible. With eyes wide open, we can often gauge how it has been received. That might mean silently, and the only clue we get is in the minor facial changes, like a minor eye roll for instance or a quick turning away indicating resistance or avoidance. Be observant of bodily responses and reactions, they tell a story, and sometimes they are the only clues we get, so pay attention. (This includes our own face, and the way we are holding the body when dealing with the "selves" WITHIN, so look in the proverbial mirror, often.) In the end, and from a more strategic perspective, we need to understand, NOW, in the moment, like as in frame by frame, how it works, so that we can use it and believe in it, NOW vs later as well as to know whether it is being used properly, our state of receptivity, if you will. We need to understand it so well that we can explain it to the "selves", as well as those that we love so that it is actually helpful "in here" as well as "out there". Like second nature. EASY! It will eliminate some of those less than stellar responses too. Thank goodness. YES!!!! We need the lesson, and we need it to be useful sooner, as stated, NOW...BEFORE things get heated! By then it's often too late. There is no later anyway. As a matter of fact, it has to play out at that point, right? The lesson, the understanding, the KNOWING what faith is and how to use it, from a bottom-line perspective truly has to happen, NOW! So, FAITH is especially important when we are down, low on energy, or truly need a break, something to go our way. Important is an understatement, right? Crucial, or imperative is probably more accurate. From that standpoint, it needs to be integrated, and available within, instantly. Sometimes, all it takes is one small step in the right direction, and everything changes, but if things continue to break down instead of up, the downward spiral can descend very quickly. So, let's break it down, so we can build it up. FAITH is available, and faith can be used, NOW! So, presence is key!

The idea is to get to an optimal state of mind instantaneously, in a flash, like almost as if by snapping our fingers we are just taken there, because we know how it works that well. Faith can do that, it can be comprehended, understood, absorbed and available for use, NOW! Faith, when we are in a good mood is easy right? Optimistic, energetic, enthusiastic approaches tend to produce better attitudes for sure, and quite honestly, better results as well. So, let's talk about both the positive and negative sides.

Notice that a lot of these mind processes are actually happening beneath the surface, unconsciously, until they don't...that is until we become AWARE enough to see them happening in real time, consciously. Our PRESENCE is what is required to see it. We see it because we have done the work to build our awareness skills to SEE, HEAR, and FEEL, for ourselves in a lot of NOW moments. By continuous effort, these skills are getting more and more efficient, powerful, and integrated, like a well-oiled machine. Faith is one of these skills, and we just need to use it properly. Over time this reinforces a very positive behavior. FAITH as a SKILL is launched as a foundational platform and it is a highly beneficial state. It can set in motion TRUE new focused actions that propel us into massive successes in all manner of tasks, small and large, as well as lead us into new and uncharted discovery land where major life achievements are possible.

When this beneficial skill is used, it obviously helps our "selves" evolve, achieve & grow. In using this ability to help ourselves though, and seeing how it works, we will have many opportunities to help others as well. When used consistently, life just unfolds differently, it is with a constant state of amazement... almost a state of AWE, which is truly wonderful, once seen that way. While these opportunities may not be as obvious initially, that will change too. Everything we focus on expands right? In addition, while this vantage point kind of implies that we should help people, the EGO can play games with the mind in this regard too. In other words, that may not align with our more selfish desires situationally, which can push us into negative feelings if we don't. Certainly, we can't allow that to happen. In fact, there are entire books written about this subject and the havoc that buried feelings & emotions create in our overall health and wellness. This can show up in physical and emotional ways, or both, when we don't deal with feelings properly. Bottom line is when there are opportunities to help, we need to help and be ever vigilant about watching these lower ego "selves" as we do. Paying attention in here (within) as well as out there (externally) simultaneously is where / when we will receive incredible lessons in how faith works, when it works, how it operates within us, and even the extent to which it is effective. It is an amazing education! We will see internally and amongst our peers all kinds of complaints / resistance and all manner of responses. Statements and body language can say that it's a waste of time, why bother, save your breath, save your energy, among thousands of other habitual re-actions. Pay attention to all of it, these are extremely valuable lessons in faith and all the internal dynamics / gearing that drive it and accompany it. Results matter and when we are available to see the thought patterns and "attitudes" that generate these results, it reveals the faith component. We need to pay attention as faith delivers whatever it delivers. It always delivers, what is it delivering for you? Pay attention to those around you too, not to JUDGE, but to learn. SEE LIFE differently, pay attention to what drives it to show up as it does, WITHIN and for others as well. This will open up opportunities to see and KNOW, learn & GROW, helping the people that we love, our family and friends as well as our "selves".

Pay attention, look closely. VERY CLOSELY! There is another point to this interaction within the mind though, and it is super important, that's why I am belaboring it. What we must realize and SEE is that our attitudes towards others is EXACTLY what our attitude is towards our "selves" internally. This is something that I encourage you to watch and see, very intently, but from a nonjudgmental and innocent standpoint making it almost like a game. It is also why I have detoured to explain it in various ways, so that you can and DO see both sides of it. You can flip the scene and "act as if", playing the various roles mentally as life plays out. This way the lessons can be magnified and amplified, and as they play out on the world screen, it can also play out within our minds, like double vision. We can hypothesize and analyze and LEARN from life in an ongoing and almost ceaseless manner. Ever heard the suggestion "Pray without ceasing"? This is essentially that, and the answers are provided IMMEDIATELY once we learn to pay attention. But we need training. Maybe I should state it differently:

PRAY attention!

PRAY = THINK CONSCIOUSLY!

The essence of what that means is that prayers are made up of thoughts. So, **THOUGHTS ARE PRAYERS**! We had better pay attention to what we are THINKING, or THUNK! I know that sounds funny, but in reality...that means we are praying CEASELESSLY! Makes you want to watch those thoughts a little more carefully because these thoughts that are actually prayers are being answered all the time...the result is OUR LIFE right now, which is the result of all our previous thoughts. If thoughts are prayers, we actually prayed for this. WOW! Once we break it down, it is a bit of an eye opener

Often times, the world can be an amazing mirror, and we can see our reflection in it in all sorts of ways, our biases, our conditioned thinking, our slanted ways of seeing things based on our positionalities and programming. Until we truly wake up though we won't see it. We must wake up, open our eyes, LISTEN & FEEL as we proceed through life's many moments. This must be understood and implemented. The skill must be activated and enhanced so that these answered prayers / lessons can be seen...EVERYWHERE, not only within our "selves". Be watchful, both internally & externally. Look WITHIN is a super powerful recipe for heightened self-knowledge when combined with this double vision.

Why is this so important? Because this expands and amplifies the ability to learn through our experiences, grow and evolve. It creates more chances for learning, quite naturally. The lessons are truly everywhere, inexhaustible numbers of opportunities. As we are "doing" stuff and paying attention out there, we constantly need to be aware and conscious IN HERE as well, ever present, awake and aware of what's going on in the MIND! It happens both ways. While we are focused within, we have the potential to miss an amazing lesson "out there" as well. That is why we need to maintain that exceptional "BALANCE" in the way we position ourselves relative to the mind. When balanced, and present, we are gifted opportunities for learning countless times in a day, both WITHIN and out there. This is why we hear the phrase "open your eyes" so often, it's like a spiritual type of eye that we must learn to see with in a different way, both ways, in and out, broadly and acutely. As our awareness, attention and skill improve in this regard, we see more and more of these opportunities for growth. What this does in a fairly amazing way, depending on how much we are exposed to various situations and how large our magnets are, is it amplifies our ability to grow through experience at a more rapid pace. While we help others, we have the opportunity to grow WITH them by helping them. To me that's a WIN, WIN. The world can be an amazing teacher if we are truly paying attention, and helping other people can be very rewarding. The interesting thing is that once this is realized, we WANT to see it MORE, and we want to HELP more. As we help more, we learn more.

Caveat here, the JOY of GIVING is very rewarding, and worthwhile, but the alternative is that sometimes, it can be painful, as I have hinted at above. While we are anxious and excited to help, please remember that not everyone wants to be helped. Keep in mind that there are times that we are feeling low, down on energy, sick, angry, or whatever and an emotion or situation has us captivated. In a moment like that, we can see our "selves" as they refuse or fail to see legitimate help, or maybe shortly thereafter we see it and acknowledge it. It is possible that maybe we will even apologize and accept the help moments later. We understand that it is because the EGO stepped in and would not allow it previously (bad attitude.). That person had just "pissed me off", offended me, done something wrong, or I just wanted to feel bad, for whatever reason. The result was that I didn't want to, nor would I accept anything from him or her, or anyone like them, or even affiliated with them in any capacity, their family, friends or whomever else. This stuff happens, and we see it happen. There are many reasons why we refuse help, and lots of situations where the EGO can get in the way of us getting help, as well as us giving help. The attitude is that I would accept some help, but not from YOU! Haha. The fact is, when we are in a poor state, it is often difficult to help our "selves" no less someone else. It goes both ways, it's just that now we are seeing it more regularly and clearly as it happens. So, with awareness, we see both sides of the faith experience. We see bad attitudes, faith in the negative as well as good attitudes and faith in the positive. Observation mode even includes the times where we are somewhat neutral, and we ultimately see what each of these produces in our lives as well as the lives of others. Our lives are the result of what we had faith in a month, week, day, and even a millisecond ago. Some "times" it just takes a little longer to TURN things around because once we put the wheels in motion, they tend to keep spinning for a while unless or until we consciously stop them or redirect.

Relative to other people, the same is true. Their state matters. So, be careful not to interject yourself into situations where your help is not wanted. It may be needed, but believe it or not, some people just do not want to be helped. Remember too, their proverbial "wheels" are spinning too. They may not be going the way that they thought they were. While we may offer up some incredible advice, and even try to deliver it in discreet ways, with gentleness, love, and even kid gloves sometimes, the result is going to be an array of eye openers. Timing is a critical consideration and even with precision and noble / careful delivery, a true spectrum of feedback is what we get. Along with that feedback, assuming of course that we are paying attention and balanced, we get more lessons. Wonderful, yes, but sometimes these lessons can make us really step back or JUMP BACK in some cases. We cannot be dependent on "control", or the result. It is at these junctures that sometimes we must admit and acknowledge that we have come to a point where we must retreat and let it go, feeling satisfied for having made a wholehearted effort. The statement that I think works best for me is something I heard at a sales meeting, and I apologize but I don't remember the man's name who said it, but it stuck with me:

They just haven't had enough pain yet!

No matter how much we really wanted to help, and used every opportunity, with compassion, love, and tenderness to give it, we must come to the understanding that they just haven't had enough pain yet, and let it go. That is the way it can be released / understood & processed and LET GO! While pain is not a requirement for learning, sometimes people just haven't had enough pain to wake them up out of their slumber. The virtual slap in the face wasn't enough, nor was our attempt to snap them out of it to show them something really powerful in order to help. The responsibility in this situation can no longer be ours. I would suggest that "try" in this case just flat out failed. At some point, people need to want to learn, and be open to it, and sometimes they just aren't ready yet. That is the reason for the statement. It makes perfect sense, and while it feels kind of mean, our help doesn't need to be accepted. We can't help someone that doesn't want to be helped. We can, with our amazing skills, be balanced and comfortable knowing that it was offered and rejected, just as easily as offered and accepted. It just feels a whole lot better when someone accepts the help and it helps them, and we see that it helped them. Obviously, that feels amazing which makes us want to do it more, help more people. In addition, it gets us through the situations and times where it is refused, because these are the ones that can be painful if we internalize them which makes us UN-consciously NOT want to help. (a pattern). That's how patterns & behaviors get reinforced WITHIN! We associate them with pain and internal exclamation points. It's like a virtual sticky note goes up that says to the ego, "*stay away from this down the road*", which is a recipe for what? Resistance or avoidance.

Once internalized, firmly planted in our UN-conscious, well then... there has to be something that would motivate us to take the risk to grow, right? This starts a new cycle of an old behavior or pattern. Some things to consider as we encounter more and more opportunities. We need to be able to let go of the "attachment" or NEED for a particular outcome. We can provide the medicine, but it's not always taken, even if understood. It also amplifies the times when / where we do this our "selves" internally. We see it more readily and sooner, so we recognize the internals that drive it and can change our state more easily because we know it is necessary and see it sooner WITHIN! We know what these internal states produce, so we change our mind / mindset... FASTER!) Releasing the need to control outcomes is a huge pressure release, highly beneficial and necessary element to faith. Knowing this is a warranted practice, we can be inspired to increase our mental agility and change our "faith" state.

Another one of the cool aspects of this is that for a shy person, as an example, this has a way of making the world a less dangerous place. In fact, it may even provide the impetus to step out of that shell from time to time, and it feels good. Trust me. Not just understanding but KNOWING changes things. In fact, it sparks a curiosity and a fascination with what might be perceived as quite ordinary things. It also has a way of literally explaining things to us as we experience them, in rather amazing ways. This is experiential and will be seen and integrated more quickly and efficiently as the skill grows. This growth on growth really compounds and as it does, the skill gains power. The integrations are no longer so labor some, they just happen more and more naturally. As the higher SELF embraces this vantage point, effort can amp up as well. Change can feel like it is almost constant for extended periods as we absorb what life offers and learning intensifies. Once again growth is taken to a new level, repeatedly, which requires energy. Sometimes it means that we must take the time to truly SIT and rest to absorb the countless lessons that were perceived in a short period of time. Otherwise, the tendency is towards overwhelm, which has more of a negative effect if we push onwards too quickly. Given the time necessary to absorb and integrate, it amplifies the energetic response, and that spark creates a chain reaction which fires the heart within to do more. The world is truly seen with different eyes once tuned & tapped in, turned on and fired up. It lights up as we light up. There are endless opportunities to do good.

Please keep in mind that:

LIFE HAPPENS <u>FOR US</u>!

It's kind of funny, and cool, but when we just go ahead and DO THE RIGHT THING, we are gifted back what was given, but it isn't a one for one, it is like a 10 to 1, or more! Naturally you might think that I am speaking of "out there" right? Well, of course I am, but as I said in the previous paragraphs, it goes both ways. The world is a mirror, so we MUST, and I mean MUST do the same for ourselves, as the higher "SELF"! Take the high road! To treat others as we wish to be treated works equally well if we reverse the view and look WITHIN and treat the "selves" in an acceptable manner. That's called SELF-LOVE. Please remember, as we grow, we are dealing with these "selves" more and more often, if not constantly. As the higher "SELF", how we treat the lower "selves" within us matters. This is particularly important when dealing with one of the EGO selves that refuses to acknowledge one's "worth" or "worthiness". This is an issue and clearly standing in one's way. That's also why I say that when given an opportunity to help someone, help them...it will come back in extraordinary ways, some of which cannot even be fathomed or imagined. You will be amazed, and that amazement and appreciation will also contribute to the feeling of "worthiness". Funny how things like this work. By helping others, we actually get better at helping the "selves" WITHIN overcome their hurdles. Often that means with KINDNESS and consideration, vs "tough love". The kid gloves, sugar vs spice is usually a good idea. LOVE eventually wins out above all. Self-love is a key driver of growth and an essential learned skill to implement voraciously.

The things that tend to get in the way of love are overpowering desires and overpowering fears...our DRIVES! So, let's talk about that a bit, the seeker within us. It is an intimate part of the ego selves; driven by it's wants and NEEDS!

4

THE "SEEKER"

WANT VS DON'T WANT & NEEDS!
(AND KNOWING THE DIFFERENCE!)

W ISDOM, IN PART, IS knowing which side of this coin we are operating from. With an overarching level of awareness, we can monitor the seekers WITHIN as long as we have the energy, discipline, focus, and presence of mind to do so. The seeker always has faith in something; what we need to see is what that faith is being placed in from moment to moment, with some diligence and then in the more demanding situations, we need to have the intestinal fortitude to be able to change our mind! Our patterns of seeing the moment through, how we do it, or whether we do it at all tend to repeat, particularly when the mind is stressed, emotional, triggered and / or in fight or flight mode. This can be dependent on our mood, energy level, and an array of other factors so we must always be consciously alert and aware of our state. Making mental sticky notes helps us recognize our own tendencies relative to the "Faith state".

The faith state is our internal state of expectations and our body & mind give us major clues as to what we are thinking / expecting and having faith in. Our mindset, demeanor, physiology, and even bodily positions change according to what we are thinking. Our mind / body can even show us when we are in a state of receptivity or resistance, as an example...as we approach the moment of NOW. Once we are aware enough and have sufficiently let go of the past to arrive in the PRESENT, that's what happens next in a flash forward. We "SET" our mind (mindset) for the future. In the very next moment, we SKIP right forward to where we are going. This is where presence, and the MOMENT is MISSED because that is exactly <u>when</u> the FUTURE reaches in and tries to grab us, lure us, and draw us into its grip. This is the precise time slot when the highly driven seeker, or the scaredy cat pops in for a visit, to note extremes. In fact, there are a whole host of more moderate RE-actions & mind sets that these future "selves" bring to the table which draw the mind to the future in worries / fears or wants / desires. Of course, there are many ego-related mechanisms within that will have us looking into the future with a strong wish to control, avoid or resist it. That means we need to be equally attentive to the MIND / ego so that we can be aware of these enthusiastic characters. These "selves" within are MOTIVATED, by something...what that is, well that is what we need to discover. The problem is that the want / need or don't want / don't need mental toggle is typically underneath the surface level of the mind and SUB-conscious. It is these switches within us that need to be sort of fleshed out and seen with a highly attuned awareness (IN-sight). Ideally this is captured in that time slot right BEFORE the moment, although some "times" it is seen in the moment or shortly thereafter. Assuming we catch it and maintain our presence, this is the exact time slot where we need faith to assist us with the skill of maintaining that PRESENCE! This will keep us firmly planted in the NOW vs. being diverted by our habitual nature. (The future "selves" and their attachments). The SKILL of faith enables and reinforces presence, NOW. Now is the "timeslot" when we can take appropriate and decisive actions!

It is TIME to catch the time thief. Learning to see where, when, how, and to what extent desire & fear show up in our lives is truly enlightening. We see the SPEED at which these internal toggles can be switched over, and as they are "toggled" our mental train track automatically TURNS THAT WAY! That's faith diverted, and it happens in an instant. Much of the time, that instant is completely or partially unconscious, so we don't even see the train of thought change or get diverted because it switches back equally fast...so we are mentally "back" before we even realize that we were momentarily captivated. As a result, we can go from positive to negative very quickly and not even notice that our mental tide has shifted. It is often very subtle, particularly when the balance is only slightly off center, such as a 51/49 scenario. The 90/10 negative vs positive is easy to see. Clearly, we are headed one way or the other and when everything "hangs in the balance" these mental levers can be make or break deciding factors. Having a preference for things is not necessarily problematic, however, when it becomes a NEED, it most definitely is. The balance is TILT-ed way too much to one side which throws us completely OFF. Once we see the internals operating WITHIN us as this happens and how it positively or negatively affects our lives, we can see that it has massive implications. It's super powerful to learn from these experiences as the universe via awareness sheds some light on something. It shows us where, when, and how fast these toggles are flipping on and off in milliseconds which determines where our focus and our FAITH is being placed. Fear vs desire, pleasure seeking vs pain avoidance have a lot to do with this and once we start praying attention, we can see it happen in REAL TIME!

Think about how many people are living in FEAR, all the time. This can help them...and of course, we can also be blindsided by desire. So, the "thrilled" go getter can also be derailed quite easily by the time thief. Faith over fear is a very real and ever needed skill. The same is true for FAITH over desire. We can pin our faith on the "GOOD" or the "BAD". We can be faithful to what we don't want just by the nature of how the mind works, what it is focused on, and this is the underlying theme that we need to see. The key to seeing this through is by noticing what we are focused on, the degree or emphasis, and especially when we are teetering around that 50/50 and one little mind wiggle could take us up or down that virtual road. Awareness can see that we can be drilled down on and captivated by fear, or what we don't want, as an example. Alternatively, we can be focused on desire and be super enthusiastic about what we do want. In both cases, when and where are we? Our mind "set" is in the FUTURE! That's not presence. One is definitely a more positive approach, but both lack execution capabilities NOW because in that mindset we are NOT PRESENT! We are attached to an outcome, good or bad. Presence is key. NOW IS HOW we will get to that future, so we really need to GET PRESENT to be watchful so that we can see what we are having faith in and to make effective decisions that are "GEARED" towards that desired future vs the one we "don't want"! What we have faith in is what we are drilled in and focused on. FEAR or DESIRE, and the many variations of these elements within us determine our state and / or which way we are facing. Our gears or internal "drivers" within are determining our overall state. In other words, if you put all of that together as a package, it determines if we are headed north, south, east or west. That typically breaks down to pleasure seeking or pain avoidance to one degree or another. FAITH plays right into that ability to be present and make decisions in the moment and by monitoring our internals we are CHOOSING our overall magnetism as we make life changing choices from the preferred angle. Ideally, that is a balanced one. Catching the internal time thieves on the precipice of the NOW moment is a recipe for attaining and maintaining presence, this is where / when and how we can make life changing decisions.

So, we need to be aware of our STATE, our MAGNETISM, our demeanor, physiology and our internals which is what drives this, right? So, what does that tell us as we are watching this? It reveals to us in a highlighted sort of fashion our attractor-factor. It shows us what we are attracting and bringing into our lives AS we are bringing it in, like REAL TIME! Another way of saying that is that it shows us what we are having faith in AS we are doing it. That can be really good, or really bad, and our mood / energy level has a lot to do with that, right? Heck, sometimes we don't even want to help ourselves because we are in such a poor state of mind. Isn't that accurate? Well, not everyone is intended to do the same thing, but whatever we are doing, we need to do it with awareness...and when we mess up, forgiveness. This applies to the "selves" as well as others (internal & external). In other words, we need to understand the human condition, on a moment-to-moment basis as we are doing it. What gradually happens if we do it with enough awareness is that we learn the underlying themes, the storylines, the beliefs, motivations, programming, and whatever else drives us to do the things we do and then we see the result. More and more, we learn our motives, our passions, our drives...these things that make us tick and then we truly understand the consequences of each "tick" or each "gear" that is activated and administered within. We begin to see the result of these internals as they generate OUR LIFE! What we inevitably see is that much of the "time" we are on auto pilot and / or UNCONSCIOUS!

These internal unconscious states ultimately break down to "Pleasure seeking" or "Pain avoidance". This is a very basic toggle, and we can see it happening in our own mind as it is happening in the moment once we dissect it, slow it down, and really pay attention. It shows us exactly HOW and WHEN we are being blinded and operating on autopilot from an unbalanced state of mind within which our internals are "tweaked" one way or the other. It shows us, with awareness, where we might have been wearing rose colored glasses (blinded by some future ideal) or we were doing the opposite. We entered the moment carrying some baggage from the past and the stigma, or emotion that was carried forward from it has influenced our ability to access the present moment because the emotion carried us away and we were NOT IN THAT MOMENT. Instead, we were in pain avoidance mode without realizing it...or whatever else took us out of the moment. We were attached, the balance had shifted, and we were NOT free to make a choice. It is an either / or scenario which could be positive or negative but, in both cases, one of the time thieves got us. ☹ This happens in milliseconds, and we are toggled back n forth so fast that without this heightened, energized & focused awareness we don't even see it happen. Fear and desire are the primary drivers of this push / pull within. A lack of energy, or physical pain can also be deterrents, de-motivational or cause a LACK of the necessary drivers to maintain the level of presence required to move forward. These internals TRY to dictate what we do, if, why and how we do it, as well as what we think and how we think it.

By paying very close attention, we can see that these elements of mind (The "selves") are the "players" in the mindscape and the "drivers" of our GEARS within. We can also see when they're in alignment or disagreement, balanced or not. These "selves" tend to flip flop between pleasure seeking and pain avoidance which equates to stress or internal conflict. These are both possible and they are both projections in the future mindscape. This "toggling" happens FAST, and causes confusion, just like when the mind flip-flops from the past to the future. Either way, we get caught up in it...and <u>NOT</u> present. It can be like vertigo where it takes a second or two to regain our balance...but what happens in that lost moment or two as life slips right on by? We need to see when this happens. The time thief is a very real phenomena...IT HAPPENS! In fact, it happens a lot but we don't see it because it happens in very small incremental moments. That is why we need to be on high alert watching these very small time slots in an ever-present and focused manner. Milliseconds matter, especially when we are vulnerable to an equilibrium shift.

Pay very close attention, it is Like the proverbial angel on one shoulder and the devil on the other, and here we are in the middle as the higher "SELF" overseeing this virtual battle within amongst these conflicted lower "selves". Smile/Frown, Good/Bad...back n forth, like a ping pong match and "I" am the net. In one moment, one "self" is going to tell me that I am the king of the world, and then smack the ball goes to the other side and the very next moment another version of "self" steps in and that one will be digging my grave or criticizing / demonizing / playing devil's advocate, sheesh. What a show! What we must do is wake up and see it happening, moment by moment and DON'T LET IT HAPPEN. We can't let these lower versions of "self" steal our life. We must WAKE UP!!!! From above, the ping pong match can be enjoyable, even comical and entertaining to watch for a while...until we just end up telling them both to turn in their racquets. Finally, some PEACE!

What if I am the net though, without an overarching awareness of this going on? YIKES! Confusion, STRESS! What do "I" do? Who to listen to... Not only is it confusing watching the ball (argument/justifications) speed back n forth, but sometimes you get hit right in the face with the ball (i.e. reality kicks us in the teeth because we were not awake and aware in the moment.) The reality in these momentary blips back n forth is that in these isolated timeslots we are always on one side or the other. Some "times" we are on one side of the net (moment) and other times we are on the opposite extreme...Sometimes we are only slightly on one side or the other. The net is the isolated moment in time called presence, but we don't spend a lot of time there at all. We are always speeding back n forth over that extremely narrow stretch of time called NOW!

So, if I am right smack in the middle of the argument, at the same level, that's what happens. I get beat up, or exhausted, or both. We need to be above it, for that reason. Higher Self-control. This means less stress, because we are above it. It also equates to less lost moments and less mistakes. While looking at this in fractions of seconds, it seems as if we are only talking about a moment here and a moment there. The thing that we need to understand and see is that these can be life changing moments some "TIMES", PIVOTAL! These life altering opportunities have the potential to elevate us to new heights if we seize the day / moment! So, I encourage you to make it a "pass-time" game...to watch the ego "selves". That is a game totally worthy of some added attention. Watch as the MIND is placing its bets FAITHFULLY!! Might want to keep an eye on this ever-changing mindscape, and awareness is a key tool / skill that will greatly help in this regard

KEY NOTE: Watch the mind and observe "PASSING TIME"! This is not to say, in general, or watch a clock, but specifically relative to this back n forth mind maneuvering ACROSS the moment of NOW. This means noticing when the mind crisscrosses from the past to the future, or the future back to the past, while NOT maintaining presence IN THE MOMENT. Be watchful of how long it can maintain PRESENCE, <u>IF</u> it can attain and maintain it vs getting locked in the past or the future. Presence is KEY!

Note to higher SELF: what is preventing or removing presence?

Without these abilities, the skills we are building, the true problem really does reveal itself. We do not have the presence needed to make choices based on the truth because the truth is not available in the past/future and that's where we are when we RE-act as the "selves". The selves ARE the time thieves! It is about "TIME", not where we are necessarily, but WHEN we are (mentally)...and when we are there, in the past/future as a moment slips by, we are LOCKED OUT of the REAL moment, NOW. We are quite literally BLINDED by our "selves"...the little ego selves in our mind that we have yet to overcome. It is in the moment with awareness that we see our "selves" and the attachments they hold dear push & pull us to the past & future, towards or away from what we want. They literally slam the door (the gate) in our face and shut us out of the moment as these toggles are "triggered" to flip back n forth. Are you going to let that happen again and again for the same reasons without seeing it? It is the internal selves that are pulling your "triggers" and flipping your switches.

Presence is the ability, OUR ABILITY, to be in the moment, the ETERNAL PRESENT! The Eternal present is the "NOW". NOTHING else is real, it a mere mirage created by falsities…LIES…essentially EGO generated illusions, generated because we are asleep at the wheel, captivated by some past or future. That is why I say it is a SKILL, because with practice, we can get better at it. In order to BE PRESENT, we cannot succumb to the lower "selves" and their attachments. We need to look under the surface of this pattern at the mechanics or internals to see what's driving it, to see the juice, or the satisfaction we are getting out of it. Whatever it is that is being valued in the past / future needs to be SEEN so that we can disconnect / DETACH from that level of self. That's the seeker. We need to be above that level of self in order to see and understand 100% what it is seeking and why it is seeking it. What is driving it to do what it is doing? Is it seeking as in desire for something "wanting" or in resist / avoid mode, as in "don't want"? Is it positively motivated or "geared towards" the negative? Which way is it pointed? On top of that, is it seeing the truth, presently? Am I present, seeing from a balanced state or am I in self-protection mode, as an example? Am I a little too excited? That would be the alternate side of that coin. Positive vs negative / balanced or "tilted". We are favoring one side or the other, like a see saw, and the extra weight leans the see saw to that side. Key observations: desire or fear, want or don't want. We need to know which of these has the POWER of our attention. That's our "attachment". These are often <u>TIME</u> related which means that the mind is captivated in the past or future! That ultimately means that no matter how momentary that captivation may have been, the mind was in relationship to the projection vs reality (mentally in the past or future).

Either way, with massive awareness, the question becomes: do we want to respond to life while seeing and hearing illusions that these "selves" are attached to and projecting onto the mind screen? …or do we want to REALLY COMMIT to our life and to "<u>BEING</u>" present to see and hear the TRUTH? The truth is available in the NOW once we are FREE from these "selves" and their attachments. That is PRECISELY where and when the still small voice can be heard, and where we can SEE life unfolding moment by moment by moment in REALITY. So, what exactly is the still small voice? I'll leave that up to you to put a label on if you wish to do so, call it higher guidance, the higher "SELF", Jesus, GOD, angels or whatever else. Other religions give it different names too, which is fine. Call it what you will, I say GGITM, God guides in the moment. If you prefer not to use the word GOD, that's fine, just substitute the word with whatever you choose to call it, the universe, the ether, whatever works for you. It is GUIDANCE, and it is available for us to use in the moment once we are PRESENT. This is key to see and hear / feel because once this happens FOR US it also highlights the places, times, and situations that it DOESN'T happen for us. The reason is because we get taken out, we are elsewhere, else TIME. I.E. We missed the moment and now we know that we missed the moment because we see it happen ALMOST real time, but like milliseconds later. We see one of the "selves" as it steals the moment, and it happened in that fraction of a second called "time". It is quite literally a millisecond before now...that is the time slot we often get taken out.

The interesting thing that is seen over and over again is that <u>the moment is where all change happens</u>! Without access to it we are essentially cut off from it... from growth, cut off from that level of instruction. The guidance in the moment can't be seen or heard if we are stuck in the past or captivated by the future. It is a time / timing related issue. PRESENCE solves this problem. Explained from a Biblical perspective, it is just like the words in the Bible... We cannot hear, and we cannot see. Why though? Because we are NOT PRESENT, we are in one of two other places: the future or the past. We need to GET PRESENT, GAIN PRESENCE, NOW! Work to become more AWARE...awareness will turn these light bulbs on, over and over again. With the ability NOW to access the moment, naturally we progress to higher states of living, of being. Can you imagine having such awareness that you could respond to any and every situation, moment to moment, with UNCONDITIONAL LOVE? I am going to lay it on the line here and say that <u>THAT</u> is the God response, and that we have the ability within every one of us to HEAR AND SEE the God response. We truly do have the ability to be "an instrument", but we need to hear and see from the truth, without preprogrammed biases and weighted influences from former and future "selves" that put illusions in our windows (eyes and ears), blur our vision, and amplify falsities in the mind so that we cannot see / hear the truth. The GOD response in and through US is not an option if we are not in the moment, (in the zone) awake and aware, because our programming (little selves) will get in the way. With faith and trust, fully conscious, awake, and aware, it can be different, NOW...we can BE THE INSTRUMENT of change, and this can change our lives. It can change the lives of those around us as well. The world can be a better place. We can help, and it starts WITHIN each and every one of us. If you don't want to do it for God, per se, this strategy and skill is equally important if you want to ACT in your own best interest to get what you want vs what you don't want. Once this skill is mastered, the choice is there...Be LOVE and respond with love or choose something else that maybe one of the little "selves" is more "self"-ishly attached to. The point is that a CHOICE is being made. We need to SEE it being made.

Conceptually, now we do understand how this is a possibility, once we are FREE to SEE and CHOOSE wisely! We just need to work on the actual skill of DOING IT! Let's face it, we miss the mark a lot. So, let's talk more about the actual implementation of the skill from some other angles. Faith is a key element, a very necessary one. As we dissect this, it becomes more and more accessible, so let's continue down the river, FAITHFULLY!

Let's talk about the mechanics and implementation of faith.

5

THE MECHANICS: IMPLEMENTATION

OF THE "OVER-SEER" AND FAITH

T HE MOMENT IS WHERE change happens, where we become NEW. For that to happen, we obviously need to be PRESENT, awake and aware, IN THE MOMENT! To do that requires focus, energy, self-management, and a more elevated perspective. This higher-level view gives us a more productive awareness of this mingling mish-mosh of states within us and that elevation helps provide a better angle on things. In my experience, this is from ABOVE vs IN the mind, and it's actually BOTH! Watching the mind from above while we are also INSIDE the mind processing in the moment is a powerful perspective enhancing view which includes a more broad-based awareness. It's like we see our "selves" from above as we are in the moment AND we are also in the moment operationally at the same time, the timeslot called NOW! So, we are totally dialed in to the content as we are focused on what we are doing, and yet we are also completely AWARE of context from above so that we have all the details and scope dialed in to paint the whole broad-based scenario / picture as we are going about our business. Double vision, but in a good way, fully integrated. The view from above, once truly mastered can be seen as a view from above TIME, as well as the doingness of the selves. It is a place / vantage point that allows us to watch the moment unfold as a progression, almost frame by frame if we can truly drill down on it at that level of detail. It's called being in the ZONE, and the zone is accessible with an extremely heightened level of focus. This section is about drilling down on the mechanics of this as we are able to see life evolve right in front of our own eyes. The overseer is a very POWERFUL vantage point to be mastered, for sure.

Consider this. It's basically like enhancing the mind functionality from a single core machine to a multi-core, multi-threading processor with oversight capabilities and error protection built in. We just got a major upgrade, not only in computer power and hardware, but life enhancing software as well. This processor upgrade and functionality needs to be implemented, integrated and practiced, which takes time. As we integrate this and use it, the time element can be seen as a tick, tick, tick and the unfoldment of the moment can be dissected and blown up, if that makes sense, so that everything is more easily seen as a progression. That is what it means to be "ABOVE TIME", seeing the evolution of the moment, with IN-sight. We are literally seeing WITHIN, as we are handling life, and doing what we do. Life can be seen as sequential time slots...very much like a series of pictures blended together into a movie, we just slow it down. With new eyes, imagine even seeing ahead of time. Just saying, while we are playing with time, we may as well play hard. In the mean-time, let's focus on the mind, watching and understanding what it is doing. This overarching awareness captures ALL! It has massive power, a lightning-fast processor, cameras facing every direction, feeling that is dialed in to the sixth sense / intuition, and stupendous hearing, such that we could hear a pin drop in an earthquake. Awareness sees, hears, and feels EVERYTHING!

This is where the overseer comes in and can be very beneficial. Once tuned in and framed in mindset wise, this can be considered a super enhanced state of MIND, ABOVE the mind and above the time slots. It's actually the awareness component that is often described as "The watcher". In the last chapter we referenced a river, and this is talking about the same angle, really. Watching the river from above the river, assuming the river water is clear, we can see what is in it, what makes it TURN, as well as what is causing it to swell up, bubble up, or even make incredible waves and formations in the water. The overseer enables this feature from above the mind, watching thoughts do the same thing in the mind as the rocks would do in a river. Now again, assuming the mind is somewhat "CLEAR", we are simply using that powerful vantage point to investigate thoughts as if they are traveling downstream in a river fashion. This way, we can see where they are headed. Whatever floats your boat is a very real consideration.

First and foremost, though, the mind / thoughts must be somewhat visible. A cloudy mind makes this very difficult. Many things can make the mind "cloudy", so by all means, pay attention to what does this to you. Things like prescription drugs, or mood enhancing drugs & alcohol come to mind and can affect the minds performance during and long after their use. Certain foods and supplements, and even water intake, or lack thereof can have an impact on our energy level and the mind's "clarity"...remember that everything affects everything. Relative to the river and thought though, picture this: "I" from a higher level of MIND, above its "self" am able to watch and see the actual thoughts that are running through it from ABOVE the river of thought. YES, the river is running through the mind and of course, the flow varies based on what those thoughts are bumping up against. Envision the rocks in the river as our "attachments". Let's refer to this vantage point as the higher "SELF "and it can see the lower "selves" and where these attachments make the river turn. The river is ME, my thoughts streaming with my attachments, and as a result, I am turning...which makes other thoughts bubble up and form new thoughts. Thoughts upon thoughts, bobbing and weaving, twisting and turning down the river WITHIN. Watching the whole thing is glorious, and miraculous as this unfoldment and gearing is seen as it develops, stalls, stops, turns, and even picks up speed sometimes. All WITHIN! This higher SELF sees as the overseer that everything is affecting everything. This rock makes me turn here, that rock makes me turn there...and that boulder over there stops me in my tracks making all kinds of internals kick up and bubble to the surface in this pool of thoughts that just keep circling around and around. WOW!!! Makes sense right?

This perspective is extremely powerful, assuming it can be energetically maintained, and this is a key part of attaining that elusive FREEDOM. This is a skill we can use to empower and maintain presence of mind and as a result, we are mastering the "selves" from ABOVE! It's like a big roundup. This is also a key element and skill that is referred to as "transcending the ego". This is in no small part, a broad-based understanding of the mechanics within the mind / ego. Awareness has the capacity to integrate and understand these dynamics as we lasso one ego element after another to truly appreciate it more deeply relative to how it affects us. We pay attention to where, when, and how it diverts the water, as well as how much water is shifting within the river of ME!! Of course, then we pay attention to the results, the outcomes that are generated, which is our current life. We see it as it is developing as a process of unfoldment, just like the moment as time slots. Tick, tick, tick by tick...these "selves" step into the river and divert the water. NOW we see it with awareness where each thought in the "flow" affects the next...so this train of thought can be seen as sequential time slots progressing and we have the power & presence of mind to interject at any "NOW" point in that sequence. When we change and divert the river of thought it changes where the river goes and that ultimately affects the final destination. Net, net, thoughts shape our lives and that affects where WE end up. So, as we develop the ability to see in this manner, we can see much more clearly where we are headed on a moment-to-moment basis.

I think it is interesting that a lot of artists speak, write or sing about "The RIVER". You see it more often than could be a coincidence in my opinion. **Esther**

Hicks talked about going with the **"FLOW"**[4] of your stream. The message is very powerful. What I gained from it was this enhanced vantage point with which I could assess thoughts. The logic made sense to me, I was to compare thoughts in order to know if they were going upstream or downstream. She said this in various ways, repeatedly, on her audio CD's as well as in her books. To determine if a thought is going with or against the stream, what must we do? First, we need to be awake and aware enough to ask the question. In other words, we need to be present to ourselves. Wake up, be aware, be CONSCIOUS! Once we wake up, we can then be AWARE of not only the thoughts, but the state of the body, emotions, tension, ease, etc. That, in turn is "processed" in the moment with our multi-core / multi-faceted mindset / awareness skills. Once the net of all that is "understood", the translation shows us what that thought, or line of thinking, is aimed at...up or down. By asking the question such as: "Is this line of thinking headed upstream or downstream?" I am asking a very pointed question: which way am I heading? Do I feel pressure? Where? AM I pointed upstream and / or resisting the FLOW here? In paying attention, we get a fairly quick answer internally by assessing our overall state, physiology, demeanor, stress level, facial expressions, tone, energy, etc. It could be the thought itself, or the underlying THEME of thoughts, that is driving our STATE. I think that this offers a really cool vantage point and allows us to go with the flow more easily from a more analytical mind angle...as if asking HOW, exactly, can I do that? What is required right this second, and this is a way that works. It helps us kind of back up, and strategically dissect it to reposition things if needed, like mind "SPIN". HOLD ON, PAUSE, let me get in the trenches of my mindset here to make sure that my mind is geared right, I am "aligned", and all systems are GO. The machine is not bogged down, adjustments have been made, gears are not going to be grinding, I am ready. I am basically re "optimized" before proceeding. It is at that moment when we are prepared and ready that faith can be implemented, as our state is maximized, IN THE MOMENT.

By changing our state, whether taking a deep breath or whatever methodology works for us to RE-focus and re-Optimize, we can meet life as a new "SELF". We ready our "SELF" and whether stated or not, we essentially press the GO button from that momentary "pause" and proceed. With a major vantage point change, we can watch / take action from a completely different perspective. As we watch life happening, we can be fully engaged, from this more elevated vantage point, above vs in the river. We are constantly attentive, present, and able to adjust / tweak our own internals as needed. We can see the different levers that are being pushed and pulled within us, and then with understanding, the natural progression is to a more curious, educational, empathetic & balanced demeanor vs a more erratic emotional status that can swing to both extremes easily diverted by an overpowering stream of thought (attachment). In essence, the result is that we are completely, 100% ready for life. Wide awake, eyes wide open, totally dialed in with unwavering presence. In this state, we are optimized and maximized as our BEST SELF! The lower "selves" and their distractions / attachments are no longer problematic. In fact, they are seen as outside of this "scope" time-wise. Even what would be seen as emotional disturbances or "pain" would be "time-locked" and so we have essentially removed it from the river. As a result, there is no more crying. Even crying can be watched, understood and then, it is as if instantly, the lesson is received and the crying just kind of stops. The reason for the pain isn't necessarily erased, but It's essentially the same thing really, with understanding there is no more suffering associated with it. The rock in the river disappears which eliminates the resistance. Pain is relative, and we removed the connection or identification element of it. Yes, we can CHOOSE to identify with the pain if we really want to choose that option, but it is seen as truly optional at this point. We can put the rock back in the water if we want to, by choice, but that is not in our best interest, and we know it. Once it is seen, it can't be unseen. Nothing can bother us from this overseer position, it is all SEEN, understood, and simply processed. More of a matter of fact type view... like Oh, yeah, I see that. That's really Interesting vs. OUCH that hurts, make it stop!

We can see a pain point, or a point of resistance as a rock within the river inside the stream of thought. By removing the thought (rock in the river) and understanding what it is teaching us as we remove it, we gain valuable IN-sights, and it removes pain & suffering. Life and the river begin to flow more easily and naturally as we LET GO which means seeing and removing more and more rocks with focus and awareness. Everything makes perfect sense, the lessons are learned, and we move onwards, all the better for the lesson. Another step forward. Pausing to "optimize" is something that can be very productive. We can think about it as a personalized strategy session with our "selves", and it takes just a fraction of a second. Consider it this way, suffering relative to pain is optional, once seen from this new and more elevated perspective. Makes sense, right? With a quick adjustment, everything can change, if we have the power of MIND control. Our frame of reference makes all the difference, we could be enjoying a little mind movie in our own fairytale land, or just as easily "suffering" from a different mindset that is stuck in a visualization of a negative past event / situation. Equally possible is a mind occupation within a dreamy future or captivated by a worried / negative mindset that is "producing" a bad future related movie on the mind screen. While positive or negative, the movie we are captivated by is in "time", and so we are essentially lost in the past or future as we take these momentary vacations from our position within the PRESENT mindscape called REALITY...and reality keeps playing while we are absentees. The problem in these scenarios is that we were not present to play & grow, we skipped class at the earth school in this world of "reality". Lessons are NOT learned because we miss a lot of moments this way. If we miss moments, or skip class, then we stand the chance of not graduating because we missed valuable lessons. (Not graduating means that "life" does not move forward, we stay the same. Growth is not possible when we are unconscious!)

PRESENCE IS KEY!

Please take a moment to really think about this and explore TIME, in depth. They say that time is a human construct, right? What does that mean? I encourage you to ponder that and not just glaze over this section and this idea. If you don't understand what this means, take a time out here and really try to digest the concept of TIME and the possibility that we can pause, slow it down, or even freeze frame a moment if needed while we process and re-stabilize. It can happen in a fraction of a second with a powerful enough processor. This could quite literally mean the difference between getting and digesting a lesson or missing it all together! It can happen in literally milliseconds, and change can happen instantaneously as a result. This is something that really jumped out at me back in the days when I was trading "in the zone" and it was insanely helpful in enabling the repeat / rewind functionality WITHIN! I mean, seriously, what if we could really slow time down like a digital data recorder and replay it in order to "catch" the time thieves in their tracks and gain the associated lessons a little bit easier, faster? Kind of like they do in the movies, freeze frame, or going back and slow rolling through a scene to catch the culprit, red handed, so to speak, or see something in the background that we missed. That's what we are doing to the EGO!!!! Wouldn't that make this process a lot easier? It would be like catching the ego like a thief in the night, and all of a sudden, we turn the light on! Super en-"LIGHT"-ening. We are educating our "selves" / teaching them lessons, evolving, growing. At a minimum, we must observe when the ego elements within draw us to our past or pull us to the future within the mind. This is where / when the time thief steps in...to the mindscape. It's like a game and it can be FUN vs painful, perspective matters.

If you really start to dissect the way that the mind processes, TIME can be seen in a different light, so to speak, as it is slipping by ridiculously fast. Each experience we meet, in the moment, is an opportunity to sort of capture a lesson. Unfortunately, the lessons are missed quite often because in the heat of the moment, stuff happens so freaking fast, we just can't keep up. What happens is that we completely miss moments when our mental circuits get jammed, overloaded, or whatever else takes our attention away. We get distracted, and all it takes is one freaking BLINK, or that we are looking in the wrong direction, focused on the wrong thing. Any number of other scenarios can happen, and then we have the potential to miss a lesson. Our eyes go over there, and we miss something over here. I heard something, but I didn't hear it quite right to really capture the lesson, it wasn't loud enough, or it didn't hit me the way that I needed to hear it to "understand". When I was trading, years ago and learning this "stuff", I was literally asking for time to slow down so I could see these "opportunities" better, among other lessons. I wasn't doing drugs or anything, but as explained, when in the zone, it does feel as if time slows down. In addition, because of this insight, I was totally working on my eyes, ears, and senses to be able to see, hear and feel BETTER, quicker. Naturally though! I was not artificially trying to enhance the senses chemically, with the exception of caffeine to heighten my focus. Admittedly, coffee is something that has helped me stay focused longer. I WANTED the lessons! I asked: "Please show me", I begged!

What if time were to stand still just for a fraction of a second, while we got a personalized lesson, before moving on. Could that happen? That is exactly what I am talking about, pausing time, freezing moments. I really looked hard at this. My take is that we can, kind of sort of by hitting the virtual pause button, for just a fraction of a second. Conceptually, assuming some incredibly powerful mind maneuvering tactics, we can revisit a mistake or a moment that just flew by too quickly and we missed something. There was a time where this kept happening to me, repeatedly. At that time, I asked, begged even for the universe / GOD to SPEAK LOUDER in a way that I could hear or see better. I asked / prayed: PLEASE show me so that I can SEE, I pleaded! Fact is, I kept missing REAL opportunities, but I could see that I was missing them, I was seeing them only after the fact. So, I was basically begging, PLEASE slow it down so that I can see it, I can't see quickly enough to act on it at this point, it's going too fast. My mind was not seeing it fast enough, or my processor was too slow! I would have to wait for that same scenario to happen again so I could see it faster the next time. So, either I would be faster, my mind would see it quicker, my processor got an upgrade, or time would move slower, so I could be faster. Either way, conceptually, it is essentially the same idea. If time were to stand still just long enough though, like a frame-by-frame type scenario, I wouldn't miss anything, hypothetically of course. This is the equivalent of learning a lesson, and in doing so, there is no longer any pain associated with that lesson. I can see the whole progression, but I want to do it in a lightning-fast manner, like milliseconds. I see everything this way—every last detail.

In addition, since we aren't always 100% present like that, isolated to that time slot with a laser like focus, how do we make a sensation or an impression stronger, or more easily seen, heard or felt? I am asking for the universe to SPEAK LOUDER / QUICKER / SOONER so that I can hear, see, or feel it in a way that my processor (the mind) can perceive it REAL TIME! Almost like I can see it coming in advance. All of a sudden, I AM just READY, like never before. Please, powers that be… Enhance my vision, hearing and senses. I am missing too much stuff, and I KNOW that I AM! Help me, I am begging you, for the love of GOD, help me to see with more clarity, focus and SPEED!! I need to see all the details, and in particular…make the most relevant information the most prominent for me so that I don't miss it. It would almost be as if that stuff was digitally highlighted by my new "lenses" as they are processing all of the information real time. On top of that though, my processor can't be stuck in processor mode without the necessary resources to process. My RAM can't be maxed out or throttled down because it is busy on other "tasks". The machine must be constantly updated, optimized and ready, maximized free and clear in the moment. Mindset wise, we are available with presence, FREE and READY to process at MAX speed.

Please take a moment and explore this idea in detail. The concept is useful, even if delayed. Time is a very interesting consideration and if we can slowly replay a moment and watch it unfold, it can provide us a powerful vantage point. In the real world though, things happen lightning fast. Take this opportunity to step back and think about it for a moment relative to watching the mind as it processes "stuff". Bottom line is that once the universe speaks up, or we learn to process BETTER in one way or another we will HEAR, SEE, or FEEL a lesson come through LOUD AND CLEAR, so to speak. We truly do "GET IT" and we get it faster. We have the capability to learn the lesson as a result. Whenever that happens for us, then what happens next? We implement this new understanding in our life, it is processed, and then it's no longer holding us back. From another perspective though, and this is important: We can't IGNORE IT anymore either. We are no longer "innocent", so the next time we see it, we better see it good. LOL. That's what helps us to prevent mistakes Some might call this "sin". The point is that failure happens very quickly, as we speed up and crank up our processor power we make less mistakes with amped up awareness and focus all dialed in.

So, life is a river. Looking at the river from a bridge above it is a powerful and enlightening vantage point. "I" watch the river of thought go by in the mind, right? I am seeing INTERNALLY, while experiencing life, EXTERNALLY. From this perspective, I am literally ON THE PROWL, for lessons. I am determined that these thoughts will NOT deceive me, no matter what I am experiencing externally. Not only that, I want to maintain my presence, in ALL SITUATIONS! I do not want to "lose myself" or rent out my mind leaving it vacant for the little "selves" to run rampant in there. HAH! After all, by paying close attention, they are the ones that are providing the lessons. I want to be watchful for when they attempt to take my mind over. As long as I am seeing them from above vs being drawn in and captivated by them trapped IN the mind, at least I have a chance, assuming things aren't moving too quickly. The replay feature is a super powerful eye opener, and so is the overseer. Two very powerful "watcher" functionalities. One is from above; the other is more of a "Time-catcher" and they work together to oversee the operations of the mind.

The way I see it is that the mind is very much like a river. If it is raging along at a rapid pace, it is going to be a little more difficult to see what is contained within those RAPIDS. That is especially true if they are kicking up some muck and muddying the water which affects our internal "CLARITY"! We must figure out a way to slow it down and keep it CLEAR. This does NOT mean damming it up. It can be moving fast and still be clear. What I am saying is that we can establish a vantage point from ABOVE to be ever watchful regardless of the speed / turbidity or the river. From this elevated level we can see into the water. Being able to look WITHIN the river shows us where the river is turning. We can see the rocks & sometimes boulders that are causing the water to be so turbulent. Being ABOVE IT, vs. IN IT, is the beginning of that process, and it is a much more powerful position to observe from "REAL TIME". We can SEE, HEAR and even FEEL with exceptional CLARITY as the river moves amongst and tries to go around these "obstacles" within, one way or another in the moment. That is where we can SEE the day's events happening from that overseer perspective, unafraid and unattached, just AWARE, observing. This is that vantage point ABOVE MIND, not stuck and trapped IN IT. From this vantage point, we are the proverbial TIGER waiting to pounce on its prey, the lessons are continuously provided, moment by moment... courtesy of the selves as they work their magic in the moment and do what they do, provide lessons. Over and over again, they bob and weave, as the EGO and it's "self" generated THOUGHTS try to push and pull the river. It is fascinating to watch a river, is it not? The EGO, once seen in this way, is equally entertaining with its remarkable maneuvers and its cunning manipulations. BE WATCHFUL....it is a true education. Watch the ego mind from ABOVE! Look WITHIN!

KEEP THE WATER CLEAR w/ PRESENCE and SEPARATION!

BE WATCHFUL, FROM ABOVE!

That's the overseer, the watcher. Detach, this is what creates the separation need-ed to see what we need to see, WHEN we need to see it. The reason is because we are FREE TO SEE, PRESENTLY from above the level of thought.

BE FREE TO SEE!

Create the separation, ELEVATE...NOW!

The idea behind this freedom concept and being the instrument of change idea is that we must be aware enough to know that we are NOT free and NOT even aware enough to be the instrument first. We are not present, or going against the FLOW, not changing, not even conscious a lot of the time. I know that sounds rather obvious but knowing that we lack the ability to change the vantage point because we are essentially lost in thought or resisting / avoiding something is a key revelation. Fighting against or trying to dam up a raging river is not only counterproductive, but it also takes a ton of ENERGY. Doing this makes the battle even MORE difficult because we lack the energy to use the skill. The river has drained it because we are mentally fighting against current events and THOUGHTS in resistance / avoidance modalities. Changing the perspective dis-empowers the little selves, their thoughts and attachments are revealed, which further EMPOWERS the higher "SELF". That means powerful insights and an education that builds on itself in a seemingly parabolic fashion. It is also providing more resources exponentially as energy is preserved more rapidly with each lesson. Like that proverbial snowball rolling downhill. It's gaining speed and bulk. The higher "SELF" is gaining SPEED and SMARTS, a true education and SKILL that is useful and progressively beneficial not only to the person who gains this ability but everyone around them. It's something that they can't help but share, it's just too good, and too much fun to not share. How can we possibly keep this to ourselves, it is insanely powerful. I can't even imagine life without it. Once seen, it can't be unseen, it just keeps getting better with practice and skill as we enhance our own abilities to maintain this presence. When people can't see though, it is frustrating to try to explain...that is why I belabor points sometimes, because I truly with all my heart want it to be understood, at a depth of understanding that is unequivocal. To make it experiential requires practice though, and lots of it. No matter how focused we are, it still seems like we miss stuff. Speed enhances the skills we are working on. Once known and understood, the how of it all can be handled faster and faster...much more efficiently using less energy because one of the biggest clogs has been un-clogged...resistance. Once resistance is seen and the river is allowed to flow again, the river speeds up. As the river picks up pace,

WE NEED TO STEP UP FASTER, we need to OBSERVE faster, process faster, ACT faster. HOW? With awareness and separation, ELEVATION...seeing from above.

There is another angle to try that may enhance this functionality as well: How about as we are seeing from above, we sort of part thoughts. Hypothetically, let's say we can separate the thoughts or the streams of thoughts, like a virtual A/B testing scenario, now there's a concept. As a biblical example, **MOSES** was able to **Part the SEA**[5]! How cool is that? I believe that to be symbolism also, whether a river or a Sea, **we must part the river of thought in the mind to be able to SEE and HEAR** more effectively. This creates the separation we need. That ability leads us to freedom, just as Moses led the way to freedom. The key is seeing the mind from a perspective that allows us to see where we are NOT FREE, and why. We have the keys, and the ability, we must use the skill. To me, it's not as much between thoughts, it is more like from ABOVE thought all together. From this perspective though, it can be seen as sequential time slots in a way... once it is broken down. This can't be seen though if we are trapped in the river of thought at that same level. So, getting elevated for some perspective, above the normal "level" of thought is key. That is the vantage point that works for me. It is kind of elevated, and behind, like a bird's eye view. For me, that works. It may be slightly different for you, just try to use a heightened awareness to adjust the perspective in order to enhance your "IN-sight" as you are watching the mind, looking within. We need to FREE our "selves" from the ego's incessant attachments to thoughts as it weighs them and judges them. We can do that by being above the thoughts generated by the ego, watching. But it's not only watching, it is SEEING THROUGH them. This vantage point not only creates the separation, but it also generates a level of transparency so that we can see what they are up to, their schemes, or schematics relative to the scenarios they are projecting /re-acting to. Their motives & DRIVERS are translucent like the river, we can see what is STEERING them, diverting them, stopping them, where they slow down and speed up. This is the way out of the "dark" in the eye of the storm so to speak, leading to FREEDOM. Just as Moses led the way to freedom, however, the higher "SELF" is shining the light in the darkness, shedding light on the lower "selves" and learning the associated lessons by processing that "intel" from above. The higher "SELF" literally sees what's going on inside us as the storms are moving through us real-time, now and now, and now. That is how education and understanding happen so quickly. Awareness, as described, sees ALL! These internal selves can put on quite a show. It is entertaining, for sure

Speaking of storms, if I were to intentionally insert myself into a storm, to be sort of safe within the storm, but I could see what was going on from a better vantage point, where would that be? To me, it would be in the eye of the storm, because that's the calm place in the center. Seems like a good place to be, to see, but why? From that vantage point the storm would literally be all around me, I could totally see EVERYTHING! That's what I WANT! But that's typically not what the ego wants, and not what it does. Not without some direction anyway!! The ego tends to resist and / or avoid storms by running or hiding, going around it vs. facing it head on. We close our eyes, don't want to see things that disturb us, so we put our head under the proverbial pillow. That's NOT a great way to see a way THROUGH the storm, which is what we need to see. We need a GUIDE to be above these storm clouds watching as the thunder & lightning clash. We need to pay even CLOSER attention to the swirling winds as they start to move things around inside of us. This is how we learn, by paying attention to these fierce internal clouds as these storms start brewing inside the MIND. We remain highly alert, and see when they start bumping into each other, as well as how the many external forces impact us and how that plays into the whole internal light show going on. By staying present through the friction & conflict, agitated and maybe even fearful, we keep our eyes WIDE OPEN so that we can see all of these internal dynamics play out from start to finish. Wide awake and fully aware from high above the various winds & penetrating rains, we remain watchful as emotions, and energy emerge, escalate, peak and then dissipate. High and dry, from far above the eye of the storm, we maintain our steadfast position as the observer of all that's going on WITHIN, calm and unaffected by the storm beneath & within us. That is how we can remain detached and unaffected, seeing every detail and taking notes as these massive waves of emotion rise and fall within the mindscape.

Whether we see thoughts and clusters of thoughts as clouds, or waves, the point is that we SEE THEM. As waves, awareness allows us to see them as thoughts within thought waves, and waves of thoughts. Some of these can move a lot of water...that's why we see waves of emotions. Sometimes we even see swells of waves and even huge TIDES that can be emotionally overwhelming. This is one methodology that can be used to attain and maintain detachment or NON-attachment. In a momentary lapse mentally, it also offers us an opportunity to reel our "selves" in, maybe after a deep breath, as an example. It is the separation that accounts for, enables, and highlights the IN-sights and growth opportunities. The same is true with storms WITHIN, we see the clouds from above, AS THEY FORM!

One way or another, we need to see what's happening within as the storms show up in our lives. A storm can make it really dark, so we need a light in that darkness. I surely hope you can use the light of awareness to find the door / gate I refer to so often in order to see these opportunities. It requires TRUST and FAITH combined with the light of awareness to highlight them. We MUST get to, and BE IN THE MOMENT because the alternative is that we are in the past or the future, and that essentially means in the dark. What needs to be seen is HIDDEN from view because the time thieves got us again, the ego "selves". It's like two cars driving past each other on the same road but at the moment they pass each other on that road, there is a barrier of some kind, like a tunnel wall, or bridge so they'll never see each other as they pass by. They are either blocked from view, go over or under each other and are unseen. There needs to be a "flash of IN-sight" where this meeting IN the mind happens, where these "selves" see each other, but from a higher "SELF" awareness perspective. In other words, not a CLASH of insight from within the battle (internal conflict), but seeing the whole thing from above and untouchable, unaffected...not taking sides. AWARE, but unattached. With NON-attachment comes balance...because now the emotions are not involved to carry us away or distract us. So, with massive awareness from above, we "See the light" from above, just at the right moment, which is right when the lightning strikes...cloud meets cloud & BOOM, huge flash of IN-sight shedding light on everything inside of us that is currently on the mind screen super bright and highlighted!!!

By the way, this elevation tends to CALM the emotional tides / storms just by the nature of the elevation and separation. This also adds to our ability to see more clearly. The goal is to get to and through the door, the gateway to NOW isolated and FREE from the "selves" and all that weighs on them (Their attachments)!! The narrow gate is right after the past, and right before the future and we need to see it NOW on that razors edge in TIME! Could I say outside of time? It is the separation between us and the promised land. FREEDOM is on the other side of the gate/door. Part the sea of thought right up to the gate and monitor the gate from above AND within. The "selves" are only a step behind, and we are faster now. We absolutely MUST be faster to have choice. That's my take anyway. In this progression, we see the ego "selves" on the precipice of the moment when they try to steal it. With this super heightened awareness & focus from above with this amazing vantage point and access control, they can't, because we see it happening and can interject. So, instead of the "selves" stealing the show and our TIME slot, we maintain our presence, NOW. Here and NOW is where / when we have CHOICE!

CHOICE IS AVAILABLE...NOW!

WE MUST BE IN THE MOMENT, MENTALLY!

That means NOT in the past, and NOT in the future, from a mental mindset perspective. The only place where change happens is in the moment, NOW! We must be there watching, within, and seeing the internals as they are stirring, brewing, escalating in tone and the emotions kick up a notch. This is what creates the internal clouds, and as they draw in more moisture, and energy, that's what makes these dark clouds dark, but now we see it. As we see these dark clouds forming and then bump into each other, it creates these flashes of IN-sight as the lightning strikes. That is why it is so important that we figure out a way to get there, to the moment, and then STAY there so we can watch our "selves" IN THE MOMENT! Internal conflict is these "selves" bumping into one another and where they bump into life externally. The moment is where we see these "selves" show up IN THE STORM. Heck sometimes they are the storm. With awareness and presence, we allow our higher SELF to beat them to the punch. By showing up to NOW ahead of them, we make new decisions, NOT STORMY ones. Some of these decisions can be very impactful, life changing choices that truly change our direction and the elevation of our lives. We elevate our life by elevating our "SELF" (higher SELF). These can be major turning points, and / or BIG momentum swings for us. We must maintain our presence, particularly through life's many storms and not put our head under the pillow. These are the moments when the "selves" take us over., we are at their mercy, powerless. Not anymore, right? Eyes wide open!

Our future is at stake each and every moment. Pay attention to the storms in the mind, they are typically lower "self" generated and then further fed with their emotional attachments to personalized outcomes and NEEDS. Many of these are anchored to the past, others can be mighty tempting invitations to very alluring or frightful futures. These are very impactful "storms". These internal past / future & present clouds are bumping into each other in the exact moment of NOW. Unfortunately, a lot of the time, we are unconscious, not paying attention to how that affects the mind / body. We get snared, ambushed, tempted, tricked, enticed, attracted, seduced, trapped, by all manner of ego related desires, wants & needs. These can be activated by all kinds of things; they generate storms / disturbances which arise within us as annoyance, frustration, anger, impatience, etc... Lots of conflicting emotions STIR us into these stormy battles. We fight them, and they fight back internally as we look forward. They build up energetically and tend to climax at a decision point. The conclusion, assuming we are present to see it is generated IN THE MOMENT when we are decidedly CHOOSING "pleasure seeking" vs "pain avoidance". THAT is what determines our magnetism and can bring out patterned or "automated" responses. These determine our FATE, and IT HAPPENS FAST. These can be mighty forces that draw the mind INTO the future and KEEP us there longer than we should stay there because we need to be PRESENT to make the decisions that get us to the preferred future, not the other way around. Want vs don't want. Either way, we can't have TRUE CHOICE if it is pre-determined by some kind of internal automation generated by an unconscious mind (the selves).

That is where faith comes into play and acts as the TIME buffer to protect us from the time thieves (the ego selves). We need this protection to STAY consistently PRESENT when real time decisions are being made by our highest and BEST SELF! If we get the automated response generated by the storm, NOTHING CHANGES! We need to be present with massive awareness, hyper focus, and intense concentration in these critical moments to make decisions IN THE MOMENT! That is the difference between ACTION and RE-action. RE-actions are generated by the ego and its attachments. NEW ACTIONS are where change takes place, PRESENTLY. That's fleeting, a nanosecond...a blink of the eyes and its GONE! Pay very close attention. Did you make the decision as your BEST "SELF" or did one of the lower "selves" step in and take the mind over in that moment?

MAINTAIN PRESENCE, with FAITH!

Succumbing to fear, desire, emotions and the "selves" is putting us in the past or future relative to time. That is the "time-lock" when we can become a prisoner of the mind. If we are caught up with some level of attachment and that "captivation" takes us away mentally, then we are not present. We are in fact, LOCKED OUT of that moment in TIME! Mentally we are in one way, or another shackled to the past or tethered to the future. Time is the bandit, and its accomplice is the lower "self".

The future is coming, FAST! So, let's play this out and understand the vantage point from within the mindscape. If we are "attached" to and envisioning the future, then tomorrow's illusion is on the mind screen. That's NOT being consciously awake and aware PRESENTLY. In fact, it is far from presence, and we have no choice.

If I am living my life with super ridiculous awareness, I am seeing outwardly / experientially as I walk down the street, float down this river, or whatever else (an external view). As that happens, I am also watching thoughts as I move forward in TIME (an internal view). This is all happening at the same time. So, we are seeing from above internally, and OUTWARDLY as well, externally. That **IS** the overarching presence It's a sort of double vision, with this level of awareness and I am SEEING from the central part of my mind as the overseer of the mind, seeing literally everything from this amazing vantage point. I am watching ALL that is going on from this fun perspective, this wonderful, dreamy place... virtually UNTOUCHABLE (detached from the thoughts themselves). It's kind of like "I" as the higher SELF could reach in there and grab a thought, pick it up, spin it around and look at it from different angles while truly assessing it in the moment to see what it is doing to me and / or for me at the same time. That level of IN-sight also offers the perspective of foresight in that now it knows experientially what that inner "attitude" of thoughts is likely to produce relative to outcomes. This is the equivalent to waves of thoughts and swells / tides of waves. "I" can also see those around me / situational details contextually. As I see my thoughts of the future, I also see the worn patterned thinking which puts me in the past, my memories, TIME! Who occupies the future and / or the past as far as space goes in the mind? The ego "selves" right"? And what do the selves do? They fight for what they want, like soldiers. I can see them fighting for what they want...AMONGST THEMSELVES in the mind. Yikes! They are pushing and pulling Me in different directions. They all want to stay and continue to be ME, so they fight for what they want, like soldiers or warriors...THEY ARE DETERMINED TO GET IT TOO!! These little ego "selves" (Silly, naïve, uneducated children in some cases) are in the future and the past, IN ILLUSION LAND. In fact, when they don't get what they want what do they do? They cry and make a fuss, just like little children, arguing, carrying on, acting out...justifying, and clamoring for attention. Meanwhile, where / when are we mentally? NOT PRESENT!

So, where is the answer, where does change take place? In the MOMENT, right? NOW! Once we see them and the storm clouds that they bring with them, we simply leave the little "ego" selves behind. With all their little wants and "needy" demands, along with all their shenanigans, manipulations & tirades we listen, consider their perspectives, understand them, and then leave them at the gate. The past "selves", the future "selves", and all of their incessant attachments are let go, left behind, dismissed once and for all. That's freedom. The dark clouds dissipate, and as a result they are not bumping into anything. No clouds, no storm. POOF it's GONE! Clear skies, sunlight...a breath of fresh clean revitalizing and energizing optimistic air. So fresh you can almost taste it. It is then that we have access to the moment because we are not stuck in that thing called time, LOCKED OUT of the moment by that virtual wall the selves create when they are stuck in a mind illusion(time)!! We have gained access to the moment, REALITY...in the moment, NOW... where it all happens. NOW, we are positioned extremely well, opportunity meets possibility in a state of mind that is OPTIMIZED and MAXIMIZED, full of hope, and possible change in my opinion, permeable to the moment and its needs. We BECOME truly brilliant because we can see all the information, a complete data set, nothing is partially omitted / no blocked details due to unconsciousness. All of the options are laid out in front of us, seen, absorbed, processed, understood and available. Undistracted, and focused we are FREE to CHOOSE amongst these AMAZING options, our highest and best choice. RING the FREEDOM BELL in the MOMENT with peace of mind. Change takes place at that moment, when we arrive there because that is the only place where choice is possible. We must listen and HEAR. We must look and SEE. The vantage point MUST change to see this way. IMHO. NOW is how with elevation & separation which allows IN-SIGHT! LOOK WITHIN, this is how.

Credit to the Scorpions for their song "Winds of Change". Years ago, I played this song over and over and over again conceptualizing this vantage point in my mind. The song, in my opinion, explains this mind angle extremely well with symbolism and it was very impactful for me to see it this way. Not only that, but it's also a great song. As they say in the song: **"The winds of change blow straight into the face of TIME!"**[6] We can use this incredible perspective to BREAK FREE. The time lock is a prison of sorts and it is a place / time that we visit "unconsciously" because without awareness we don't realize we go there, nor do we realize that we have the key to let our "selves" OUT! The key is having enough presence of mind / awareness to snap us back into the moment of NOW! With presence, we ring the freedom bell in the moment. Presence is attained and maintained with FAITH! This detaches us from the time lock that the "selves" and their future outcome-oriented attachments create.

I encourage you to arrive in the moment with eyes wide open, and ears with which you can listen and hear with exceptional clarity, as well as senses that are dialed up and tuned in to feel with every ounce of your being. It makes all the difference. With this skill, I hope that you are ringing your own freedom bell, NOW, BEING in the moment, FREE to see, hear and feel. This will also heighten your intuition.

Notable, if we find a way to get to the moment, that "secret door", we can ring that freedom bell, OURS! It is our FREEDOM that's at stake, claim it! We do that by waking up, with PRESENCE, we gain peace of mind because we can finally SEE and HEAR from that new perspective, free from the "selves". Freedom offers CHOICE, to choose new thoughts and / or a new direction, not one that is dictated by a mind that is stuck, frozen, or operating from patterns and programs. These can predetermine our outcomes, which is what we need to see. That all seeing perspective is THE SKILL we have been working on...and quite possibly, that just may be the change we needed if the opportunity is seized. Just what we needed, right when we needed it. Life happens FOR US, not to us, right? We see this OVER and OVER again as we watch from above. We see the flashes of IN-sight via the lightning strikes within, in the moment. Momentary glimpses that provide an education with vast far-reaching consequences. We must be awake and PRESENT, being watchful to SEE and gain the IN-sights.

With all the lights on from the flash, an almost overwhelming display of brightness shining light on everything around us and within us, we can literally see the content & context. We get the complete picture, inside and out. As we exit the past and the present is arriving, we see the whole thing unfolding right in front of the wave of time. SO, the millisecond that we arrive in to NOW, we CAN seize the moment assuming one very important detail. That detail is as follows: at that exact millisecond we are entering the moment, we MAINTAIN our presence vs being DRAWN into the FUTURE, skipping over and through the moment and missing it with unconsciousness no matter how momentary that blink of an eye happens. VERY POWERFUL! We must not miss the moment. With our freedom and PRESENCE, we can ALLOW... we can be an instrument, which changes all the "TIME". We need to find a way to BE an instrument of CHANGE, NOW, for our "selves"!! It's the ME! I need to change! Without growth, and learning, or getting the lessons provided... we are a more primitive instrument, just as depicted in the song **"winds of change"**[7]! Of course, that primitive instrument may not sound that good and time is fleeting. Ha-ha. We just need to be tuned in a little bit to be able to play better music. Changing our "tune" requires presence. That means being able to hear and see the guidance in the moment and then we would be able to CHOOSE to play a different tune, a GOOD ONE! The universe, or GOD is showing the way in the moment, we need to tune our instrument, the BODY / MIND so that we can see, read, hear, feel and play it out. We can **BE THE INSTRUMENT**! Find the door to the moment...and then we can be the change we wish to see in ourselves and the world because we are FREE to receive the brilliant guidance that's available NOW! Basically, we see the notes being played and have learned to read the music ahead of "TIME", the one called the future. That's faith "exposed". All the internals are seen. It's beautiful...all of it. Enjoy the music...PLAY! While playing, watch the interplay of the vast number of forces that are affecting everything. Everything affects everything...it is AMAZING! What a symphony...

Recommended Chapter Task:

Watch the river of thought from above as a teaching mechanism and enjoy it. It is an exceptional, and sometimes comical opportunity to learn, process, grasp and understand the "selves", (the little "Me's") and the ego vantage points that tend to "BLIND US", turn us, stop us, start us, scare us, get us excited, overwhelmed, sad, glad, etc... That's the music they are playing...HEAR IT, read it, LISTEN, understand it and LEARN from it. It's actually a fun way to learn in this discovery mode. It is less stressful from this stance; we can be entertained & educated at the same time. That's a win-win. We need to just pay attention to what we see and hear and work hard to assimilate as much as possible from everything WITHIN. Always be on the lookout for a new aha moment as the "selves" are trying to STEER towards or away from what they want / don't want. At a minimum, it should inspire a lot of chuckles and grins, even a smirk or two once in a while. It is a comedy show sometimes. As we see familiar patterns, it is kind of like reading an educational book, we learn more the second or third time we see it than the first. In fact, we see it faster too. Each time, this higher "SELF" perspective gains an IN-sight or two from listening and / or watching. BE WATCHFUL! The same applies to music, we hear more WITHIN that music as we see it or hear it "played" over and over again. That's the vantage point. We listen, watch, see and hear as the "selves" play their music. As they play, our internal "tune" changes and we see / feel it. That tune translates to attitudes, demeanors, and they change our overall state which affects our magnetism. Our magnetism affects our "attractor factor" and that determines our outward results. The internals affect the externals. Our internal music generates our life and our outcomes, and this can change lightning fast...as our life moves, and we move through it. See, feel, and hear with this more discerning oversight to potentially get a better understanding of these underlying themes as life happens and as we experience it with this higher level of awareness & presence. Often this might indicate a different meaning vs just the surface level views. This will show us the cover emotions that may be hiding something that lies a little deeper within our core. There may be more substance to them, underneath the surface of these "covering" emotions. These are the emotional distractions that take us out of the moment which keep us from true "IN-sight" via presence from above. That's what the ego does, and it is quite good at it, a specialist. Possibilities are endless of course, as all the internal "drivers" of thought reveal them "selves"...and of course, all the various "out there" possibilities are also affecting this charade. Have fun with this. Let it lead wherever it leads, hopefully that means to a new level of freedom. By all means, stay out of the time-lock, DO NOT become a prisoner of the MIND courtesy of the ego "selves".

Freedom is earned, not by avoiding the battles, or resisting them, but by fully engaging with the storms. We enter them willingly, with massive awareness from above, watching with IN-sight. LOOKING WITHIN! That's not to say we should be out there picking fights; the battles are WITHIN. Be watchful and look within for these life changing insights, They are always delivered right on "TIME"

STAY PRESENT!

Watch the internal music as it is playing and be amazed at life and what it produces.

The amazing thing about this higher level of watchfulness is that we see where we are bumping into and creating our own limitations. The underlying beliefs are EXPOSED! The storylines & subscriptions we are living out based on habits, laziness, comfort, and / or some level of unconsciousness truly come to life. It is as if they jump off our mental screens with this enhanced level of focused awareness for us to see in full color and highlighted in a way that is quite remarkable. Once you see it, you can't unsee it...it's certainly an experience to behold. It's like living in a constant state of amazement. Just being able to see our limitations as we are living life is extremely powerful.

So, let's talk about LIMITATION vs Open ended BELIEF, TRUST and GUIDANCE.

Hack Your Reality
7 Days to Unbreakable Faith & Limitless Potential.

Are you tired of feeling stuck, limited by fear and doubt? Do you dream of living a life of unshakeable confidence and limitless possibilities?

What if you could unlock the power of faith, not as a vague religious concept, but as a practical skill that you can use to transform your life starting today?

Warning: May Cause Spontaneous Enlightenment.
(Side Effects: Joy, Confidence, & Ridiculous Success).

That's exactly what "The 7-Day Faith Accelerator Program" is designed to do. This isn't just another empty promise – it's a powerful system, based on the principles found in The "F" Word: Faith book, that will help you:

• Identify and dismantle limiting beliefs that are holding you back.
• Master the art of forgiveness to release the past and create space for a brighter future.
• Cultivate unwavering presence to experience the power of the NOW moment.
• Become the "Over-seer" of your thoughts and take control of your inner dialogue.
•Connect with your "Higher SELF" and make decisions that align with your true values.

Ditch the Doubt Demons
The 7-Day Faith Reboot
That Will Transform Your Life!

Imagine waking up each morning with a sense of purpose and excitement, knowing that you have the power to create the life you truly desire. Imagine effortlessly overcoming challenges and setbacks, because you have unshakeable faith in yourself and your abilities.

Get Your Copy
TheFWordFaith.com

FAITH: Not Just a Word.

It's a Superpower. Unleash Yours in 7 Days.

This is your opportunity to break free from the chains of doubt and fear, and to step into a life of limitless potential. This isn't just for people who feel "spiritual". This is for anyone who feels they have untapped potential. This is for YOU.

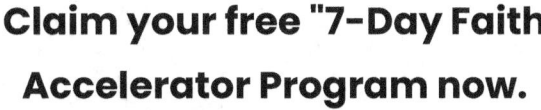

Claim your free "7-Day Faith Accelerator Program now.

• Daily exercises and activities that are easy to follow and implement.

• Guided journaling prompts to help you deepen your understanding and integrate your insights.

• Proven mind hacks to reprogram your subconscious and eliminate negative thought patterns.

Get Your Copy TheFWordFaith.com

6

USING FAITH TO UN-LIMIT OUR "SELVES"

I N LIFE, STUFF HAPPENS fast, sometimes lightning fast. So, how can we remain consistently positive, productive, peaceful & secure in a state that is balanced, stable and FREE to make effective, loving and profitable decisions to stay afloat in this crazy world? That's a tall task when there are so many distractions in the world today. Day in and day out, it is a barrage of data, and we are constantly being fed more and more propaganda, it seems. ANSWER: PRESENCE, with 100% trust and 100% faith, IN THE MOMENT. This is key because it offers us a vantage point from which we are completely FREE, balanced & unattached with clear vision, and so we literally see potentiality emerging REAL TIME. This vantage point, with presence UN-limits the potential selves and ACTIVATES the highest "SELF" as us REAL-TIME, moment by moment. From the overseer position, we can see where we are about to get in our own way, so we don't. Instead, we GROW into our BEST SELF by taking new actions extremely fast with a mind that is so nimble that we amaze our "selves". Tell me that's not powerful. It's like a giant vacuum that sees the storm clouds brewing and just by understanding the drivers of the formation of the clouds and what is blowing them around, it sees the "causes". By a stupendously fast & miraculous assimilation process, this understanding happens whereby the SELF "gets it" and sees the reason the dark clouds are dark. By process of understanding, in fractions of a millisecond, it sucks all of their darkness into this giant dissipation machine from above. As a result, the dark clouds simply disappear, IMMEDIATELY. GONE. We are good to go instantaneously. POWERFUL understanding is assimilated in a lightning-fast manner as we see this way. That's what happens when presence is attained and maintained.

So, instead of accumulating negative emotions and allowing it to build these internal storms, we are constantly just "shaking them off" and maintaining our presence as an imperturbable state of mind. That's what my coaches used to advise when I had made a bad play or something, to **"shake it off"**. In other words, don't let any negative thoughts get into your head, land in there, and start brewing into frustration or anger which will weigh on you and bring you down for the next play. DROP IT, let it go NOW. Stay in the game, mentally, here...NOW. Instantly dissipating life's negativities is truly uplifting, it's like they never really land on us at all. If they don't land on us, not only do they not accumulate for some highly negative future blow up, but these "stormy" unconscious internalized attitudes can't generate negative behaviors or further mistakes / errors because they didn't create the unconsciousness to begin with. The "foul state" that could have happened didn't happen which would have caused us to miss the next moment or enter it with a crappy attitude which attracts more of the same negative stuff.

SHAKE IT OFF

This means we are arriving to and into the next moment FREE from that "bad play" or mistake, and we are open & ready, fully awake and aware, ready for the next play without the unconscious "attitude". The attitude is what causes the "BLIND SPOT" via a lack of presence. So, by losing the attitude, we regain consciousness, and we are capable of letting it go. Letting it and the past go allows presence. We enter the new moment focused with an "empty cup" as opposed to being full of our "selves" and all of their attitude problems which are the result of the internal storm that was just averted. We are ready to be filled up with whatever is needed in the moment, ready to take a NEW action, with a blank slate, make a great NEW play...and WIN. That's a true victory over one's "self". If we really want to master the "selves" as this higher version of "ME" then this would be the actual moment where we could and MUST take a really negative attitude, stabilize, re-optimize, and LET IT GO! Miraculously, at that moment, we are able to insert a balanced and redirected and maximized mindset ready for whatever the next moment has in store for us.

We have to be aware enough to see this way first, as well as be flexible and adaptable "state wise" in order to be receptive to the guidance that is available in the moment. (The still small voice) As we are successfully guided over time, in ongoing moments, it builds <u>TRUST</u> within us that it will continue to happen. First, we make our highest "SELF" available in the moment (empty cup). Then, as we maintain our presence, we get the IN-sights that are available and needed IN the moment. (filled up) As we continue to see this process unfold and we are delivered what we need, as we need it, we begin to believe in it. Belief evolves into TRUST. Trust means faith was used to activate it, or build it up, right? It is at a bare minimum a component of faith. As we are "delivered" exactly what we need in the moment and we see it happen with oversight, feel it internally, this trust factor evolves into a "knowing" experientially over the course of many moments. It builds on this BELIEF factor that we always get what we need which is what creates and reinforces the "knowing". This "belief" is not fixed though, it is ever evolving like an understanding of a process. The "knowing" is a knowing that we always get what we NEED! It may not always be what we want, but it will be what we need and as a result of this understanding, we become more trusting, if you will. Trust becomes more trusting. More trust means more FAITH, right? If we have that, then where is doubt, worry or fear of the alternative? It doesn't exist, not in our mind anyway. THAT IS BELIEF which is essentially unwavering FAITH or KNOWING!! It's a progression. The "clouds" or dark thoughts / life's situations don't seem so dark anymore...they begin to dissipate or weigh on us less dramatically and quite honestly, we really look at them differently. At a minimum, they are not quite as intimidating as they once were. We are looking at them with different eyes...the ones that can truly SEE! Over time, this means we can remain more balanced and stable throughout life's storms because we are taking them on head on, by choice fully involved, balanced and ready. Many of these EXTERNAL storms dissipate quite quickly as a result of this assimilation process as described in paragraph #1 in this section. No internal storm means that the external storm is handled with grace under pressure. Mainly because the pressure relative to these attachments and controlling outcomes has been released in favor of 100% FAITH & PRESENCE!

Jesus demonstrated this principle. He had no question that life would respond to him the way that he wished it to. It responded because he never doubted! He understood and KNEW what was needed in the moment, THAT is presence! If we go into the moment "KNOWING" that whatever is needed in the moment will be provided, how can we fail? That is FAITH! 100%! When people needed food, it was provided abundantly. Fisherman needed fish; they were provided abundantly. People needed health and they demonstrated belief, it was provided, ABUNDANTLY! INSTANTLY, no doubt

"GO, it shall be done for you as you have believed."
-Jesus

Can we believe like that? When? Can we "BECOME" our best "SELF" in this moment? That is what I like to call the GOD response, or the highest and best response to and in the moment. Can we become what is absolutely needed in the moment vs what the ego dictates? This is the difference between a RE-action, and a NEW action. We come into each moment, don't we? Do we actually see it through though? Do we actually arrive in the moment mentally focused 100% at that precise moment of NOW without a whole lot of baggage from the past and / or an itemized agenda weighing us down with a predetermined outline for outcomes set on a specific detailed future timeline? Do we arrive in the moment full of our past / future "selves" (full cup) or are we arriving with an empty cup ready to be filled. This matters BIG TIME because that determines whether we are getting through the gate with the light of awareness shining in all its glory on all that we need to see. (The guidance.) Pay attention, pay very close attention, with laser focus, massive amounts of awareness, HUGE amounts of energy...NOW, and NOW...and NOW. With these new eyes, with these new ears...in the exact moment of NOW, without being distracted by our "selves", we can see and hear the TRUTH. They say that the truth will set us free. I would say that we see the truth because we ARE FREE...to see it. We must be FREE to SEE! This actually helps us to understand WHY:

The truth sets us free because we are free to see it.

It is mainly because we are no longer blinded by our "selves" in the "TIME-LOCK" and a prisoner of the mind. Then, and only THEN, once we are FREE, we can see and we can BECOME what is needed moment by moment as the fully comprehended reality of this moment is clearly visible and taken in. That is when we step into our POWER! NOW! Now is always how! We become what is NEEDED! The term selflessness comes to mind and often that is the difference. Selflessness vs selfishness. The ego thinks that it is all about me, but it is in GIVING that we receive. If we can find a way to give our BEST SELF to every moment...WOW, the possibilities We receive what we are, and that is another reason why being attentive to SEEING what we are becoming as we are becoming it, is so important. Sometimes it is at the last millisecond that we can optimize and maximize and redirect as needed. A course correction, real- time. Real time guidance provides real time solutions. As we arrive and GIVE life our BEST "SELF", life gives back.

"self" – less – ness" = Less "self", leaving the lower selves at the gate to NOW!

In doing so, we also leave their LIMITS at the gate. Said slightly differently, when I say, I AM _____ or I AM _____. The moment we fill in the blank, we become THAT, in the MIND, and from that microsecond forward we are LIMITED to being that version of "self". So, if we are limited then what life gives back is ALSO limited. THAT is exactly what keeps us from the moment, we are locked out by time, expansion is impossible. Our cup is full, and we are full of our "selves". ON THE WAVE, at the very moment it is crashing forwards, that microsecond, between the past and the future is when the false self (former me / future me) steps into the moment, BECOMES me, and ACTS IT OUT as me for me and STEALS IT. That version of "self" is LIMITED. We need to Un-LIMIT it. First, we must SEE IT limit us by being attentive to the mind, watching. Then we must see it sooner the next time, so that we can arrive in the moment to CHOOSE differently... It's like we see that version of self TRY to step in and steal the moment and we simply don't allow it to happen. By watching attentively, we can see the progression well ahead of the choices, so that we can make new ones.

We have to see that Instead of us ALLOWING our highest and BEST "SELF" (The GOD response) to take a step forward and provide or BE the best re-sponse, we became limited by something else that former me or future me was ATTACHED to and THAT is unfortunately the response that happened in the moment. (that's the EGO re-action / response). That, once seen, is the equivalent of EDGING GOD OUT! ("EGO")

Consider it this way: The light (SUN) comes from above. The dark thoughts are the clouds that are blocking out the "light". The EGO creates the clouds. We can be watchful of these as they are created within AS the clouds are forming. We can literally see the storm brewing. With awareness we SEE as these emotional "clouds" are forming. This is what creates the internal storms. As these storms happen "TO US" we edge GOD and "CHOICE" out with our own internal cloud building software which blocks out the sunlight from above. When we begin to see things differently, it is as if the playing field has been changed as the vantage point is enhanced. When we understand that **the storms are happening FOR US** vs TO US, we begin to look at these emotional clouds with different eyes, different ears. We even feel them differently because they are not "hitting" us, landing on us, or becoming us. The perspective changes. We can then be watchful and affect this process in NEW WAYS as we see these storms shape and form us into the clouds we become. We are the storm in our unconsciousness. However, with awareness we can avert the storm, grab the lesson it provides for us, and move on. This also gives us an opportunity to preserve and redirect that amazing energy! Meanwhile, the storm simply dissipates which is our opportunity to become something NEW, make a new choice. We see where & when we create these edges, and it is at these edges where we EDGE GOD and the ability to choose OUT. With mindful awareness we can see it happen and learn the lesson vs becoming the storm. These are the lessons we learn as we inadvertently allow the ego access to the moment, which happens at the extreme EDGE of NOW, we:

EGO =

Edge

God

Out

That's when "time" is NOT on our side, and we lose our ability to CHOOSE because we are not mentally in the moment TO CHOOSE! In fact, with awareness, we see it in hindsight quite a bit before we start to see it REAL-TIME! It had us LOCKED OUT of the moment. That's the time-lock. When we are in the zone, we literally SEE IT HAPPEN on the very edge of the moment as it happens. That miniscule sliver of time is where the ego tries to edge God out (and US as the higher "SELF" too.) and so the perfect response cannot happen because we can't see it to be it. CHOICE is unavailable. Narrow is the gate, and we missed it, we got locked on the other side of the gate with the selves in their illusion called time, the future or past. The EGO won, that time. Seeing this happen is that proverbial light bulb turning on. It is shining the light on the internals that are making it happen / or NOT allowing it to happen so that we can see it faster and sooner the next time. We can then step into the next moment with a new vision, a new "SELF", and a KNOWING what must happen. We need to get better at seeing with these new eyes because we are missing many opportunities otherwise. We are missing many opportunities because we are missing many moments. Choices cannot happen if we are not present to make them.

Taking this to the next level, as we step back or UP to see this perspective, we uncover something truly insightful. These edges can be seen or felt IN ADVANCE! It's like seeing the future. We can almost "cheat" on our "selves" if you really think about it because we can see them coming. It's an unfair advantage, like counting cards, from this higher perspective because we know their tricks. In essence then, we are gaining a better stance as we enter the moment with a more balanced and neutral attitude. It's more stable as we are preparing for the "TEST". At first, this is a bit uncomfortable as we are stepping into the moment because we feel somewhat naked, identity wise. We are not only entering the unknown, but we ARE the unknown. This is a totally new experience for me, a totally new ME, and a totally new moment, so it's ALL NEW. Perspectives. The human mind doesn't like the unknown so this may take a little bit of adjustment, practice, and getting used to it. That uneasiness is quite natural at first because if you really think about this, we are truly NOT "identified" with anything. That's the nature of the empty cup and it feels weird, kind of like we are hollowed out. As described previously though, over time, faith and trust build as we are filled up and we see it happen. It becomes an experiential "knowing". We believe in it, so we **know** what we must do, leave the former lower "selves" behind at the gate (empty our cup) in order to be NEW (GROW). This is how, where, and when we **TRANSCEND THE EGO** (vs killing it) on the very edge of NOW. Semantics really. We literally leave it and the lower selves behind at the gate, in order to get present and STAY present. With presence, we have TRUE CHOICE, and we can **Edge GOD IN** and with that choice, we can grow through each experience. We edge in as the higher SELF and ALLOW the highest and best (God) response to occur through us, as us. This absolutely 100% REQUIRES faith to take the step because we are leaving all of our "selves" and what we know behind, trusting that our highest and best SELF will be "delivered" what is needed in the moment. Choice is available; however, we are no longer making the same choices that we formerly would have made by habit or unconsciousness!

After we are hollowed out like this, empty our cup, we lose, transcend, and / or grow out of our "selves", there can be a bit of a "dark night of the soul" whereby we go through somewhat of a mourning process as we are letting go of the lower selves. Fact is, we have been with these selves through thick and thin, because we WERE these selves, until we grew out of them. As this process escalates and unfolds faster and faster, we do get "hollowed out" quite quickly sometimes, for lack of a better way to describe it. Periodically, that can leave a feeling of emptiness, like "loss". It is a bit of an identity crisis and can be felt as a sense of bewilderment, loneliness, or sadness in some cases. Others, quite frankly, it is more of a "good riddens" type feeling. When we were really identified and kind of liked who we were and know we need to let go of that aspect of ourselves though, there can be episodes of a weird kind of grief. It's like who we once were, and what we once believed, and what we once wanted are just GONE, not true anymore, and we know why but it feels like it just disappeared because it happened so fast. The problem isn't acknowledgement, it is more or less a processing issue similar to losing a loved one. The higher "SELF" must step in and be the bigger SELF, presence is the key. Who I was is no longer ME! Looking backwards invites the time lock and while we know it, there are intermittent periods of reflection as we are in the process of being "filled back up". It may take a minute to regain our footing so to speak. Before that fully develops as a knowing, the human mind can feel lost and even abandoned some "times". This dark night is a much deeper subject and probably the recipe for another book at some point because there are various intricacies with it. The dark night is talked about in other contexts as well, so there are lots of caveats and many perspectives to consider. For now, please understand that we must empty our cup in order to be "delivered" and filled up. It takes faith and trust and it is a process

WITH FAITH & PRESENCE: WE ARE GUIDED!

GGITM: GOD GUIDES IN THE MOMENT!

With 100% trust, 100% faith, and 100% awareness IN THE ZONE, IN THE NOW moment, we can get out of our own way, become a better version of our SELF, and ALLOW the GOD response (the needed response via our highest and best SELF.). With choice, the "RIGHT" response is an opportunity through us for a NEW ACTION, vs a re-action. Instead of our own patterned LIMITED MIND slipping in and making the choices for us we are BECOMING NEW. Potentiality emerges through us. It happens in a lightning strike of a fraction of a second, and without being there, precisely at that moment, we are unable to make a better choice. Change can only occur NOW! LOVE is only available NOW! UNCONDITIONAL LOVE, in my opinion, is the GOD response, but when is that choice available? Can that choice be available through us? How? Answer: YES, NOW!

NOW IS HOW!

Check this out, from another spiritual philosophy, and an amazing book: "I am THAT"[8]

Nisargadatta Maharaj:

"Absolute perfection is here and now, not in some future, near or far.
The secret is in action—here and now.
It is your behavior that blinds you to yourself.
Disregard whatever you think yourself to be and act as if you were absolutely perfect
—whatever your idea of perfection may be.

All you need is courage."[9]
-Nisargadatta Maharaj

I'll add, and AWARENESS / PRESENCE, because with these implemented, fear disappears. So, technically, courage is no longer even needed when there is nothing to be fearful of! Presence solves the fear dilemma. In the beginning stages though, courage is required because the presence is not fully integrated and trusted!

"As you watch your mind, you discover your self as the watcher. When you stand motionless, only watching, you discover your self as the light behind the watcher. The source of light is dark, unknown is the source of knowledge. That source alone is. Go back to that source and abide there."
"I Am That"—pg 188"[10]
-Nisargadatta Maharaj

CAN YOU BE THAT? Didn't they call Jesus the light of the world? How bright was that? More importantly, how bright is your light? Can you see it? Be it? Share it? Is it Limited, or have you UN-limited it? What is the status of your dimmer? What % light is getting through? How do you know?

As an analogy, we need to check our dimmer switch at the gate. Our mental circuit breaker cannot be "tripped" by a trigger or anything for that matter. If it is, nothing is getting through, NO LIGHT can even get to, no less through the dimmer switch. We are giving away all our power. First, we must be the watcher and SEE, then we are the watcher and HEAR too. After a while we SEE, HEAR, FEEL and KNOW because the instructions are crystal clear. We have been guided and we become the light. Think about it, we don't need to know "ABOUT" something if we are it. Jesus was an example of a SUPREMELY bright light...the light of the world. That's not DIM. He also said that we would do even greater things than He was doing. Seriously. We need to make sure that we are not dimming our own light. We are, and now we can see where, when, how, and how much by watching the storm clouds as they are forming...WITHIN. They are creating the "darkness". These storm clouds are blocking out the light. The clouds are LIMITING what we can see, which is limiting what we can BECOME. That's the internal DIMMER affecting our magnetism, our POWER. The POWER WITHIN us is not making it through these clouds which are dark thoughts, and dark, negative patterns of thoughts. OUR LIGHT isn't getting through US. Remove the clouds and the storms dissipate which reveals the SUN that was shining all along but HIDDEN. This way OUR LIGHT can shine brightly. Did you ever hear of someone talking about the dark cloud that follows them around?

This is how to make it go away, it is a deliberate and conscious LETTING GO vs pushing on it or resisting it which just makes the clouds darker. You can't push a cloud anyway, but with a bright enough LIGHT it will evaporate. YOU ARE THAT LIGHT! See the clouds, and they basically just go "poof" and disappear which reveals this massive internal power and then the internal light shines brightly BEAMING everywhere.

BE THE LIGHT vs the potential darkness!

Darkness can mean many things and show up to challenge us in all kinds of ways. Life provides us lots of opportunities to "STEP UP" and overcome obstacles personally and professionally. When dealing with a personal challenge, and as an example, sometimes we need to deal with some fear and / or "stress" relative to that thing that is standing in our way. An obstacle of sorts, whatever it might be, shows up on our "path". Whatever it is, it represents a ceiling, or some kind of limit / challenge we have yet to get through. First, we need to stop looking at it as a roadblock and start looking at it as an opportunity for growth, one way or another. A challenge can mean "GAME ON", which changes the way we look at things and often times that means we can see a way through because we are looking at it with different eyes. So, if you want to try a different approach, try being a plane metaphorically, what does a plane do? It flies right through the clouds as if they aren't even there. Make like a plane and FLY! (Obviously not a literal suggestion, don't go jump off a tall building expecting to fly.)

What I am saying is that many of our obstacles, limitations / ceilings are a mirage, we need to walk right through them, alert, fully awake and aware with PRES-ENCE. As a plane, we would fly right through them. Some of our internal clouds are going to cause some turbulence, that's for sure. Especially in dealing with something that we have not yet overcome because it is "stressful". We know it and we see, hear, and FEEL IT too. Don't "TURN AWAY!" Don't fly around the storm. This is the moment you have been waiting for, your moment, this is YOU TIME! So, keep flying straight into the storm, eyes wide open! This is FOR YOU! Act as if you are a plane, does a plane have a choice once it is IN THE CLOUD to turn around, NO...so keep flying. Do your best to manage the bumps, and rough ride relative to the various emotions that are most definitely going to cause a stir if not outright panic / fear internally. Butterflies, shaky or sweaty hands, jitters, etc. ALL of this is NORMAL...Take one more step with faith and MASSIVE awareness paying attention to all the internals, just watch, and keep flying. On the other side of the clouds is calm, clear and stable air. The SUN shines brightly. Just make sure that as you are flying through these clouds and these internal storms are telling their stories, that you listen up so that you can hear all the "STUFF" that it is bringing up inside. This is a MAJOR BREAK THROUGH MOMENT, and it is here FOR YOU to learn a key lesson. You are about to have a breakthrough so you need to keep going so that you can BREAK THROUGH a personalized and emotionalized LIMIT! These clouds represent a ceiling or a LIMIT, and they are showing you something ABOUT YOU, an obstacle you are about to put behind you once and for all. Their story is just that, a story...by seeing the story for what it is, an ego generated illusion, that limitation / ceiling can be erased...and it IS ERASED as you fly right on through the illusionary cloud. SOAR, like an eagle or a plane Above the clouds the sun, and YOU shine brightly. It's easier to see, and the air is fresh and clean. You sure are a bright light now. The inner turbulence was overcome, and the effort was worthy of this steadfast persistence...so pat your "SELF" on the back for a job well done. This was an amazing "self" mastery moment, a victory over one's "self" and worthy of celebration. Don't look back for too long though or you will fly into something. LOL

How bright can you let your light shine? Where and when do you want to start? How? NOW of course. Just realize that your light is BRILLIANT...just remove the internal CLOUDS as you fly through them with awareness. (Limits, ceilings, negativity, etc.) Once the clouds disappear, your light shines on, BIG TIME! In addition, without the clouds interfering, things appear that were "unseen" previously. "IN-sight" and "OVER-sight" are super powerful, they allow presence. There is no other time that change can happen, NOW is the only time. It is literally NOW or never as far as change is concerned. We cannot change anything in the past, that is for certain. We also cannot change anything IN the future. We can only change things RIGHT NOW which will lead us to a potentially different or "changed" future. That future has "changed" only by a decision made by us in a previous moment. In other words, that future moment is the future moment of a NOW moment that happened before. LOL Our NOW moments are ever unfolding, and every NOW moment matters to every future moment. Hopefully that makes sense.

Our PRESENCE ability matters to our future. No doubt. We discover our highest future "SELF" as the watcher, with AWARENESS, NOW. We literally have to practice this skill and make every effort to arrive in the moment... over and over again. This may be more difficult in the early stages and require seemingly MORE energy. Seriously, it is a challenge, so keep making that effort. From a mental, emotional, energetic, and awareness standpoint, putting all the elements together requires a massive amount of focus. That level of focus requires a TON of energy, and from an operational standpoint...unfortunately, it is really hard to see it through at first. Failure happens a lot in the beginning. The BIG difference now is that we SEE IT HAPPEN! That's GOOD, not BAD...so don't get frustrated. Seeing this is AMAZING, this means more and more opportunities. This should be exciting. Seeing our own failures means GROWTH! Make every effort to see it through and it will happen more and more frequently. Successes and failures will happen. Ultimately, seeing it through will be the norm. The goal is to be the NORM in the STORM. By norm, I mean balanced & ready, completely awake, aware, focused and PRESENT. By seeing that we need to see our own failures in order to learn key lessons, it kind of takes the stress out of it, in a way. We just need to see it in a detailed, focused way, with awareness so that we can see where, and when we "erred", failed, or simply could have done better.

Until this is true for us consistently, we are more often NOT the norm in the storm. The cool thing is that we can see it when we are not. We realize this as our awareness factor kicks in and shows it to us, just moments afterwards. In fact, it amplifies the fact that most of the time we are NOT capable, NOT present, NOT aware, and NOT making it to the moment. While we are behind the wave of thought so to speak, or not in the moment, the best version of "I" (me / you)... the highest "SELF" is not making it to the critical juncture and decision (NOW)! That can really taunt us, as it is seen. We need to use that "taunt" energy to amplify, manage, and DIRECT the energy. This is productive use of "bad" energy vs the many alternatives, like allowing it to siphon off energy in frustration / anger. We need that energy, and so we learn to tap, channel and use all kinds of energy by optimizing & redirecting it to where it is needed, such as towards focus and awareness. Forgiveness of that lower "self" that I was just a moment ago allows me to recapture that energy immediately so that I can use it. More on that later...

Back to the point though. In the moment now, consistently with presence we realize that we are still getting caught mentally on the other side of the gate, shut out by time. The MIND circuit breaker got cut off at the breaker box again. It is then seen from above with awareness that when we are finally capable of arriving IN THE MOMENT to meet the moment as the higher "SELF", change can happen. Then and only then, alert to this reality and NEW possibilities, we are READY and ABLE to BECOME NEW! It is at that moment that IT, THAT...whatever you want to refer to it as meets us there. It is seen that with TRUST and FAITH, in that MOMENT it can happen, the pieces fall into place and the answers drop in our lap so to speak, from seemingly out of nowhere and the possibilities are endless. In that moment, choice is available with IN-SIGHT and GUIDANCE! We can ALLOW the best response; I call it the GOD response. You can say the universe, the powers that be, higher power, or whatever your philosophy allows. The point is that it can occur through us, and we must ALLOW it to happen through us in an instant. From inside "THE ZONE", in that moment, we can BECOME the best version of our-SELVES by allowing "THAT" to FLOW through us as we are GUIDED!

The key element to grab from that last paragraph is that the jump from the past to the future doesn't SKIP past or through the moment of NOW without our awareness. It USES AWARENESS to create that momentary presence with trust & faith in order for the "RIGHT" answer to arrive **FOR ME** in the moment as the best ME is receptive to it. It happens THROUGH us. We must "have faith", be receptive, perceptive and malleable like a chameleon and be able to transform our "selves" with speed, and agility with the guidance we receive. We become THAT which is needed and that happens NOW, there cannot be any delay. We do not have time to get caught up in processing mode because "TIME" is not on our side. It must happen NOW!

As **Nisargadatta Maharaj** states, **"I AM THAT"**[11]! (great book)

In other words, I AM what is needed right now, in this moment. I am just becoming it in every unfolding moment. I am THAT! "THAT" is ever evolving, ever changing. NOW is when that happens.

Ernest Holmes says it in a similar fashion below. Here are a few of my favorites:

"All limitations are self IMPOSED"[12] (Note: lower "self" imposed)

"Peace comes from the absence of FEAR, from a consciousness of TRUST, from a deep, underlying FAITH *in the absolute goodness and mercy, the final integrity of the universe in which we live, and of every cause to which we give our thought, our time, and our attention."*[13]

So NOW we know, and understand that to get into the ZONE, it often requires forgiveness, and to STAY in the moment with presence requires FAITH, right? That means LETTING GO of the past AND future... Let's dig deeper. If we have achieved presence and neither the past nor the future is weighing on us, then wouldn't that explain why we feel so peaceful, as described in the above paragraph? The peace in the above statement comes as a result of attaining presence because in that moment we are FREE. Having let go of the past and future, presence offers us that unique perspective that is unattached to both. Relative to the FUTURE though, and all those mischievous WANTS, what happens? Instead of fretting over it, whether that be in the desire of having or the fear of

NOT having, with FAITH and presence, we stand STRONG in the moment with a deep underlying FAITH and TRUST instead. That's HUGE!

Once seen in this manner we can see that the "stressors" are the "selves". The past selves and future selves alike each relate to things differently, but BOTH are attached to their vantage points and trying to project them constantly on the mind screens. We have to simply turn off the projector with awareness and let go. The past is somewhat easier to let go, in a way, because it already happened, so we know we can't do anything about it. The future, on the other hand, well...WANTING IS HABITUAL! It is truly a bad habit, anchored in LACK, and we are so accustomed to doing it that it takes a lot of energy and a different way of looking at things to CHANGE. Change also requires PRESENCE, being in the moment, and as we already know that is NOT a constant. We want outcomes, situations, and things...because we feel that they will make us HAPPY, so we "project" them along with our "selves" into that future and imagine the time when we either HAVE or DON'T have it. That is where and when fear and desire take us over. We become "attached" to some future outcome, or fearful of its opposite and presence is lost. In addition, the emotion that took us out of the moment is the ANCHOR which constantly proves to the mind that we don't already have it right now. When it comes to BELIEF, that's actually our "vice" because the belief is in NOT HAVING what we WANT. In fact, we know it, and with this really bad wanting habit we keep proving it to ourselves with an emphasis based in FEAR and DESIRE. With faith and trust all that goes away. That turbulent cloud called "stress" VANISHES! With a higher level of mind mastery, we let it go. PEACE at last. Calm, fresh, clean, light, and bright air is seen, felt, and experienced instead.

In the first sentence of Emerson's "The Over-Soul" he states:

"There is a difference between one and another hour of life, in their authority and subsequent effect. <u>Our faith comes in moments</u>; our vice is habitual"[14]

BRILLIANT! ...and now we are seeing this happen right in front of our own eyes!

The "VICE" is living our lives via the lower unlearned "selves" in this constant state of STRESS! Let it GO! This kind of shows us the same thing, right? BE-WARE, or be AWARE! We are being aware of our patterns and habitual responses as they become us in life. As these lower "selves" try to take us over, and become us, we see it...and that offers us an opportunity for change. These patterned selves may not be serving OUR best interests, nor the world's best interests either. Not only that, but they are stressed all the dang "TIME"! NO WONDER! That is brilliant. Seeing it happen is the key. That enables CHANGE. Lessons = growth opportunities and as we BECOME new instead of our patterned "habitual" responses, we expand, get better...GROW, faster and faster.

As human beings, we build patterns, and those patterns become us...that's a HABIT! The habit is through our unconsciousness and habitual behaviors. That is allowing these little ego selves to run the show. Our life is being controlled by them and they are having their way with us. Our habit is subscribing to the known, or what I refer to as our internal "programming", and often this is a comfort zone. Is that not the ego? So, to the extent that we have a learned response to anything, that learned response, or software "program", will represent us in the moment until we learn to step into the moment without the "support" of the habitual or "unconscious" self that wants to represent or react for us in that moment. (As the lower "selves" vs higher "SELF") **That requires FAITH**, to step out on a limb like that and BE NEW. Being new means being consciously in the UN-KNOWN vs the known. This means uncertainty, and possibly being uncomfortable, momentarily. Nerves ratchet up a notch, a little internal turbulence comes into play, the jitters, etc. and it is in these moments that we MUST be able to walk through that to become NEW! CHANGE can't happen otherwise. The internal component that enables that next step is FAITH! Faith eliminates stress, fear, desire, excitement, all of the emotions which take us OUT OF THE MOMENT and put us in some future scene, imagery, having or not having. Faith turns off the projector so we are no longer relating to the projection, we can FOCUS, IN THE NOW!

So, you might think, patterns are not an issue, we need to learn how to do things, right? So, is this good or bad? Well, both really. In the situations where learned skills are necessary, such as repetitive trade skills, life skills, routine everyday tasks etc. I'd say good, so we don't mess them up much. However, the ability to act on new information, and BE NEW, in the moment is something that the mind is generally incapable of doing consistently. Why is this? In its design, it is programmed to STOP, research, and RE-act. This is how it works, and it all happens in a FLASH, I mean really fast. So fast, in fact, that it is mostly invisible to the mind that is asleep (lost in thought), or unaware. So here is what the mind does, it arrives at the doorway to NOW and it:

1. Stops time, momentarily...while it "thinks". (Based on its own positionality, reference point, vantage point, knowledge, wants & needs.)

2. Research, while on pause, to find the closest match to the current "input" (information, situation, etc.). Just be careful here though because this is where it can get tricky. It could be a similar situational thing, a similar person that looks like this person so that you match them with someone or something that you knew "like that" in the past...and this is why we can instantly like, or not trust / not like someone and never have met them before. It can also be intuition, so be just careful here. The point is to observe and SEE with awareness that the "MIND" is trying to gather information from the PAST, so that it can use that information as a basis to RE-act as it did the last time from what it "Knows". It is just searching the mind database for the best alternative in order to:

   a. Get what it wants / needs.

   b. Avoid what it doesn't want (resistance)

       i. That is the A/B toggle, and something to be observant of. Specifically, the drivers of want vs "don't want" activate the internal gears within us and that is where the emotions get involved. So, on to step 3.

3. Using the information that it just gathered in a fraction of a second in step 2...The MIND will RE-act. RE- means acting from a previous version of our "selves", from our knowledge base or "program". A memory is stepping into the moment to act as if it were us. Again, this RE- sponse is based on a biased vantage point FROM THE PAST, perception in this case is NOT reality. It is a curve fit solution based on previous decisions that is expected to work in this one. The egoic responses.

Faith, is relative to our ability to wake up from our psychic sleep, and to be present...NOW.

The above process is SLOW, mentally. While I am aware that this is happening in fractions of a second, it is still slow relative to faith. FAITH is faster, and here's why. The first methodology, the slow road, goes like this; We are faced with an event and need to do something, the mind goes in search mode in the database to find the solution, in the past. That requires energy, and TIME to process. It takes us BACKWARDS in time, out of the moment, and then once it finds an appropriate solution, assuming it actually does find one, it comes back to the moment to "do it". Whatever that "old" pattern was, it isn't new, and it took forever to go find it. Faith mentally is already PRESENT and anchored in the moment with trust. That's why faith is faster, it is unshakable. It is already there, IN THE MOMENT! It isn't bogged down in "processing mode" nor is it caught up in "TIME" illusions. It isn't "cramming" for the test, and then bogged down with data, and then stuck in "search mode" looking in the past for answers because it KNOWS and TRUSTS they will be provided in the moment. So, the result is that it STAYS present, rather than being caught up in some illusory past or future time-loop, flip flopping incessantly in a desperate attempt, running the mind back n forth and all around to find the answer. FAITH = TRUSTING that in this next moment that is juuuuust about to happen that "I" will be delivered ALL the necessary information, data, and skill required to ACT! This is the key role for FAITH because it eliminates the "attachment" to the future. (the outcomes we want or NEED as the ego.). Whether that is driven by desire or fear, we recognize it, wake up, remain conscious and see it through, instead of getting "locked up" in time and delivering a "fixed" or static predetermined response to the moment. Instead of being diverted, or locked in that illusion in the future mindscape, we are leaving that in the cinema and arriving to the moment without that egoic baggage that the "selves" bring with them. This SKILL needs to be practiced to become experiential. The answers are IN THE MOMENT, but we cannot drag our former or future "selves" into the moment and BE NEW at the same time, it's impossible. We are either mind **FULL** of the past, or mind **FULL** of the future, or we are PRESENT, NOW! Mentally, we cannot be in two places at once which in this case means two "times" simultaneously. To open the mind, we need to be free of those "selves" and be NEW, presently. Being New means being new, it's UNKNOWN, unknowable. We have become un-identified with the "selves". That can be uncomfortable, that's why it requires FAITH!

Sometimes that means we need to OBSERVE emotions as we progress through the moment...FEAR is a good example of this. Observe means watch carefully from above, SEEING with a level of detachment. Being unattached to whatever is driving it is the key to SEEING fear vs BEING fear. Observation mode, seeing emotions vs being caught up in the emotions (in time: future or past) is super empowering. There is a big difference in what we see by being above the cloud called fear watching its edges as they bump into life and other clouds within! Fear is just one of many storm clouds within that we need to be watchful of and it is amazing what it reveals as we are getting more consciously aware of its lessons. The lessons are provided FOR US as we bump into life, fully awake and aware of the internals WITHIN us as they are activated which translates into waves of thoughts and possibly some physical trepidation as well. The clouds and internal patterns within form and sometimes start to escalate before they are SEEN! Once seen, we simply dissipate them with awareness and skill as we educate the lower "selves" and move on, all the better for the lesson. As long as we are energized, awake, and aware, we are able to do this early in the process and the potential storm never actually becomes a storm. We neutralize the clouds with resolve which requires skill, awareness and PRESENCE! Pinpoint timing can often be the make-or-break element.

The answers to life's problems, or obstacles arrive in the moment. We resolve them by dissolving them as we learn lessons with presence and awareness in the moment. We are always given exactly what we need. Call it GOD, angels, the universe, your spirit guide, or whatever else. I call it GOD. GOD lives in the eternal present. God is omni**present** and omnipotent. Trustworthy? I would think so, I challenge you to take a chance and see...and you MUST arrive in the moment to find out! That is why faith is required...and also why we must know what faith is **experientially**!!!! Unfortunately, our habitual nature is to flip flop between the past and the future searching for "ANSWERS"! That, of course, depends on which one of the ego selves we are captivated by and what that ego self is focused on, which is carrying the weight of that moment. Our prior selves want to step up and react from our past, or programming(knowledge). Our future selves, our projections, which don't exist yet, also want to step up and act on our behalf and that would be based on their vision in the future. The ego wants and needs are driving this. That's what throws us into the time-lock. Depending on where our focus and energy is, which is being driven by the ego attachments, that will determine which version of our "self" will arrive at the gate. You SEE the problem with this right? In both cases, we are seeing an illusion, a virtual projection onto the mind screen of that past/future. The EGO and its' "attachments". Depending on how driven the ego is, that will determine the level of attachment. That can be seen as it moves from want to "NEED", or want to don't want, resist, avoid, and other negative modalities. We can see very clearly that mild wanting is much different than MUST HAVE! "Must have", as an attitude, takes it one step further which equates to darker clouds and MORE BLIND! Darkness hides the light, OURS! The sun can't get through these dark clouds. Dark clouds create unconsciousness. We can't "see the light"!

In a lot of mundane situations, this does not present a problem, especially when life is "easy". Life is "easy" when we are in the same or similar situations and the "pattern", our habitual nature can respond and that doesn't cause an issue. It is when we live life to the fullest and challenge our "selves" to do better, to overachieve, in new ways, putting us in new situations. If life throws us a curve ball, so to speak, we need to be able to adjust. That requires us to be NEW, and we are not accustomed to doing this. That is also when we run into resistance that turns us. We are in unfamiliar territory, and that may be uncomfortable. In the moment (just before the moment) it turns us from being in the moment to either past me, or future me, searching for solutions. In both cases, IT doesn't have an answer, AND we are not present to get the answer because we are bogged down in processing mode "searching" in the "time" database. Let's further dissect this and repeat that there is no state of trying.

Marshall Sylver[15] showed me this as a pretty cool demonstration in his course. He basically put a pencil in his hand and instructed someone to pick it up. The point was that either you picked it up, or you didn't. So TRUE. There is no state of trying, it either happens or it doesn't.

It is the same with presence. We are either present, or we are not. It's an all or nothing deal. If we are not present, then we are living from either the past me or future me. (an illusion!) Unfortunately, this is driven by the same emotional baggage and storylines that comes with them (the ego). So, for instance, if we are mentally in the past and being driven by the emotions relative to that past, we will enter situations in which we experienced something, either good or bad, and we will carry that past with us into the next moment, situationally. Most times if we are carrying it forward it has some kind of charge to it, positive or negative, which locks us into that cinema of the mind, right? We get caught up with it visualizing some kind of fairy "TALE" instead of being PRESENT! It could be a previous pain, and / or it carries a type of stigma with it, possibly with a fear of a bad result or the alternative, like as in over optimism/pessimism. Similarly, if we are visualizing in the future and entering a situation where we have never been before, we may be anxious, or fearful, that it may not turn out as desired...which also may be relative to our previous track record. So, what our mind does, is it creates an ideal, and then becomes attached to that "illusion". So, our mind flip flops from searching for answers in the past to imagining and anticipating future ideals, "wants", desires or anxiously captivated by their negative alternatives, such as fear, worry and catastrophic thinking. Imagining the best or fretting about the worst...lost in "TIME", that's what the ego mind does. Again, depending on what is carrying the weight, and where our attention goes, so goes our focus, and energy...so that will determine WHO (what version of self vs "SELF") arrives or doesn't arrive in the moment to make the decision. This is why I call it a "RE" action vs a NEW ACT-ion. CHOOSE to ACT! "RE-actions" are responses to life that are generated from the old former little ego selves, or our projected future "selves", basically our habitual nature or an idealistic "self" generated answer. That's the EGO automations from the database or hypothetical "idealized" and scenario based illusory projections that are based on some imaginary "future" created in a mind that is not present and basically guessing. ACTIONS are NEW,

NOW based on REAL-TIME data, all of it! That's why ego-based reactions are often wrong, because the RE-actions are automatic and / or based on programming, either way they are generated and delivered courtesy of the ego, thank you very little, from fantasy land (NOT HELPFUL!). We may not do anything because the mind was trapped in the TIME capsule in the illusion still. It was either caught up in it searching for answers in the past or captivated by some emotion relative to a good or bad future. The mind is flip flopping in an endless loop, back n forth, but NEVER PRESENT! We need to wake up and see it happening, GET PRESENT, and STAY PRESENT! That's how the F-tools help us

Using the F-words, assisted by awareness, the higher mind sees where we are in time, and the version of "self" that is responsible because of what that level of self is relating to. Depending on that lower "self" and its attachments , it could be driven by desire or fear (in a projected future). It could also be relating to something in the past and caught up in some other emotional response. The emotionalized "weight" and RELATIVITY of this life situation changes our internal state, and our magnetism. It brings us up or down, smile or frown, and all kinds of different mannerisms can emerge as a result. That state we are in then sets the stage for our RE-actions from WITHIN our internal GEARING, which is often the result of our PROGRAMMING! It is a cycle and / or a progression, each of which has certain mechanistic "norms" or "habits". The ego "selves" are the reactor factors within us that RE-act these patterns out and so that could mean acceptance, avoidance, resistance, or any number of internal propensities, quirks & tendencies. We call these all kinds of things, like idiosyncrasies, predispositions, etc. They are basically habits & behaviors that we are "programmed" to react with and as our "selves". Some folks are quite eccentric, and others are somewhat mild mannered, we are all unique and these differences all change who we become / how we RE-act situationally moment to moment. These "selves" become us moment by moment when we are not present to represent as our higher self-aware "SELF"...the one that is conscious and PRESENT, NOW...with FAITH!

The point in seeing this evolution of the moment internally as a progression from above is so that we can see these RE-actions developing, as well as where / when / how and from whom they are being generated. In other words, we are being watchful of these "selves" and seeing their patterned responses develop within us as thoughts and waves of thoughts are forming (The clouds are building.) It is within the structure of the ego that we can see "that" which is generating these automated reactions within us to various life situations. As we begin to see these as automations earlier and earlier in this process of formation and unfoldment, we see the thoughts within thoughts and the attachments that they are tied to...which reveals the underlying themes, "code" or programs that are associated with that particular sequence. This equates to the deep core source code: our programming / behaviors / the habits of ME. The point with being aware of this at this level of detail is that we can actually see that these behaviors are RE-actions vs NEW ACTIONS! As the clouds form, we become the storm. The storm is what causes the RE-actions as these internal clouds bump into one another and life externally. If we don't see it with awareness, then the storm becomes us and then it basically plays out in our unconsciousness which can leave wreckage behind and quite a mess sometimes. With awareness, we can basically STOP any storm in the beginning stages, or at any point in which we become aware... and it simply dissipates. The clouds disappear and the storm never happens. This allows NEW actions to take place from a more peaceful & balanced state. The storm did not become us, so the storm did not respond, WE DID, but as the higher and better "SELF", a NEW SELF!

NOTE TO SELF:

RE-actions are NOT new ACTIONS!
They are habits, or patterned responses!

This requires a level of intense focus and awareness to be able to see life as a pro-gression like this. It is worth it because we want the PRESENCE ABILTY to be able to take NEW ACTIONS, make new choices and CHANGE! Change, once these habitual natures are revealed, requires releasing these patterned responses, the attachments that generate them, and entering the moment with a clean slate, unbiased, balanced, and FREE to make new decisions. That's called LETTING GO of who we were a moment ago, what we know, and our comfort zone. OMG, that means the unknown, and UNCERTAINTY! YIKES! STRESS...LOL

I would argue quite the opposite, actually. Uncertainty is living from a state of being that is at the mercy of these internal storms, and OUT OF CONTROL! Certainty, from a mindset perspective, is operating from a rock solid unshakable foundational trust, KNOWING our core is stable...and SHOWING UP in an ever READY and adaptable state. It is a state of mind that is receptive and highly aware, balanced, AVAILABLE and PRESENT to become NEW. That's the FAITH STATE! The funny thing is that this state of KNOWING is NOT knowing but having the faith and confidence to TRUST in that not knowing. That's why they call it a leap of faith. We are willingly stepping into the UN-KNOWN, GULP! (ha-ha!).

THE FAITH STATE ROCKS!

You will begin to love it, count on it, cherish it, and believe in it. It is present, conscious, and focused at the highest level. In the initial stages though, as this confidence is building, it requires energy to power it up, and some persistence to persevere through a little bit of trepidation physically or some extremely negative self-talk some "times". We may need to push through some negative internals and "turbulence" as we adjust to the new platform. STABILITY doesn't happen overnight, it does require some practice and experiencing these growing pains is a part of that. The internal emotions, or turbulence we are experiencing is due to the fact that we have not fully disconnected or let go of something. The "time-lock" has not been released; something has not been fully let go. What we need to see in these moments is what we are hanging on to. What has us "captivated"? We are locked on to fear, or desire, or some imagery that is either wonderful or awful. The prevailing emotion is the clue, and the answer is underneath the emotion...that's the attachment. With awareness it is revealed as we shed light on it. Either way, whether positive or negative, we must let it go in favor of FAITH. Once seen, for what it is, that's easy...because all it is, is a false image, a scene, a movie...a complete ILLUSION. Faith allows us to turn off the projector and experience the NOW, in the moment. Presence is attained and we can CHOOSE something NEW! We become NEW in that moment!

So, that would kind of mean that I am entering this new moment WITHOUT everything I have ever learned and KNOW as well as whatever I am expecting and projecting. Wait a minute here, so I am supposed to arrive at this new moment without KNOWLEDGE? I can't arrive to this new moment and not KNOW exactly what to do before the moment arrives, I need to know what to do ahead of time so that I am prepared...what do you think I am, crazy? That's ludicrous...Well, yes, I get it. That sounds sort of NON-sensible when we look at it like this, so let's look at it the other way. If I bring everything I know into the moment, am I not bogged down with all that "knowledge"? There's just too much "weighing on me". How is my processor supposed to process NEW information if it arrives with all that baggage? It can't...that's the point. I must LET IT GO. Life is not a jigsaw puzzle, the pieces of our lives from before don't quite fit into the next moment because every moment is DIFFERENT. We can't bring the exact piece of the previous puzzle into the next moment. Not only does it NOT MATCH, but it would also take us forever and a day to dig through the database to find a close enough match to get a reasonable outcome. That's what the mind is trying to do. It is looking in the past to fill in the pieces of the puzzle in order to find answers to the future... they'll never match 100% because no two moments are the same. We may not find a similar moment to reference at all, meanwhile, the processor (my mind) is bogged down TRYING to find that exact match or trying to locate the "recipe" in the database. Given this dilemma, we do pretty well, don't we? I will say though that we do have a better way to proceed.

So, rather than that option, bringing all of our baggage, hoping for an answer in the jigsaw puzzle database of previous moments trying to find old answers to new problems and challenges, what else can we do? BE NEW, BE HAPPY and COMFORTABLE being NEW! What does this mean?

We must learn to be comfortable being uncomfortable! We must be comfortable NOT KNOWING!

What would that require? Let's say that I start with a rock-solid foundation, relaxed, balanced, stable, unbiased, firmly planted, settled & confident. I am NOW ready to begin with an unyielding TRUST that everything I need and know is going to be available to me at this very next moment, the precise moment that I need it. Even though I recognize that every new moment is new and may very well be different than every single one before it, I am going to bring my brave self with every ounce of courage I can muster and TRUST that what I need is already within me or that it will be provided. That's where and when the persistence to push forward and take that next step comes in. We must have FAITH and the intestinal fortitude to take the step that we KNOW we MUST. Wide awake, 100% present and watchful, for the sake of growth, if nothing else...I must TAKE THE STEP! What we want is on the OTHER SIDE of that wall of fear, or whatever it is that is standing in the way of that "step". That means pushing through the "psychobabble" (negative self-talk) and / or the physically shaky internals that tell us not to do it. We must do it with massive awareness though, because that lower version of self will want to do ANYTHING other than what we must do. It will want to turn, run, hide, get under the desk, blanket, tuck behind someone else...NO! It's time...OUR TIME, to step up and SHINE!

This is where and when FAITH provides our backbone to stand up straight and take it on, that one more step. As THAT higher "SELF", we can and will arrive at the next moment open and ready for whatever it brings, even if it is something new. Awareness converts nervous energy into FOCUS ENERGY, awareness is amplified as well by the nature of this infused energy. The transformation is AMAZING, and we EVOLVE with RESOLVE! It truly resolves the emotional energy issue by USING IT productively. The relationship with fear and other kinds of emotion changes. The negative or anxious emotions dissolve, the fear vanishes but the energy produced is still there and available for us to use it. The crazy thing is that the fear factor is not even a factor anymore. It's not that all of a sudden, we just magically come up with this incredible amount of courage, although it does feel like that is necessary at first because we see some kind of obstacle in front of us. Once seen in detail, by being watchful with ultra dialed in awareness...the fear actually vanishes by the nature of what we are in relationship to. In this case NOTHING, because the "future" illusion is no longer being projected on the mind screen. Prior, we were in relationship with a future image that was being cast on the mind screen...which brought up fear or excitement. The projector self that is casting the illusion is SEEN with awareness and shut down with faith and presence. So, what would that mean? FAITH turns into TRUST in that moment, it has to. "WANTING" goes away, FEAR, goes away...quite naturally. Maybe only marginally at first and that is why UNTIL WE KNOW this to be true, we get the quivering and / or hesitation and still miss opportunities.

Once faith evolves to TRUST, in the moment, I can and will arrive as my highest and best "SELF". My MIND processor is completely ENABLED, and my integrated electronic circuit board is FREE to process at MAX SPEED! What came first in that sequence? FAITH! I must be able to step into the moment ahead of me with this one key element. It is the key that opens the door. I MUST free up my processor to be able to PROCESS in the moment...and LETTING GO of the past "selves" and knowledge is what allows us to enter the moment without all that baggage to BEGIN WITH. BEGIN = NEW!! This is a super-fast progression, and so being alert, awake and aware as it unfolds is essential. The basic equation though amounts to the fact that once we get to the moment and we are IN THE MOMENT, faith KEEPS us in the moment where new choices can happen with a processor that is free to choose, as well as powerful enough to make quality life changing choices. Faith is the key, and it acts as a guardian of the moment. So, "letting go" of the future to establish and maintain presence in the face of fear or excitement releases our attachment to outcomes / ideals, and anxieties relative to the future. It also serves as an interrupt to this perpetual and incessant state of "WANTING" which requires FAITH. Have FAITH!

As a quick summary, in order to achieve PRESENCE and FREEDOM to ACT in the moment as our highest and BEST SELF, what do we need to let go of, and what are our tools to do so? With understanding and forgiveness, we are letting go of the PAST! With faith, we are letting go of the FUTURE and our insistence on trying to CONTROL the next moment. This allows us FREEDOM and with PRESENCE in the moment we can be adaptable, receptive and focused. Rigidity is not freedom, it is defining, limiting, and NOT receptive, not flexible. It's more like "My way or the highway", right? Does that sound like a state of receptivity and being highly aware of what the situation / moment needs? NO, in that moment we are quite literally FULL OF OUR little "selves", the ego and its' identifications, beliefs and the associated definitions / LIMITS. We are not adaptable at all.

Keep in mind that this does NOT mean we should not PREPARE and ready ourselves. By all means, GET READY, for sure...because the next moment is coming, seemly faster than ever. So, remember the top 13 P's for "self-mastery" and performance under pressure:

Patience, **P**ersistence & **P**erseverance are mandatory, and often come first, and then ultimately, we come to a new moment when we must PERFORM, so add:

Proper **P**rior **P**lanning which allows **PRESENCE** & **P**recision (with faith & trust) in order to:

PREVENT a LACK of PRESENCE, which would result in:

Piss **P**oor **P**erformance under **P**ressure!

That's a lot of PEE! "P's"! LOL, So, remember, always take 13 P's before going into the moment. Haha! Being properly prepared for LIFE is often a key elemental factor that allows us the confidence, installs the FAITH factor, and then unwavering TRUST kicks it up another notch to maintain the presence we need to perform under pressure.

Then we are fully letting go of the past & future "selves", availing our NEW higher "SELF" to arrive in the moment with what? Amplified FAITH!!!! Taking a leap of faith requires huge amounts of what though? ...TRUST! Faith and trust go hand in hand. As trust becomes more trusting, faith is enhanced. They build on each other. It is a progression, so let's play this out.

FAITH is dependent on our ability to TRUST, but also delivers that trust which is a little bit confusing because it is kind of circular. It builds on itself. Faith builds trust and then the added trust builds more faith progressively. So, what are we trusting though? Are we trusting our higher "SELF", GOD, the ether, the universe, the probabilities? Let's break it down to components, it may help. Let us say that maybe in the case of "faith" there is a state of trying, for kicks and giggles. To the extent we can "try" to remain present will be the equivalent to our "FAITH" ...and remember that faith represents our ability to TRUST. It is my belief that with presence, FAITH and TRUST convert to "LOVE" or at least they have the capacity to...and unconditional love is GOD, right? It's like a super-fast metamorphosis. If you prefer to leave the GOD element out of this equation, then just say with faith "I" can arrive as my best and highest SELF to ACT. All new actions are the key. ACTION = the ability and freedom to CHOOSE.

RESOLVE to EVOLVE!

This is the internal gearing broken down so that we can see the actual components. This reveals the various interchanges where faith is not converting to 100% trust or BELIEF! We are not trusting enough, YET! So, what does that mean when we can't seem to convert that, or generate enough faith to produce 100% trust / belief in the moment? Something is getting in the way. That's where awareness comes into play...in fact it is required to see WITHIN the progression. Being in observation mode shows us what that something is. US! We as the "selves" are that something that gets in the way. We are the fly in the ointment. We are the PROBLEM, and now we see it.

As an example, a situation presents itself that has an emotional component to it, I have been there before with a negative result, or positive, doesn't matter...regardless it is a very important event to future ME. For whatever reason, this event has a stigma attached to it, so I am either somewhat, or VERY "attached" to the result of the next moment in TIME. That means baggage, right? PRESSURE! OMG...Stress. Where does this come from? THE IMAGERY in the mindscape which the mind "projector" is projecting onto the mind screen; so we are temporarily "occupied" while looking at a potential future. The mind is speculating because we are ATTACHED to a particular result, and outcome. Something the ego WANTS is driving the desire FOR it, or the alternative if focused on the negative. So, the alternative is fear, driving us away from what we don't want. In BOTH CASES, it is driven by a lower ego self and its weighted attachments. So, we can see in this progression that it is self-created, either way. The weight and the STRESS of this is self-created, drop it...lose the attachment. Easier said than done, right? Let's assess then.

What if scenarios. OK, let's talk about that. Desire vs fear, want vs don't want—THAT is the "occupation" and the balance changes based on which one is carrying more "weight" in the mindscape. The weight is the ego and its "attachments". So, the ego / lower "selves" are also the "time thief". That version of self is the one that steals the moment because it puts us in the TIME-LOCK! (The future or the past). Once seen in retrospect, the dots can be connected, and the progression is understood. In addition, it is seen more quickly the next time this scenario presents itself or something similar because we are aware of it. It is now on our radar to be more watchful for it. The attachment is the cause of the fear / desire balance disruption which is what ultimately generates the response. This what I refer to as the RE-action by the fearful or excited "self" and that is "the takeover" (time thief) which then takes the mind over in that lightening flash of a moment. This happens extremely fast, that's why I suggest breaking it down...sometimes into incre-MENTAL time slots, like milliseconds. As we become more aware of this particular elemental habit, the progression can be seen earlier in the time sequence and basically prevented, or optimized as far as a response goes, allowing new actions because we were essentially NOT taken over. We saved our higher SELF from the "time thief", maintained our presence, which enables a better ACTION, better choices / decisions.

Let's back up though so that we can see this as an evolution of the moment, time slot wise, tick by tick, moment by moment... What happens when we are "attached"? With various degrees of self-created "attachment", AKA "NEEDS", let's propose some scenarios:

When we are not really attached to the result such as a mild want vs a NEED, our ability to be present is amplified tremendously. In other words, presence in unemotional situations is easier. Less baggage, and minimal energy to manage. We are more than capable of handling the energy involved here, so "overwhelm" is certainly not an issue. So, past me, and future me are less likely to intrude on my moment and BECOME me for that moment. The demanding "selves" are behaving. LOL. In this scenario, we are not really "attached" to the result, and therefore we are able to TRUST in a reasonable outcome... "whatever happens...happens" is our mindset. (a state of detachment) In these scenarios, we ordinarily get a reasonable outcome, do we not? That is because potentially, as an example... 1-20% of ME may still be in the past, and maybe 5% is hoping a certain future thing happens, but I AM 75% or more unattached or primarily present. We basically trusted in a reasonable outcome, something good would happen, and it did.

Let's introduce a different scenario with a more weighted and "attached" situational and "personal" BIAS. In other words, we really want one thing to happen vs another. It has almost developed into a NEED, but not quite. Again, as an example, there may be 30% of ME that is thinking through past examples searching for solutions, I remember previous versions of myself and the associated successes and failures. There is another 60% of ME that is considering possible outcomes in the future, projecting this imaginary "good" or if focused on fear "bad" result on the mind screen. So, what we see is a series of "what if" scenarios and variations of future "Me's" being broadcast on the mind screen with whatever variation of "me" is necessary to make that result happen, good or bad. The mind is busy running projections trying to "play out" and KNOW the next moment ahead of TIME! When the answers are not there it flips back to the past searching the "time" database for answers. This back n forth churning is a huge distractor factor and also equates to stress, mainly because it isn't finding exactly what it needs or wants. The ego mind wants a GUARANTEE that what it comes up with will work or be the right answer. There are no guarantees in life. There is always "risk". Never-the-less, that's where the mind is, lost in "TIME" flip flopping from the past to the future, but never PRESENT! It is looking for the sure thing. In that scenario, "TIME" is occupying most of the mind space, which only leaves only 10% of ME to be present and process information in the moment...with "faith". That is NOT a whole lot of processing or manifesting capacity. In fact, I have reduced my ability to focus and decide how to take action IN THE MOMENT drastically because my processor is nearly maxed out. 30% in the past and 60% in the future. Is this "trusting"? NO! It is trying to control outcomes, and by doing so it has lost control of the processor. 90% of it, which means that there is only 10 percent left to process "reality" and a very small chance we actually get it right. The odds are not in our favor, are they? That equates to 90% RE-actions and only 10% of the time we have more favorable probabilities to get it right by pure luck or by taking a new action.

Unfortunately, if that situation does not occur exactly as our mind projected it, we will be very much like a deer in the headlights, because the future me is here in this moment, and future me did not project this, so future me has no idea what to do. It is RIGID, inflexible and full of its "self". While past me and future me have been scanning the mind for a similar situation like this, and / or projecting scenarios that may or may not work, they are eating up a huge amount of bandwidth, MINE: 90% of it. My mind space is occupied & my cup is full of the "selves" and their alternating projections. They are projecting their videos for how things were OR ought to be so they can re-act accordingly. Meanwhile, the moment has passed, and a decision was made either for me or by me, but it wasn't the highest and best ME that made the decision. I was sidelined by the lower "selves" while I was all "stressed out" and because my processor was maxed out. Bummer.

When we are taken out of the moment by the weight of the moment, choices cannot be made by our highest and best "SELF" because that SELF is not even PRESENT! Due to our unconsciousness, these life altering decisions are made by:

1. The situation (or someone else.)

2. Past me (old knowledge, stale inaccurate illusory and personally biased

data, a RE-action.)

3. Future me (A rigid and inflexible RE-sponse based on trying to control OUTCOMES. An illusionary and personally biased projection that is predefined and LIMITED!)

The result here is predictable, isn't it? YES...dang it. I dropped the ball again. I was not present. I got "PRE-occupied" by the "selves" and taken out of the moment. So, because I got my mind hijacked, I either had the situation answer to the situation, a former self stepped in and acted the same as the last time it was in a similar situation, or future me guessed based on a projection. The projection was based on who "I" projected that I should be, which was formulated in the mind based on a very specific illusion. So, my RE-sponse was identified before the moment even happened. I, as the lower self, was responding to the illusion, which is completely inflexible, 100% PRE-determined by a mind that was temporarily inside of a fairy tale. In each of these scenarios, I was not even in the moment. (i.e., I was blinded by my "selves"). HABIT, or guesswork. Is that our highest and best self? Is that the best we can do? NO! We need to make decisions on REAL TIME current information so that we are basing our choices on REAL DATA vs illusions, projections or old stale data.

Net, net, we can do better. Let's face it, we get caught up in the past and future a LOT. The "task" at hand doesn't even need to be a difficult task. Even in small seemingly meaningless tasks this can happen, such as picking up the salt, or pepper...or something out of the refrigerator. If our mind is elsewhere, do we drop things? If the mind was not "occupied", is it really all that difficult to grab the ketchup without dropping it on the floor? NO, the mind was temporarily not present. This is stuff that happens when the mind gets sidetracked, and it happens all the "time".

Did you ever really drill down on where the mind was that moment that you dropped something? What was it "thinking"? Where was it in relation to TIME? It was more than likely in a projection...mind imagery vs present. That mind imagery is where? Typically, it is past/future oriented, or envisioning something on the mind screen, but not here, NOW! Daydreaming, projecting, remembering or whatever else. That is NOT presence. While we are PRE-occupied, which can be a momentary blip and boom, spilled milk, or an exploding bottle of ketchup. If this happens performing routine tasks, imagine if there is a life situation, or a competitive / demanding situation and something is really on the line, with EN-ERGY, and more DATA throttling in. How much more bandwidth is required performing a complex task, in a fast-moving environment, and how quickly can this type of scenario happen? Life happens fast, a snap of the fingers and the moment is gone...it would not take but a fraction of a second and we will have missed it. That is why we hear the statement: "narrow is the gate". It's not a gate per se, it is a time slot, essentially NOW. With awareness we can see this. We can also see when we missed it. That miss is often the snap of the fingers on the precipice of the NOW moment when we get side-tracked and in that momentary blip, we end up missing the moment of now. We got TIME-LOCKED out of the moment which is when the decision was made. The "higher" choice was unavailable because the higher "SELF" was muted out or LOCKED OUT. CHOICE = NOT MADE, not by our highest and best SELF anyway. One of the "selves" took us over.

We can do better; we have the key. If we really pay close attention as awareness sees the evolution of the moment unfolding in real time, it reveals that trust emanates from faith, which enables and empowers it. It becomes more "trusting" as it uses the key and opens the door. As it does, it gains access to NOW, the moment. It empowers by giving it FULL access, all alone, without the "selves" and their limitations, concerns, projections & attachments. It has eliminated their distractions by letting go of these, which eliminates MISTAKES because as the higher SELF, we are focused unwaveringly in the NOW. That's one of the reasons why it becomes more trusting over time. The "selves" would have taken us on a detour, out of the moment, distracted, elsewhere in TIME which is why we make mistakes. We have to let them go. By doing so, we have essentially given this higher version of "SELF" ALL of the power vs none of the power. Without faith and trust, the moment was inaccessible, NOW, it is. I'd certainly call that empowered. If we take the selves out of the picture with awareness and skill, add faith and trust, and then amplify it with all of this new- found ENERGY, then we have a pretty solid game plan. We just got the key to the door and USED IT, finally. The lower selves are always preoccupied, so they'll never get this key. It is reserved for the higher "SELF" because it knows how to gain access. With effort, awareness, concentration, energy and presence, we can BECOME this higher "SELF"! "Becoming" can be a highly empowered "state", and this is a learned skill. We need to enable and empower it though. We "will it" to happen and that's why they call it WILLPOWER! What WILL BE will be and we will it to be by becoming it.

"RESERVATIONS" DON'T WORK!

When I say reservations, this has multiple meanings. First, this means entering the moment with hesitation, apprehension, a level of anxiety or fearful. It means that if we are full of our "selves" that are full of FEAR, we have no room for something else. How does it feel to have reservations anyway, NOT GOOD! So, it is actually a big relief to just let the fear, worry, and "reservations" go. Thank goodness Secondly, I am referring to a reservation as a projected reality, which is NOT really reality. What I mean is that the future "selves" try to make a reservation in a future moment to BE something or DO something that is PROJECTED to be exactly what is needed in that moment. This happens with not only fear, but excitement too. So, the past "selves" try to reserve a spot in the future moment to be exactly who they were and do what they always do in that type of situation. OR They project who they have "identified" that they "should", "WILL BE", "WANNA BE" or "need" to be...which is trying to predetermine or make a reservation for whom I am to be in that moment. Here we go "wanting" again. Of course, this is "assuming" that a fixed response to an up-and-coming moment (in the future) will be the exact right "answer". It is "projecting" who I will need to be, while not KNOWING all the variables. (context). That's probably not going to be the best solution / answer. How can it be? It is certainly not optimized or maximized. Neither of these scenarios can be 100% ideal in an ever-changing landscape. Our world moves too fast, changes too quickly, and no two moments are alike. We must be more flexible, less RIGID, less DEFINED, and less LIMITED! By waking up, we can see these limits and front run them...

So, instead of being captivated by desire /excitement, or by fear / anxiety / nervousness, maybe even a little "EDGY", we cancel that "reservation". We must do that NOW! This is a moment, as they all are, that we need to step up as our HIGHEST SELF to over-ride these lower natures, the patterned responses to life. It is these NEEDY lower "selves" that are trying to CONTROL outcomes and make reservations. CANCEL their reservations. Get prepared to BECOME NEW! We do that on the very EDGE of the now moment as we catch the lower selves trying to reserve their spot ahead of "TIME"! Just remember, reservations don't work!

LETTING GO of the "selves" ENABLES the state of BECOMING!
NO RESERVATIONS REQUIRED!
FAITH and TRUST replace reservations!

They are actually much more accommodating. In addition, we can expand into and through the moment rather than identifying some limited and defined application of our "selves" ahead of TIME!

Let's introduce a third scenario, we have paid attention, and with a lot of hard work, we have GROWN tremendously by seeing, hearing, and feeling life happen with extraordinary awareness. As a result, with our enhanced SKILLS, we have become better and better at meeting the moment as the moment occurs in a receptive manner understanding that life happens FOR US, not to us. As a result, we have been practicing this vantage point for a long time. Many moments, years and years have passed, and we have become brilliant at TRUSTING and "allowing" while seeing these "timeslots" evolve. We have grown to understand that whatever situation we are brought to, we are bigger than, can handle it, and we have **full faith** in the fact that the answer will arrive in that moment to assist us (trust).

FULL FAITH = 100%
Is there any room for doubt?

We are completely and unwaveringly NOT attached to the outcome (future me), and we have completely released the past (past me: no regrets, no delusionary biases or baggage.) In this scenario, we are Zero percent limited by the past versions of "me" because they have been slowly and surely RELEASED in favor of growth and learning in the moment. In other words, our older more limited selves have been seen, understood, and LET GO in previous present moments. We have seen and know all their tricks. LOL. Releasing them is what allows us to ACT as the higher "SELF", the BEST SELF in this moment. We have seen this happen so many "TIMES" that we NOW believe in it. These former versions of us have been "integrated" & updated with new information, and the new software that is more optimized deletes the old. We are gaining NEW skills moment by moment and current methodologies that are necessary relative to THIS particular challenge, which helps us to feel confident and READY. This essentially UN-limits the "ME", increases the trust factor, amplifies faith, and maximizes My ability to be present this time. NOW! Faith & trust build on each other. As we arrive through the gate and stay in the moment, the "SELF" we bring into it is balanced, highly alert, poised, present, focused and READY for life. Bring it on!

As we aim for success in whatever it is we are dreaming of achieving, we have grown to accept that whatever situational information arrives in the moment will be met by a ME that is able and qualified to ACT in my own best interest NOW (trust). While I (you) don't necessarily have all the informational components, nor have we been in this exact scenario, whatever this moment brings, the "I" will be awake, aware, and PRESENT to get the guidance needed to make the best decision. Life happens FOR ME, not to me. It's NOT about the "little" me anyway, it's about the BIG ME, and this is where it becomes FAITH-FULL (Full of FAITH!). In this process of understanding, there is a huge pressure release because it is NOT about little me, and this is SEEN WITHIN the release, which opens up the space for trust & faith to fill it up. When we have released the past and all the little selves that have the potential to affect an outcome, we have ZERO situational biases pulling us to the past. Likewise, if we are unattached to the result because we have learned that ANY "outcome" is OK because it is "FOR ME"...it will be met with a "ME" that can "SELF" correct as needed in "acceptance" mode. It is then that we have ZERO situational bias pulling us into the future bogged down by all the various "considerations" / analysis paralysis. In this scenario our ability (hypothetically) to remain present and TRUST, and to have FAITH is 100%. In this situation we have the opportunity to BECOME the best version of our "SELF". We are capable of "being the instrument" of CHANGE! New choices and avenues of "BECOMING" are seen and available in that moment. Since choice is available presently, change is possible NOW! Our processor is 100% ready and able to "receive", accept incoming information, process and ACT! As this progression happens, our highly aware and focused state is managed, overseen, available and receptive. So, we are PRESENT and ready to be "filled up" with guidance, which is EXACTLY what is needed in that moment. Since we can see it NOW, we can be it NOW...so as far as answers go, we have the opportunity to become it in that moment. An unwavering presence is possible as long as we can maintain the energy level that is necessary to power it up. Not only that, but it is also clearly seen that we cannot enter this time- slot / space with "reservations". A reservation would be "identified" or "attached" and thereby LIMITED! Limited is NOT FREE to become new. Even "AI" is LIMITED, based on its programming. I am new now, undefined, un "identified", and thereby UN-limited.

Let's just say that the sky is the limit, or better yet UN-limited. As far as answers go though, let's take the highest road possible in each and every scenario or life situation. What would that look like? What would it mean to BE the changeable and adaptable instrument in the moment? What is the fastest and most reliable "AI" relative to the human mind, or a reference for instantaneous "PERFECT" decisions? What is the answer? Isn't it LOVE? LOVE KNOWS! If we become the instrument of LOVE, it is never wrong. Can we do that UNIVERSE-ally? That would mean basically making LOVE our universe. WOW, so without the selves stepping in front of us at the gate, and without our "baggage", we can trust, we can "allow" and we can BE PRESENT, NOW! GOD meets us in the moment to ACT. Our focus is FLAWLESS, our faith is unwavering, and our ability to act in our own and others' best interest is PERFECT. We are presence. YOU ARE THAT! Love is the answer. I AM THAT! To the extent that we can make our highest SELF available and ready via FAITH like this, we can become our BEST

SELF. As our best SELF we BE what we wish to see in the world. We become it. That's our ever-expanding universe. That's letting LOVE answer THROUGH US! Amazing things happen. It is quite an experience. We arrive as our highest and best "SELF" every moment.

As a result of this happening, and the higher "SELF" seeing it through, we begin to TRUST IN IT. That is how faith & trust build on each other. Faith builds more trust; trust builds more faith. What we focus on expands, right? So, LOVE GROWS! We are making love our universe progressively. Not only that, but it also FEELS GOOD!

What does that make us? LOVE, we became it. We get what we give, right? That's our magnet. Quick and very serious question here. Can we do this unconditionally, or universally? Idealistically, with effort and practice, we could become love unconditionally. Wouldn't that be advisable? Isn't that what we would preferably give to our "selves"? So it has come full circle, the understanding, it begins WITHIN. We MUST give our "selves" SELF-LOVE and practice this so hard that it becomes UNCONDITIONAL. We give what we are...if we BECOME LOVE, then that is what we respond to life with, it is us. Life gets LOVE, because we became it. We get what we give, it comes full circle right back to us. GIVE LOVE! Isn't that what we all want and NEED? Be that. This is how. First we must become it, else we can't give it, because we don't HAVE IT to GIVE IT! So, gradually, over time, we fill ourselves up with it. How do we do that? First, by giving it to our "selves". Once this becomes a priority, it builds rapidly. Every moment from then on, we practice BECOMING IT. We BE the answer, and the answer is LOVE! We become LOVE and ACT it out in the moment. Love basically comes through us in a miraculous progression. The SPEED of LOVE is incredibly fast.

CHALLENGE: Make <u>LOVE the answer</u> to life UNIVERSALLY! UNCONDITIONALLY!

What's the reward, because we always want an incentive, right? Easy...what's needed as a driver for the behavior is a new pattern and life responds to what we give it. If we give it love, it answers with love. So, that's the reward. What that means is more loving people show up in our lives. WE GET LOVE! If we meet life with a smile, CONSISTENTLY, life gives us smiling and happy people. The alternative is also true. When we meet life with resistance, complaints, and / or animosity, well... "Ask and you shall receive." Be careful what you wish for. Our wishes are granted by what we are putting out there, like clockwork, you can count on it. You have to see it to believe it, so pay attention. Be "bad" get BAD. Be angry, get ANGER. Be "good" get GOOD. Be love, GET LOVE!

Now that we understand the "recipe", we must accept the challenge and implement it in our lives. There are many opportunities to reflect ugliness and respond to life in ways that might not equate to "Be LOVE, Give LOVE, Get LOVE!" so now that we SEE THE CHOICE, we can BE THE CHOICE!

With great power comes great responsibility. This choice is available, every moment of every day. It is an amazing realization; however, it comes with expectations, doesn't it? Suddenly, we are slammed straight into the wall of reality, face first, and it states something like this. HOLY SH**! Where and when am I NOT being my best self, to my "self" and others? At first, it might be a LOT...but we learn to do better. That begins with a massive focus on SELF LOVE and self-understanding. The "selves" need to be coached and loved. Be watchful for the less than desirable alternatives, when we respond to life and ourselves with less than unconditional LOVE. Let's face it, we make a lot of decisions in a day...how many do we make with PRESENCE and LOVE guiding our decisions, and responding with LOVE, LOVINGLY? Seriously, step back and be watchful. Is this what you would prefer to be "given"? Ask and you shall receive. We are asking every moment... by what we give life and the people around us. As we become more and more aware and we see this progression as it happens, we get better at giving life what WE WANT in return by giving life what it needs, us. Smiles, happiness, love, and kindness show up through us. Call it selfish, but this is a SKILL, and as far as unconditional love goes, we can "TRY". By trying, we catch our "selves", and educate them when they fail. This process, with empathy and self-love via appropriate and timely coaching builds on itself as the higher "SELF" becomes more of a commanding PRESENCE within the mind.

Becoming faith and love is relative to our ability to TRUST and be present. They all go together. GOD lives in the NOW, in the eternal PRESENT, that's why presence is needed. We need to be PRESENT to get the guidance. That is where / when we can BECOME the best version of our highest SELF. That is where / when we can **ALLOW** the love response, our BEST SELF response. When can this flow through us? NOW. This is the one TIMELY response where / when we can become ALL THAT we have and all that we ARE learning to BE. That is what we give the world in that moment, and we must become it because it is always NEW! Narrow is the gate, it is right after yesterday and right before tomorrow, that time-slot is called NOW! It is always the right time to step into life and represent as our highest and best SELF!

As an example, remember that "YOU" that you always wanted to be? It's that one that you INTEND to be in your heart of hearts as your highest ideal. It's the same one that brings tears to your eyes when you see a projection of that potential self in life, a movie, or someone you admire. The moment, NOW, is where / when YOU CAN GROW into that version of YOU, the one that you have not quite become yet in previous moments. That is where you can ACT in a way that is TRUE to yourself, and not make the same mistakes repeatedly. That is when and where GOD is truly on your side, instructing, and the ability to "SEE" and "HEAR" is guiding YOU instantly because finally YOU are in the moment to actually hear and see the guidance with presence. This is timeless guidance; it is NOW and NOW and NOW! It is a constant state of BECOMING!

You finally "get it". The reason you receive the guidance in the moment "all of a sudden" though is because of this more open and receptive FAITH state. It is like a light bulb went on because suddenly you see the evolution of the moment... faith, belief, and trust via presence happens. That equals the receptive state where the DELIVERY can be perceived and received. WE ARE DELIVERED! That's also why it doesn't happen all the time, because time is the issue. Sometimes our state of receptivity is BLOCKED out by the emotions, time, etc. We are essentially locked out, NOT DELIVERED, stuck in the time warp / time lock, "captivated" by some emotion / illusion on the mind screen. Once FREE, and receptive, allowing it to flow through us is a choice as we are in that state of becoming. Complete LOVE and complete faith are always available; however, we must meet the moment to receive the guidance and BECOME IT. We become our own best "SELF" and in fact, our own best friend by cheering our "selves" on to do better. As discussed previously, sometimes that requires a little forgiveness and SELF–LOVE, some hand holding and encouragement from time to time can go a long way and is a much healthier alternative than some of the other options we tend to choose when we make mistakes. Make SELF-LOVE a priority, the rule and the standard in your life. Practice it "religiously". In fact, try to accomplish this major feat "unconditionally" and remember to BE WATCHFUL! When anything less shows up, use the F-word, FORGIVENESS, QUICKLY! Learn and grow, and let it go with forgiveness and then immediately implement faith. This is the key and the recipe for a function. The functional aspect of faith in this application is to maintain the presence that was just attained.

As a reminder, if we are 10% present, and 90% asleep at the wheel, we are losing 90% of our ability to hear and see the guidance that is available in the moment. Our faith in GOD, in "SELF", or in the universe, whatever... to help us in this moment is a mere 10%. 10% is not unconditional, is it? In fact, if we really think about it from the other side of this equation, that will mean 90% LIMITED!

Yikes, that doesn't sound favorable, does it? That's why we make mistakes in the first place. Ten percent trust = a 90% chance of errors the way I look at it. That could mean some vicious negative cycles and a lot of frustration. That equates to the same ole same ole. Certainly, a wake-up call SHOULD be in order.

If we are 50% asleep at the wheel, and 50% present our chances are increasing dramatically to "TRUST", have faith, and ACT on the guidance we receive. BUT there are problems with 50%...it's basically a coin toss. What will we HEAR and SEE? There is a good portion of the time that what we hear or see will be the wrong side of the coin, especially with all that mind chatter going on to distract us. Why? Because the little "me" that meets the moment is a hypothetical version of me, a projection by past or future me, which is bringing an illusion into the present and acting on it vs what is really here in this moment. Past me brought a past situational response to a similar situation and just made the same decision, or future me projected a scenario and based its decision on a guess what might work. Think about all the cross currents too, all the mind chatter and the bandwidth that it's eating up. These decisions are all based on an illusion, a projection on the mind screen, we must see this. If we are seeing the past or future on the mind screen BUT deciding in the now, then is that decision based on an illusion or reality? Our decision is based on an illusion / a LIE. How well can that possibly go? If a patterned response is required then it may go just fine, but not if the next moment is different.

If reality is not exactly the same as the previous moment on the mind screen, then we are deciding based on an illusionary projected reality. That isn't reality. It's like referencing false data or reading the wrong music. The puzzle piece that I just pulled forward from the database of previous moments doesn't FIT exactly the way it should, but we still try to nestle it in there because that's all we could come up with. That's all we "KNOW". That's what happens when we respond to life with a false or LIMITED data set or guess based on a hypothetical. Result? We err. Mistakes are made...and disappointment follows. There is a better way!

As an alternative, in that state of "becoming", what if the higher "I" ACTS on the information received in the moment without the involvement of these past / future "selves". Forget the puzzle pieces. As my highest "SELF" available to date, I am going to step into the moment alone, no baggage and CREATE the puzzle piece that this exact moment needs, right NOW!! That would mean I AM more available, present, awake and aware and REAL guidance would have a chance to reach me because I AM listening, watching, seeing, feeling and RECEPTIVE to it all. As a result, we can decide NOW, based on current REAL information, what or who to become, based on EXACTLY what is needed NOW, right? That's basically enabling or "ALLOWING" a "REAL TIME" ACTION, and it is that higher "SELF" within us that must show up to take it!!!! ACTION vs RE-action. We become NEW. Becoming is a skill. We become the puzzle piece that fits where nothing has ever been before. Of course we need to create it, this moment has never ever happened before...so we absolutely must be new, else the puzzle piece doesn't fit. We are providing the answer. Furthermore, the puzzle pieces build on each other as we create them. How exciting is that? The puzzle becomes our life, but it's not puzzling. We are creating it piece by piece, moment by moment, faster and faster by becoming it. How FUN! Kind of a different outlook on life, right?

As we increase TRUST in our "SELF", the "UNIVERSE", or "GOD" our faith increases. GOOD NEWS...our ability to meet the moment and BE in the moment is also amplified. This happens faster and faster. Therefore, when we gradually quiet the mind, the number of "selves" making suggestions drops dramatically. The old voices in our head are fewer and fewer because we have educated them "lovingly" and LET THEM GO, so the "NOISE" level goes down. The likelihood we hear the correct voice (See / hear the truth & get the guidance) is amplified for sure. As an example: when 45 people are speaking in the same room (our mind), at the same time, what do we hear? It's a mish mosh right? It's hard to make sense of it. Exaggeration, yes, I get it, but seriously, without carrying all that baggage and hearing all that NOISE generated by the "selves" in the mind, the "Still Small Voice" is going to be a lot easier to decipher. In fact, with a quiet mind, it can be crystal clear. Because we will experience this ability and the messages get clearer and clearer, we learn to trust this ability, our faith naturally increases. Imagine hearing ONE voice in a packed house, the virtual stadium is FULL of our "selves", cheering, yelling, screaming, objecting, condemning, etc. GOOD LUCK hearing that still small voice amongst all of that crowd noise. That's the unconscious mind with a "full cup". It is full of its "selves". We quiet our minds by educating them and letting them go. A quiet mind is much more receptive and adaptable.

Continuing with the example. As we eliminate more of these old former "selves" and their associated programs and attachments, it reduces the "NOISE" level, as well as the need to attach ourselves to the outcomes in each situation. We expand our presence even more as the raging fans filter out of the stadium called the mind. We empty our cup, which results in a quieter mind overall because it is less CROWDED in there. The demands of the "selves" are a little more manageable. As this progresses, we attain a quieter MIND, so we can HEAR better. Faith grows as a result. Our FAITH becomes more "trusting" as we enhance the skill. They are basically feeding one another, like a turbo compressing them through those final few stages just prior to the gate. One is fuel, the other oxygen. Our faith is increasingly being injected into the engine by us with our new skills. **TRUST** and **FAITH** are adding fuel to the fire. Our ability to stay present is being amplified as a result. With more presence, we are not flip flopping back and forth from the past to the future eating up bandwidth, so that added presence is adding even more fuel to fire, its purer, and responds even better to the added faith, so they both expand, building on each other. This is where we must channel the energy and focus HARD to manage from the overseer post because of the uptick in energy being thrust through the system! This is a massive amount of energy, and it is coming into the system faster and faster as we become better at using that energy and directing that energy towards focus and becoming. It needs to be distributed appropriately, and if managed and distributed properly, that converts to MORE SKILL. When our skill level is increasing to where it is climbing into higher and higher percentages of the time, we as the higher "SELF" are being present more and more, then we begin to hear and see the truth more as well (We see reality and we hear the still small voice), which ADDS even more FAITH. This experiential confidence has a compounding effect. As we attain 60---70---80 and even higher percentages of "presence", with AWARENESS, our FAITH increases in like kind because we are able to see and trust the guidance as it is delivered. As we approach the edge of NOW, FAITH and TRUST are basically building on each other really super-duper fast, like a snowball rolling down a giant hill, but remember this is our internal FIRE, combustion. More fuel and more oxygen are being highly compressed and burned IN THE MOMENT! That's ME, I am FIRED UP! Burning a lot of fuel, energized, and optimized like a turbo charged engine FORCING energy into the system. BOOM! We are lit up, charged up, fired up to take action. Success, WE DID IT…YAY! But we just used up a ton of energy.

KEY-NOTE: The massive "SELF" generated and isolated focus we need to attain "presence" and function like this requires a lot of energy at first and can deplete us rapidly!

KEY-LESSON: We need to learn how to "SELF" generate and maintain this level of focus and energy more optimally & efficiently to fuel ourselves internally for longer stretches of time. As we learn to function in this more streamlined fashion it puts less energy demands on our systems but produces the same level of focus and intensity. Awareness is not sacrificed by the surges in effort and other challenges as this is functioning at a higher level and independent of the content. Awareness is overarching perception of context AND content. It is unshakable and virtually untouchable!

KEY UNDERSTANDING and RESULT: **Energy management via this extraordinary awareness and perception helps us to maximize our usage of energy in the moment when we need it, as well as preserve, optimize, regulate, and maintain it for longer stretches of time by using it wisely and efficiently with regulated oversight and internal optimization REAL TIME!**

Higher level awareness = UNWAVERING!

They call this "STILLNESS". Once mastered, it is a core state that anchors us in PRESENCE! This requires practice in life's vast playground. That's ultimately a much higher level of SELF-MASTERY! When we are not overseeing this bigger picture schematic and managing energy with diligence, we see the result which is that we burn out too fast, and we become depleted. Firing on all cylinders is AMAZING, but it burns a ton of fuel. Yes, we are maximized for that moment, but since we have not learned how to regulate, conserve and use energy efficiently yet, we can burn out pretty quickly at first. As a result, we miss a lot of moments. In the beginning stages, it takes practice with awareness and presence in a lot of moments to see them through. We must see our "selves" THROUGH these moments, fully awake and aware. Some "times" the system gets totally overwhelmed by life or the "selves", and we do miss moments. At times, we don't get fired up at all because we are just spent and haven't preserved / managed the energy. Other times, we get all hyped up and jacked up, and then we peter out by the time we actually need the energy. So, as a result we are exhausted, sometimes completely burnt out, and we miss opportunities because we don't have the level of energy needed to perform well. At other times still, we just need to acknowledge that we must recuperate, and in doing so, we end up missing a bunch more moments. It's a real thing, our internal fire is literally burnt out, so life passes us by while we recharge. As we see this repeatedly, over time, we get better at managing and distributing this energy as well as monitoring our internals which actually preserves more and more energy because we can see where it is being wasted, mis-used, misdirected, or lost. Since that is re-captured, our day gets longer, and our focus is extended throughout much more of each day. So, the result is more work getting done quicker and more efficiently for longer durations. Consistent, timely & better-quality work yields MORE OUTPUT in a fraction of the time, which leaves additional time & capacity for FUN if that is prioritized. This is rewarding because having a balanced lifestyle yields more smiles, and like attracts like. We get more to smile about.

Energy is essential. As we learn to manage it, we spend less time on the sidelines, or spinning our wheels and more time being productive. We are IN THE GAME of life getting things done, having fun, optimized, focused, producing, creating, making an effort to BE HERE NOW with exactly what is needed, when and ONLY WHEN it is needed right now, but not before. This allows us the mental space that is required to REST when rest is needed, warranted, and possible. With awareness though, we have the readiness, understanding, and capability to energize. We can spring into action to push and persist when that is required, so we can truly focus and drill down on opportunities when they present themselves It's like we have this amazing reserve tank we can tap, as needed, when needed and it is always available, instantly.

As we progress, there is also a very cool realization that comes through to us over time. With practice, we can see that the natural faith building process is feeding the fire from <u>WITHIN</u>, which is feeding ITSELF! So, the realization comes that we do not have to be throttled up at 6000 RPM's every moment of every day. Our awareness is tuned in and these ever-ready skills can run in the background sort of "on call" and waiting for opportunities. As life demands us to show up and rise up, we can fire up the turbos and leap into action. We can rev up and show up in an instant to perform as life needs us to very quickly. We need energy to get us into the moment and this is where we find it, WITHIN!! We see new ways to light our "selves" up with tweaks and "fire starters" to maximize our internals AS NEEDED and they are also regulated efficiently. This ever-ready state is a product of the presence. It is essentially available "ON COMMAND", like instantly, even from lower energy states as this progresses. So, the system can be energized, optimized and maximized...READY TO GO out and MAX OUT in an instant.

When dealing with a highly charged system, we can be kind of "idling", basically relaxed and calmly waiting to hit the gas pedal at any time. The presence is constant, unwavering, and so getting "in the zone" is attainable very quickly, if not instant, because we are essentially already there mentally. Response times are lightning fast. RE-gaining presence relative to time is not needed, unless attention wavers, so that split second is no longer lost. Firing up, when needed from WITHIN the moment for added spark and the resulting energy is also attainable almost instantaneously as our higher "SELF" is already in command presently and can kick us into another gear THAT FAST! There is no hesitation, no transmission slips, or turbo lag. Finally, and seemingly quicker than ever before, as we fuel the fires within systematically, our internally generated and super-charged energies combine to give us a final push, like a quantum leap into NOW, if we were not there already. If we were present already it just gives us more momentum as the concentrated energy provides additional thrust from within and BOOM, it happens. We are completely FIRED UP from within at a whole new level. Presence is either attained or enhanced as a result of the progression. It's like a final flash and it feels like instantly HERE I AM, NOW and ready like never before, in the MOMENT maximized and optimized for performance, as needed, WHEN needed.

PRESENCE is a stupendous constant that never ceases to AMAZE as it is ever ready and high functioning with tremendous SPEED. At first it feels kind of miraculous, but over time it becomes easier and more routine. Being energized certainly helps fuel the internal fires though and so we learn the nature of the internal fires that truly "fire us up" in order to use that energy with an incredibly stable level of discernment. The funny thing is, and quite incredible, is that this higher level of awareness stays aware even at lower levels of energy and in extremely complex highly demanding situations alike. The presence stays PRESENT, but it requires less energetic FORCE, which allows us more longevity each and every day. Force burns too much fuel for a variety of reasons. This really shows us WHERE and WHEN we are losing energy due to the fact that we are forcing things unnecessarily. We see these "STRESS" points where and when we are pushing too hard and so, we realign with presence and oversight which is how we regain our power, balance and stability. Life becomes EASIER as we capitalize on this new perspective and maximize the moments we have with presence, poise, persistence, and with an air of peacefulness which is stable and lasting. It doesn't lose vast amounts of energy pushing too hard when it is not warranted, getting frustrated and burning up energy with emotional outbursts or running in circles physically and / or mentally. Many of these things cause us to burn out too soon because we create these imaginary timelines or are held to them by arbitrary "NEEDS". Yes, there are times when we do need to meet deadlines, however in many cases we create idealistic timelines that are unrealistic and completely unnecessary to begin with. By seeing this, we can step back and see that we are creating our own stressors via these self-created timeline projections, so we stop doing that. Life flows so much better and easier as a result. It's more peaceful, we can enjoy the journey. TRULY!

ENJOY THE JOURNEY!

Life happens NOW, while we are mentally busy making other plans and creating our imaginary timelines. It's actually funny and reminds me of the proverbs: "Man plans, and God laughs" or "If you want to make God laugh, just tell him your plans". Add timelines to that, ha-ha. I think that the universe does laugh at our timelines sometimes and now we can get in on the FUN because we are watching too. LOL. This is very true though because we can see frustration and other emotions come up and we see what they are relating to. Often, that is a self-created need along with a timeline. Requirements, demands, "NEEDS", deadlines, timelines. These are all systematic "WANTS". Wanting converts to "attachments". Mentally, these are in TIME (the future or past). Once seen, we can step back, release, LET GO, and regain PRESENCE via FAITH and TRUST. This allows us the freedom to ACT with efficiency and GET ONE THING DONE! It is actually a whole lot more enjoyable too because the mind is not trying to map out the future, nor is it anchored to the past. It is HERE NOW "Enjoying the Journey" vs being all over the map, throughout all of time (the past and future).

GET ONE THING DONE!

As we get better at energy management, we light up and shine our light in the world as needed, moment by moment with less and less FORCE, which empowers us with more and more POWER! It is peaceful and stable power, even keeled, unwavering. Some moments definitely demand more energy than others and our higher level of awareness helps us to manage this distribution. As we learn to oversee & distribute the incoming and self-generated energy, then we can appropriately allocate & use that energy wisely and efficiently. It's like this ridiculously fast chain reaction that happens; faith, trust, presence...BOOM! The internal fires light up and the moment explodes with OPPORTUNITY from virtually nothing. Zero to 60 in a FLASH! READINESS, constantly! The constant "presence" opportunity offers new choices, and the moment is infinite, which means what? It is not limited. I suggest that means UNLIMITED! Endless opportunity, how does that sound? I AM _____. Fill in the blank, moment by moment, with EXACTLY what is needed in that moment of becoming, with presence. In order to take massive action, we need massive amounts of ENERGY. That means that we must become masterful at energy management.

With energy, we create MORE, we become more, and as a result, our life expands!

Previously, It was like the moment was the puzzle piece and we were always trying to figure it out by defining it and seeing the edges. For some reason, we took this grand schematic approach looking at all the pieces of our past and then we drilled down on this ONE PIECE and tried to nestle it right in there matching it up with EXACTLY what we had defined around it...dang, that would be pretty miraculous, especially with it being a moving target. Not only that but the puzzle (our life) has a lot of edges that are intricately detailed and DEFINED, by US, with lots of words and stories. This is severely LIMITING as to where, when, or even how this piece might fit in...if it fits at all. The likelihood we find a piece to fit this exact moment from our past, pretty slim...but that's what the mind does. This is churning and burning huge amounts of energy. IT BOGS DOWN in the pursuit. The mind is busy, locked out by "time" and mentally in the past. It is trying to find the answer in the time capsule, that proverbial needle in the haystack, meanwhile, the moment flies by. Not only that, but we burned up a bunch of fuel with the endless searching. Lost in space... It's like when we lose our internet connection, and the wheel just spins on our screen but produces nothing. It is the same basic concept here, it's just that the mind is locked out by TIME vs an internet connection. It's not IN THE MOMENT...the connection to reality, NOW... is lost. Presence, gone. Poof, we basically "blacked out" or timed out.

How about instead of that charade, which is often a guessing game anyway, we start with a blank slate? We ARE the puzzle piece, no colors, no shapes, no definitions or edges...we can be anything, we start with NOTHING, and we BECOME the piece that fits. We simply CREATE a piece and as we do this, ever evolving, ever expanding, the puzzle creates itself, NOW. How's that for getting in the FLOW? Life FLOWS when we don't get in the way. In this constant state of becoming, life continues to expand, OURS! Envision a puzzle that is ever expanding with NO EDGES...infinitely growing. How does that sound? Piece by piece being laid down, step by step, our universe is forever growing, WOW! The sky is NOT the limit, it really is limitless, there is NO CEILING! As this happens FOR US, the whole thing seems to happen faster and faster...some "times" it feels like it is TOO FAST! It's like we are riding that horse, and we have to say "Whooooooh there, Slow down.". This is very exciting but dang pal; I wasn't quite ready for all THAT. LOL Life can move really fast when we are becoming new at a gallop speed...and as we light up, that's LIGHT SPEED! We feel like we need to rest up to be "READY" for the next growth spurt. Do we ever really feel ready though, ready to BE NEW? We must get ready, bottom line, because guess what...the next moment is coming, ready or not so we may as well BE READY! We may not feel ready, but we are...take that step you know you must.

*******   YOU ARE READY. TAKE THE STEP!   *******

HAVE FAITH!

So, to review, please take a moment to really contemplate this: faith and trust are what feeds the INTERNAL fire for that growth. We must become NOTHING, or as small as possible to fit through the gate...to BECOME something. That something that we are to become "next" as we are in a timeslot that is right before that moment is UNKNOWN! HOLY SH**, that's the progression, so that's why it requires faith to begin with. We don't know what's next and right now we just cleared the slate, we have to become something and DO SOMETHING! So, relative to the moment, the progression leads us right up to and THROUGH the gateway to NOW offering us access to the moment completely UN-"identified", un-"defined" (an empty cup). As we meet the moment, right at the narrow gate, super compressed, squeeeeeeezing juuust small enough to fit inside the gate and BOOOOOM, a massive opportunity opens up AT THE GATE, and this final explosion pushes us through the narrow gate, all alone, no baggage, one solitary SELF arrives in NOW! Sole survivor...all the little "selves" gone, transcended. That = FREEDOM! "I" as the highest "SELF" is the only one that makes it through the gate. ("Nothing" is pretty small!) When we arrive as "nothing" IN THE MOMENT, we BECOME PRESENCE. Our processing power / speed has increased dramatically as well. Light speed is FAST! We are FREE to BECOME! Wide open fillable space. Wait, did you say SPACE? That's the universe...OURS! We have the power, with guidance and no distractions, to fill it with what we want to fill it with because we NOW have CHOICE, and we can "process" faster to make new ones very quickly. It is from this space that we can choose more wisely :) We can make the "right" choices because we are 100% available and focused...NOW!! It is in THIS MOMENT that we BECOME, we CREATE, we ARE THAT puzzle piece that totally fits and is needed right NOW!

Translated, that means that I am the "answer", and exactly what is needed in that moment. That means completely 100% adaptable. I can be whatever I choose, such as LOVE, as an example. I can be "The instrument of peace". I am the instrument of change. I am powerful, calm, stable, and adaptable for whatever is needed with PRESENCE! That puzzle piece is me. I became it. With awareness, I SAW, I HEARD, I BECAME, and I watched in AWE as the whole thing happened as a progression in my life. At first, it can be quite astonishing, almost beyond belief. The state of amazement is surreal as the highest "SELF" is delivered and delivers. Once seen, this unfoldment is quite miraculous, and we do surprise our "selves" some "times" because they are quite literally beside them "selves". They are left out in their time capsules. Rightly so, because they don't fit into the puzzle anyway. I realize this whole thing is a play on words, but it makes perfect sense While the lower "selves" are locked out by TIME, the highest "SELF" is PRESENT, and 100% available to respond at LIGHT SPEED to what the moment needs. Look closely at the prayer below, we must BECOME the puzzle piece that fits into the moment. Totally open and ready to be guided, to BECOME new...and to "Do what's right", to masterfully thread the needle and produce the piece that fits, we must be listening, that requires PRESENCE, NOW. GGITM: God guides in the moment.

Peace Prayer[16]:

> **"Lord, make me an instrument of your peace:**
> **where there is hatred, let me sow love;**
> **where there is injury, pardon;**
> **where there is doubt, faith;**
> **where there is despair, hope;**
> **where there is darkness, light;**
> **where there is sadness, joy.**

> **O divine Master, grant that I may not so much seek**
> **to be consoled as to console,**
> **to be understood as to understand,**
> **to be loved as to love.**
> **For it is in giving that we receive,**
> **it is in pardoning that we are pardoned,**
> **and it is in dying that we are born to eternal life.**
> **Amen."**

What are we dying to though? The "selves". They are always trapped and captivated...locked up in TIME! PRESENCE = FREEDOM from the time lock, it is NOW! We have the key! The past doesn't exist, nor does the future. NOW is all that exists. So, let's focus on the MOMENT we are in...BE what we need to be, when we need to be it, that's always NOW! Always = what? Forever, is that not eternally? Just saying...is that another play on words? So, we are NOT physically dying, but we are dying in RELATION to the "selves" and TIME! The presence is outside of time as we typically relate to it, namely the past or the future. PRESENCE is NOW!

Now that we have an understanding of the time-lock and know that presence is the "CURE", let's proceed with massive awareness. Once this is seen like this, as it unfolds, it builds confidence and amplifies faith. The shock and awe have a way of sticking with us as an understanding, if it can be called that. Certainly, it is experienced, and now as life moves on and we do experience it more consistently, we begin to count on it. We may not know the intricacies of the how or the why, but we just saw it happen right in front of our own eyes with awareness and oversight. EYES WIDE OPEN, the unexplained opens us up to new possibilities and we stop drawing so many LIMITS in the mind.

With FOCUS, AWARENESS & ENERGY, we are gifted with even more FAITH AND GUIDANCE. They arrive in the moment of NOW because we have made ourselves available to receive it, we are open and ready (an empty cup, innocent and PURE.)! The "sacrifice" was our "selves" as we left them at the gateway to NOW! Narrow is the gate. As we arrive in UN-limited fashion, in that moment, our abilities are amplified with 100% CLARITY, and we can HEAR and SEE the guidance NOW available. Our processor NOW has ZERO distractions. ZERO LIMITS!

FREEDOM!

(To CREATE, to "BE", to BECOME!)

So, dying isn't dying physically, but a "LETTING GO" of an ego "self". One of the lower selves has been transcended, and so it is gone, basically "dead to us". It is no longer "ME"! This is where and when we can BECOME what is needed in the moment. From this wide-open space, no reservations or filters are required, we can see & hear the PURE guidance. The still small voice is heard because there are no other voices, they are on the other side of the gate. Presence and freedom exist NOW. That is where time and opportunity meet untethered to the past and future, we are FREE. We become LIMIT-less. The "selves" ARE the limits and they have been LET GO at the gateway to now. This is how we BREAK FREE! The chains that BOUND us to the past have been broken. We break free from our limitations. This is how we raise "our vibration", lose the negativity, challenge our "limits", raise our ceilings or eliminate them. Looking at the detailed analysis...it is by NOT DEFINING and NOT putting in a ceiling to begin with. By leaving the "selves" and all that they ARE at the gate with all their definitions, labels, edges, words, stories & LIMITS behind, we have an opportunity to become NEW! Our puzzle is an ever evolving "LIFE".

OUR UNIVERSE EXPANDS!

This is our universe expanding CONSCIOUSLY! Moment by moment we UN-limit our limits!

The interesting thing that the higher "SELF" can undoubtedly see, is that without the ego "selves" and all their programming, faith can become love in the moment to the extent that it shows up through us and LOVE answers. When faith becomes 100%, it can show up as unconditional LOVE, and anything that is met with unconditional LOVE is met with exactly what it needs in that moment. Let's just say that the choice is there, whether or not we make it is something we need to pay attention to. The "right" choice is available. This is when and where we can take ACTION with full faith and unwavering focus / confidence, in the moment. At that moment, we have REAL-TIME info at our fingertips and ALL THE GUIDANCE we could possibly need. We BECOME what is needed in the moment if we TRUST in our highest SELF and HAVE FAITH! That is what makes things crystal clear.

Check out this Johnny Nash song below as a lesson recap. While this may not be exactly what he was referring to, it is a super perspective, and I love the positive nature of the song. It is also a nice reminder of what happens when we take on this overseer perspective, obtain, and maintain our presence. Once we do, we can see the obstacles, and see the "darkness" within, with awareness and new eyes so to speak. By seeing them with our new skills, we can remove them, or let them fall away quite naturally. As a result, we can see much more clearly, and then go right ahead and have an absolutely beautiful sunny day as depicted in the song. What a great song to exemplify this perspective and use as a reminder to STAY PRESENT as the overseer. Thank you, Johnny.

"I can see clearly now" -Johnny Nash[17]

Seeing clearly gives us CHOICE! Faith & trust get us there, LOVE can answer, but we have to CHOOSE IT! We choose it with PRESENCE by BECOMING IT! We become the answer.

"Be the instrument" is a skill we can develop!

This can be very real. There are certainly scenarios where this is NOT happening in the world today, particularly OUR world. For simplicity, keep it close to home. After all, it is recommended that we "look within". Maybe there are some opportunities where we can do better. Remember, THIS IS NOT TO BE CRITICAL. Please understand that judgement is not the desired goal here. The idea is to show up in life with a level of awareness that sees opportunities, with new eyes & new ears. What I'd like to acknowledge here is that we all show up to life at different levels of understanding, and a certain consciousness level, if you will. In an ideal world, we need to pull each other up, NOT put each other down. Sometimes, an opportunity to be a light in someone else's world is fleeting, and we literally need to pull them up "by their bootstraps" in that moment to help them along. "The way" sometimes requires BOLD actions, quickly. In completing our mission, we see these opportunities externally and internally, with the "selves". We also see how fast an opportunity can scream by. We need to pull our "selves" up by THEIR bootstraps internally, LOVINGLY! That's higher ME helping lower me. That's not always easy, is it? NO, and you guessed it, sometimes that requires some tough love, INTERNALLY, as we get lessons we may not want to see or hear!

ACTING as our higher "SELF" now we can settle for no less than our highest and best in every moment, and so we see where we fall short in life some "times". We let ourselves down in moments we lack awareness and / or presence, mistakes are made, failures happen. It is in these moments where, with empathy and love, we TEACH the lower selves in order to learn & grow. With these higher perspectives, we show these lower versions of self "the light", the lesson, and how we could have done better with more "IN" sight!! The light of awareness is "SELF" powered, ME-powered (empowered!). We turn it on our "selves" so that we can SEE where and when we can do better. You might even say that these "selves" fuel the internal fire as we burn them up in the moment. The fact is that these old selves are exactly that, former selves, in order to be NEW, we must leave them behind. So, using them as fuel is the key to our growth. I.e. our internal fire burning within. We are fueling our own fire WITHIN! EMOTION generated by these selves is the fuel, if you did not make the connection. We need to learn & see where this fuel is being generated so that we can TAP IT and use it wisely. Some "times" we can even "SELF" generate it purposefully. In a lot of cases, it is just misdirected / mismanaged without awareness to harness, optimize and use it. Once we recognize the emotion that is associated with that potential FUEL, we look at emotions and life differently. We process it differently and we use it more wisely and efficiently as well.

EMOTION = FUEL

If we really drill down on it, we can see it happen. Why not MAKE IT HAPPEN?

MAKE IT HAPPEN... MAKE FUEL!

7

EMOTIONAL FUEL

W E NEED ENERGY, THERE is no question about that. It is constant, and at times, LOTS more of it is required. If necessity demands it, which it really does some "times", we must then become something or DO something! So, we do what we need to do. We SELF generate the energy required to DO THAT, whatever is needed. Generating energy internally can be fun and obviously productive, with some detailed oversight. I have to admit that when extremely overtired, this can be a challenge. Most times though, we do just fine. This chapter is about being diligent and watchful as the internal ego "selves" RELATE to one another, life, and in some cases, instigating it to provoke the reactionary emotions internally.

Recognizing and capitalizing on energy production opportunities is kind of like "gaming the system", but since we are doing this internally as an optimization technique it seems fair. It can actually be quite fun, but it takes knowing our own internal dynamics quite well. I wouldn't recommend doing this to other people though, you will probably piss them off. They will not understand the provocation and may even be offended. The obvious realization is that this can be done with others and even groups of people, but much care must be given to the delivery and methodology used to deploy such a strategy. The consequences can be far reaching. BE GOOD! Remember that when people are in an unstable state, just like us, RE-actions can be all over the map. They may not be balanced or present. That is certainly NOT guaranteed.

So, let's dive deeper into this so that we can be masterful at the "SELF" generation of energy. These internal selves rub against each other, and life, all the time. As they do this, it creates "FRICTION". Friction causes HEAT, or the emotional component. Internally, we can get a little HOT as a result sometimes. Something is generating an emotion internally. This is the opportunity. At that moment, in some folks this will convert to anger, in others nervousness, in others denial, avoidance, resistance, fear, etc. All kinds of emotions get STIRRED WITHIN. As the "selves" we become the emotion and burn it up in useless and counterproductive ways which often produces mistakes and back steps. Going backwards is NO FUN. Instead, we need to see this as the potential internal fire from a mindset perspective to take productive steps forward with the energy provided. All we are doing internally is poking the logs, maybe twisting them a little bit to spark a new flame and ignite a new fire WITHIN. You could say we are poking our "selves", but INTENTIONALLY! Seen in this way we are making our own flame brighter and hotter ON PURPOSE, which provides MORE ENERGY, not less. It is much like the other team is taunting us but we use it to get stronger, wiser, BETTER! It can fuel the higher SELF! What people can do in these instances is back down, or shy away from these opportunities, trying to squelch the fire, put it out, because it doesn't feel good. It is more energy, different energy, so some "times" people don't know what to do with it, so they waste their precious energy in fear and anxiousness or try to offload it...dissipate it unproductively. It could be intimidating or cause some inner turmoil. All this is done because we have a processing error. The mind doesn't know how to process and USE this added energy because it's DIFFERENT! We must recognize this energy as THE ENERGY WE NEED! It is being provided by the emotions of the "selves" by the "selves", FOR USE! It was given to us for a reason...we need it. Don't waste it, or put it back in the bottle, dissipate it unproductively, or squander it on whatever the "patterned" responses are that the ego typically generates, USE IT. We just found it, now we need to REFINE IT, process it, and USE IT...wisely. That also means not using the energy to run away. That's avoidance mode. We don't learn anything by running around the obstacles. Take it on, head on, take the step you know you must. Just do it with awareness. Yes, you may fail, but think of it this way: YOU MAY WIN! The odds just went up too because now you have more energy and focus to do it.

If failure happens, that brings us back to curse words like SH** and the small f-word. We all make mistakes, have "issues", fail from time to time. It happens, so instead of saying F***, think FORGIVENESS first and then realign with FAITH! As we attain and maintain presence, this can happen almost instantly. Light speed is pretty fast, and the light of awareness is forever shining in this state. So, with the light penetrating every corner of our PRESENT REALITY, we are using our F-words productively instead of dissipating that extremely beneficial energy in a tirade and offloading it into thin air or onto someone, something else. That negative use is extremely counterproductive because it drives that experience

DEEPLY into, and cements that experience in the UNCONSCIOUS mind as baggage, bad, problematic...and something to RESIST / AVOID in the future. (That's a future "trigger"). So not only did we save energy, but this also actually prevented more Karma. Not a bad bonus. Haha. So, the alternative is that we learn to tap and USE that energy and eliminate some form of negativity or a blow up of some kind down the road, that's a WIN-WIN!

So, when an emotional component within us kicks up a notch, or more climactically the system prompts us to use that smaller f-word it creates an internal alert. That alert broadcasts a new message that highlights it as an opportunity for us to USE THE ENERGY! Pay close attention, our system internally says to us the following: Here is an abundant resource for us to tap, please pay attention, come back or STAY HERE, in the here and now...we need to use this energy wisely. This is how we recognize and USE emotional fuel. When we get really good at it, we can SELF GENERATE it on PURPOSE! **KNOW THYSELF**, it's very powerful!

The alternative, of course, is to continue planting it in the unconscious, over and over again. This obviously creates more and more baggage, which results in more blow ups. In addition, think about this for a moment: Later in life when we are going to be forced to peel back this onion, dig down deep / understand and offload all this baggage, piece by piece, do we really want to add more to it? Not only that, do we really want to plant that ugly seed in our garden to grow another bad experience at some point in our future? Like attracts like and that smaller F-word is broadcasting to the universe that something bad has just occurred, please give me more of it. Seriously, we can do better than this unconscious attractor factor. Planting that seed is providing fertilizer for something EVEN WORSE to happen very soon, a larger life disturbance is on the horizon, and we put it there. Unconsciousness breeds and FEEDS unconsciousness. A better choice would be to WAKE UP and choose our F-words more carefully.

Let's revisit the cloud example. The small F-word, the one with 4 letters, is lightning in a bottle. We can capture this anger, frustration, or whatever the reactive emotional energy is that is being SELF generated, or that which caused the small f-word to be used. We just learned how to tap this amazing resource, WITHIN. As these internal selves, or "clouds" / emotions are bumping into one another, or they are bumping into life externally, we SEE IT! In fact, we can see it in the formation stages as we get better at it. When these clouds bump into one another what happens next? Energy is escalating, emotional energy is being produced. If we recognize it as "potential" energy, then we have some options as to how and when we capture and use that energy. We can use it before lightning strikes, or AS the lightning strikes by directing it purposefully. The moment of need will be recognized. If we don't get the alert, fail to stay present, or awareness wavers, we miss the opportunity and then lightning strikes, right? Out pops the F*** word! That's the energy being released...we need to set the stage, be ready BEFORE THAT HAPPENS mentally. We kind of / sort of know it's coming as we are becoming more alert and aware of the context / content...as well our state of mind / body. So, as it escalates, we see it, hear it, or feel it on the horizon. It's coming, and we can almost hear the drumroll...so we get ready to RECAPTURE that energy as it is building. When necessary, with pinpoint timing, we redirect the energy, and USE IT for something more productive. So, in the mind, we see the internal storm brewing, we are wide awake, aware, and WISE TO IT! We see it happening, and we are LETTING it happen, watching internally as it develops into the "storm". It's like we are feeding the clouds while watching them get darker. The storm is the internal "selves" bumping into one another and life, and now we are watching, waiting, and ready to interject. We are seeing this earlier and earlier in the process. As these "selves" generate thoughts, we are watching, hearing, seeing these thoughts "CONFLICT" internally, and with "LIFE". Inner vs inner, inner vs outer; both of these meet and / or rub against each other. That entanglement creates conflict and emotional "STRESS"! So as these thoughts are in the formation stages, they are creating the clouds. Clouds = stories and storylines, so now we see them. Since we are wise to it, and we see it developing, we can see an opportunity coming to redirect that "potential" energy. It hasn't been wasted YET! Because we see it coming in advance, the opportunity doesn't pass us by, we capture it. As a result, energy is preserved, managed, and directed to where we need it, when we need it, which is always RIGHT NOW! That's when we need it right, always NOW!? Haha Think about how much energy we just saved though for a future moment. Mind blowing opportunities...

Self -preservation takes on a whole new meaning when emotions are looked at in this way. Life happens FOR US, not to us. This is a GIFT; we need to use this energy that was just gifted to us. Relative to nervousness, anxiety or FEAR, in particular, we can look at this from a higher level and USE THAT ENERGY!! Energy is required to break through this internal LIMIT, that's why it was provided FOR US. So, whatever it is that is "stressing us out" or we are fearful of, we can use the energy that is generated to beat it at its own game. This is newly created energy that is being provided, however, to date we haven't used it properly. Probably because we see the emotion and that's where it stops. That's where WE STOP, or TURN! In order to see it and capture the energy, we must look to and THROUGH the emotion to the root cause. This is where we see the level of self that is producing the cause and what it is bumping into. The result is an energetic

/ emotional response which is where and when we can tap that ENERGY. EASY PEASY. Once seen and understood, it is processed, lesson learned, and then the energy is AVAILABLE for use. It's just energy, when seen this way we understand that it just needs to be identified, defined, refined, redirected and used in a wiser way. We can process fear and other types of emotions in many ways, a lot of them negative. Let's not concern our "selves" with "face values" relative to what we are being fearful of, and / or emotional about. Let's look and DIG a little deeper WITHIN, change the "SPIN" and WIN. This is a true victory over one's lower limited "self".

FEAR = ENERGY
EMOTION = ENERGY

When seen this way, fear is one of the bigger energy creation emotions, anger is another. Frustration is just anger with a different label. It is a great example of what to be watchful for because this can easily be seen as it escalates and builds more and more energy. Broken down though, ALL EMOTION generates energy, but in different ways. Why waste it? All we really need to do is see the energy, interpret it, and then convert it to useful and productive energy by directing it where it is needed. There are a LOT of emotions, from worry and fear to guilt, remorse, frustration, and many others. Frustration can generate huge amounts of energy which can be used more productively. We need to pay attention to how we are using or dissipating these emotional energy opportunities? Are we processing them at all? AWARENESS sees these emotions as they are developing, which is what makes them available for use. PRESENCE uses energy productively and WISELY! What thought clouds are generating energy for you? What are they bumping into? It isn't a question as to whether lightning is striking, it is. The question is, are you SEEING it when the lightning is striking or missing the opportunity? Sometimes this lightning is just ambient heat lightning, other times it is much more dramatic, flashy, and climactic with some fantastic noises to go along with it. The bottom line though is that it is ENERGY! One of two things is happening as a result, we either use it or dissipate it. USE IT OR LOSE IT. So, are you dissipating it, or are you directing that energy for use? Sometimes, lightning does need to strike...for us to see what we need to see, and then we are WISE TO IT. Be thankful for the lesson. Learn and GROW and LET IT GO! NEXT...

Frustration, as an example, can be interpreted internally most often as NEGATIVE, right? It doesn't have to be that way. For some reason, it doesn't feel good, and if we are low on energy, that negativity can hit us and land on us a lot quicker than if we are full of energy. We give up after a short lackluster effort, or just quit before we start. When energized though, frustration can accumulate in a negative way. If we let that energy build and fail to process it, it tends to carry through to the next thing we do as well. It's like it gets amplified and the downward spiral begins / continues. More often than not this type of energy escalation that is building up inside us ends up being released in a climax type event of some kind. Something really bad happens and makes the initial situation or whatever we were dealing with and frustrated about look like child's play. We just made it dramatically WORSE by not processing it in the early stages. This is mainly because we are swallowing the anger and internalizing it vs. "processing" the anger and learning our lessons as we go. It is landing on us, and STICKING vs. deflecting or being used in a better way via understanding and letting go. After some practice, it just deflects right off because we have already internalized the lesson previously. So, there really isn't anything left to process, we just move right on and that happens faster and faster. Meanwhile, we preserve and capture energy more and more efficiently.

Situationally, before we get to that capitulation point, we need to understand each emotion and process them. Sometimes that will require some digging to root out the real essence of the emotion. With watchfulness and the transparency of thought and oversight, we can see that frustration is anger in essence, and as that builds up inside us, it BURNS US UP along with a ton of energy. We are BURNING HOT because we keep going into the past mentally and burying a whole bunch of energy in that "time lock". It's locked up, stored up because it wasn't released. The unfortunate part of this is that the energy is NEGATIVE, we failed to convert it. Since we give the world what we are, that is negative. Being negative, this massive magnetic "INTERNAL" is operative and magnetizing as a MINUS, a NEGATIVE attractor factor is building up within us. It is getting worse and worse as we add more and more frustration to it. That is a huge amount of negativity, so of course it is generally released in a "BAD" way. We get what we give and that's what we just gave the external world. So, something really negative happens. Not only that, but all that energy we just built up is WASTED as this whole thing BLOWS UP in our face. As that happens, here comes the small f-word and we wonder WTF just happened!?! I tried so hard for that NOT TO HAPPEN! Haha. Frustration can be an enlightening experience, but a lot of times it is missed due to unconsciousness.

Where was our focus? What was the result? Frustration keeps looking forward and then toggling backwards and noticing that whatever we wanted to happen didn't happen AGAIN! (The past / future) We failed to let it go and we are still "wanting", so it accumulates. The final capitulation of emotion is not only bad, but an eruption of sorts. A massive blow up and huge expenditure of energy. What does that do? It leaves us completed deflated because we added a whole bunch of exclamation points to the event and the whole things is just, well...MORE frustrating, and so the cycle starts all over again. We keep looking backwards, and forward in time for the answers and NOT finding them. Then we are storing up that negative frustrated energy for another blow up. The problem now is that we start from an even lower point, energy wise, because after all of that, we are deflated and / or defeated. All our fuel just got burned up in that process. That feels terrible. The good news is that with awareness this whole thing can be seen and remedied with some better energy management. Seeing this is understood as a MASSIVE opportunity. HUGE! All this amounts to is: BAD AIM, and an unproductive use of energy. That alone changes our "TONE"! Once seen in this way, it can't be unseen. We look at life in a completely different way. It's just energy, instead of converting it to negative energy...DO SOME-THING DIFFERENT! We know the tendency for negative energy to produce negative results, so why keep doing that? We can just as easily convert that energy to positive and go right back after it. If for whatever reason that's not possible in this moment, then step out of the box, take a breath, refocus, regroup and take another swing after regaining your composure (this is a baseball analogy; stepping out of the batter's box to refocus). Just don't keep plowing forward in life banging your head against the proverbial wall, doing the same things, and expecting a different result. That is the epitome of forcing things. Something must change, more often than not the something that needs to change is us. Our internals need to change.

Recognizing the energy WITHIN ourselves in the moment is quite transforma-tive. It can be a good gauge to moderate and / or choose appropriate activities on any given day or in any given moment. With awareness of a certain "attractor factor" we could choose what "pursuit" is most suitable for me right now. They say, "nothing ventured, nothing gained", but when we venture into something with a bad attitude that doesn't always shake out that well. Sometimes the best course of action is to change gears and / or do something different until we can generate a better "energy" relative to whatever it is that we are trying to accom-plish. That's where recognizing the TYPE of energy that is throttling around inside our internal chambers is beneficial. At that point we can decide to change the energy, change the attitude, or change the activity accordingly to one that is more suitable. That could be relative to the type and amount of energy we can "SELF" generate.

Emotions can be used to generate a massive amount of energy, and by recognizing this vast tappable resource, we can make major strides. In amazement, maybe even

AWE, we now know: That's a lot of energy we are producing, some emotions generate more than others. What if we could redirect that energy at any point along that "TIME" line? Better question, right? We can, and we have to be focused to do so, wide awake, balanced and aware enough as this is progressing. As the "frustration" energy is building, we must see it and be able to interpret that frustration as a core "angry" energy. As we "understand" the energy, and what's driving it, we can use that momentary IN-sight to RE-FOCUS to gain our "composure" and CAPTURE the anger. Anger gives us massive fuel, and once converted to constructive vs DE-structive energy, it can do amazing work. Fear also provides an incredible amount of energy. In essence, fear gives us the energy to conquer fear. We must recognize it and use it in the same positive way that we just converted anger.

To dissect it, this literally changes our internal composition, "TONE" and then we arrive to the next moment in a more balanced, hopefully POSITIVE way assuming a higher level of "SELF" mastery. (We learned a big lesson and GREW.) This may require that we take a step back, or inhale a big deep breath, so that we can REDIRECT! As a result, the anger we just saw and processed isn't anger anymore, it's just FUEL! As a result of this internal transformation, we can use that highly energized energy more productively by channeling it and using it WISELY! On top of that our INTERNALS have completely CHANGED, and so our magnetic attractor factor has also changed in a major way, from negative to positive, or at a minimum, negative to neutral. As we neutralized the negativity, what happens? It's like a fresh start in that moment! All that negativity is wiped clean, and yet we are still ENERGIZED. So, we just ALLOWED a much more positive "SELF" to show up in our life, in a fraction of a second, that is full of energy to FOCUS and DELIVER! We basically delivered our higher SELF from the ashes of our lower "selves". We just burned up those lower selves and left them behind. The difference here is that we used the emotionalized energy they created in order to enter into the next moment as our energized, maximized and optimized best SELF, NOW!

Whether or not we can make that transition, and HOW QUICKLY we can do it, is a skill. We can develop that skill with practice, and that requires a keen level of discernment, particularly in heated situations, because not only is the energy different, it comes in at a much higher velocity. If the speed and type of energy change on us, which happens all the time, that can affect our ability to process it. This can certainly throw off our equilibrium, so we can get rattled, or feel unsettled as a result. Since this doesn't feel good, it can kick us into fight or flight mode which shuts down the processor. With awareness, the energy can be investigated as "new", with a new level of interest and curiosity, as opposed to what might have previously been a flustered or disturbed response. So, instead of generating a resistance or avoidance type response, the energy is received differently...curiously! From this more inquisitive nature, this energetic exploration develops into a higher state of RECEPTIVITY. The energy is recognized, seen, processed, understood and captured. Next is the interpretation stage, and this is where the time element can be a factor. We must be able to "understand" the energy. So that processing capability is a factor, because we must look UNDER the surface level emotions. That takes time, and it can be accomplished ridiculously fast with practice. We are talking milliseconds, ultimately, with practice. When lightning-fast responses are required, that can make or break us because the energy needs to be managed and distributed from that compressed wave in a balanced way so that it doesn't overwhelm the internal systems. The objective within the interpretation stage is that it does NOT kick us into an "unconscious" state. We must stay highly alert, present, responsive, and "in the zone" so that this AMAZING energy we were just blessed with can be used in a way that benefits us and the world we are in. Fight or flight mode cannot be "triggered"! We cannot "fall asleep" or go unconscious on the job!

This is a completely different way of looking at energy. Resisting life and our energetic internal responses doesn't work, believe me I have tried it. The results are not favorable. Avoiding them or burying them internally doesn't work either. Again, NOT GOOD, they'll come back with more force the next time, and it will be HARDER, not easier. DO IT NOW. Consider it this way. Energy is provided for us to USE IT. Sometimes we just need to understand the energy for that to happen. Since life is NEW all the time, we need to be NEW, we aren't always going to recognize the energy flowing in. That's why an exploratory and inquisitive attitude is a great platform for us to use as a centering mechanism. It helps us to maintain our balance and ultimately affects our foundational support and stability in each and every moment. So my recommendation is to adapt the mentality to one of curiosity, and to look at energy with these new eyes. Say this:

"What can I do with this amazing energy that is being provided to me right now?"

Frustration provides many opportunities, and so our ability to be centered and balanced has a lot to do with whether or not this can be accomplished in the early stages. The energy must be interpreted, understood, processed and changed, which doesn't happen as quickly as may be required for ultimate success when fractions of seconds matter. That's why it requires practice, assuming momentary responses are critical for one's success in that particular endeavor. Each opportunity must be recognized as an energetic intervention window within which we can change our own world if that energy is used in an appropriate way. In order to capitalize on these flashes of IN-sight, we need to be at the top of our game. Frustration is only one emotion, there are many, and they all hit us a little bit differently. Once we begin looking at them as a blessing vs a curse, as a fortunate tick up in energy vs an undesirable emotion that needs to be suppressed or avoided...we can change the world we live in by changing the "selves" we just were a moment ago. It can happen in a flash, but that takes massive focus when things are coming at us at a pace that we are struggling to keep up with. We need to be able to decipher the array of energetic forces coming at us and understand the patterned energetic responses within us all at the same time, like NOW! That's why having the ability to watch our own internals becomes so important.

BALANCE IS ESSENTIAL!

Emotions show up in different ways, we MUST recognize them, understand the drivers, catch the lower "selves" doing whatever it is that they are doing, and thinking whatever they are thinking. As we do so, we can dig a little bit if we have to in order to identify, interpret, capture the energy, refine it, redirect it and use it. Preferably in a beneficial way. Think about all the different types of emotionalized energy this can be applied to. Oh, the possibilities...we have all kinds of emotions running through us, all day long. OPPORTUNITIES GALORE!

As we tune in and drill down on these observations, we can take advantage of all these amazing emotions. These are opportunities to capture energy. Let me just introduce a few possibilities. If you had to and needed to, could the energy that anxiety, nervousness, dread, fright, panic, fear, scared, or just generalized "STRESS" be converted? What would that look like?

Raw fear can change to EXCITED and / or energized COURAGE. Maybe we can even stand tall with some level of BRAVERY!

Apprehension can change to a more focused and energized curiosity and a better attitude to GET IT DONE with a more fun-loving attitude.

STRESS disappears, POOF...it's GONE, and in its place is an energized highly aware and productive HAPPY & PEACEFUL "SELF" that can meet life with a sense of awe and inquisitiveness.

"Let's explore", as an internal platform, creates more of a fun-loving attitude and approach to life.

With this as a new backdrop and higher level of IN-sight, let's look at the world with the assistance of this higher vision.

8

THE HAVES VS THE HAVE NOTS

WARNING: THIS SECTION MAY generate some ENERGETIC internal clouds and may also include some sarcasm, suggestive language and WORDS! You may be tempted to RE-act or get emotional. Please be conscious and watchful as you at-TEMPT to define the words and be careful and aware as you regulate the effects (The ENERGY it produces can be used, be watchful.). This section may generate an adverse Re-action based on your internals, so BE-WARE! This is not intended to be "offensive" or judgmental. These both have the potential to be dark clouds, for sure. Let's look at both sides of this from a balanced, studious perspective, grounded, and with an open mind. The fact is, we can all be "haves" and get along just fine, IF ONLY! The alternative to that is also true, we can all be "have nots" in any given moment, so pay attention. What comes around goes around...LOL! With all that said, be diligent and stay in that watchful state. Be aware of when and where the emotions arise within, and to what the "cause" underneath that emotional reaction is. The purpose of this introspection is to recognize the emotion, see the energy it produces, convert and redirect that potentially positive energy and USE IT in constructive and productive ways.

In the world today, this have vs have not scenario is an ongoing topic. It is in the news and people are seeing this broadcast in various ways across the globe from a National and International perspective. It is clearly an issue, and the disparity or "wealth gap" is becoming quite disturbing. (This is a hook, so again, BE WATCHFUL!) The rich do seem to be getting richer, right? Oh, and well...the poor are becoming poorer it would appear, right? That is what the media would have us believe, and maybe to some extent, that is true...but is it true for you?

Is the "story" really the story, or is it slanted, and maybe some "SPIN" has been added, emphasized, with highlighted color, "noise" and drama added? Is it true that the little guy has no chance, the middle class is disappearing, and we are all VICTIMS? I see lots of success stories out there. The question is, are you one of them? What do YOU want to subscribe to? What would you prefer to BELIEVE and is that belief serving you?

Wide awake and aware, of course, these stories are **<u>NOT</u>** entirely true, are they? There are success stories all around us, and we can subscribe to whatever we want to believe is true. We can be one of the awake souls out there, that's for sure. But, in the media, FEAR and emotionalized stories SELL. That's what they put out there because ratings matter and airtime is airtime, views and clicks matter. So, they grab our attention however they can, that is the way that they, and the ego, tend to lure us in for the kill "attached", emotionalized & captivated by rather unproductive beliefs, dramatic stories, and headlines. We need to wake up. If we really step back and look at things from a higher level, we can put two and two together. We can see that the news media works the same way as the ego does. SALES! They will use whatever means they possibly can to grab our attention, and they know us better than they ever have before based on what we click, or the channels that we tend to watch, websites we visit, how we shop, etc. It's all data and by sorting it, filing it away in their databases, it can be prioritized. They know what makes us tick (just like the EGO)! Once they have our attention, they try to sell us something...because they know what we pay attention to, what we want to see. We tell them by what we click on, subscribe to, buy, view, bookmark, revisit, etc. It is not that hard to figure out from a data collection perspective. Using what they know, along with highly advanced "AI", they do their best to KEEP our attention by throwing more and more drama & propaganda in our face, and then they can amplify it with emotion. Even the advertisements can be customized to our own personalized preferences so that they grab our attention and are geared towards us with color, drama, SHOCK and AWE! You might consider it our own highly personalized click bait. BTW, that's what the ego does too. SUCKER! That gives "look within" a whole new meaning, right? YES, the ego is cunning and agile. It is constantly trying to sell us something. We need to be faster, WISER, and much more aware of its shenanigans. Wake the faith & forgiveness up...we need these tools to parse the data, so that we can see what we NEED to see. That is NOT necessarily what the ego is prioritizing or focused on.

If you want pretty faces or ugly headlines, the ego, search platforms and "AI" will gladly and automatically gear everything you see to what you "tend to want" to see. Our tendencies, even relative to social media, and what we click on, are categorized and packaged up, neat and tidy. Then it is analyzed, dissected, parted, charted and filed away in the database. Then they kick it back out to us...just like LIFE. We get what we give, in this case, we give our consent to barrage us with more of what we LIKE. We tell them what we like and authorize it by what we click on. Just like the mind "THINKS", and it records our internal agreements and disagreements. It sees what we pay attention to, what we like and what we don't like is recorded in the database. What we focus on expands, in fact we tailor it by drilling in on it and emphasizing it with higher degrees of emotion. If we pay attention to our lives tick by tick by tick, as closely as we pay attention to what we click by click by click, we might learn a little bit more about our "selves" if we do life consciously. That would require us to look within, wide awake and aware...and we watch as we get emotional and add data to the database. But we do most of this UN-consciously. So, the ego...much like the news media is a data collection device and it stores its data in the UN-conscious. That's why we get blindsided by our "selves", their data pops out when we least expect it.

In fact, when we do "LOOK WITHIN" the news media and the headlines we see all kinds of stuff that COULD grab our attention, and it does sometimes, right? Depending on our energy level, or today's events, and our "vulnerability", we can get captivated by a dramatic storyline. It can engender a sense of emotion, maybe even victimhood, etc. Stuff like, "POOR ME" stories, all kinds of VICTIMS, from all walks of life, and whomever or whatever was to BLAME for it. They are painting a picture, putting thoughts in our head! We hear these sob stories and dramatic tales of woe, and we get sucked in, who did what to whom, and all kinds of atrocities. Money is an ongoing issue, it seems and of course, this person or that company just made a billion dollars. So, the ego mind goes into measurement mode and compares what they have to what I have and then my eyes and ears perc up. Anything to keep us engaged and enraged. Keep in mind that the "stories" we hear, see, or tell our "selves" can either EM-power or DIS-empower. The news media and the ego thrive on this. Certainly, we can choose to pay attention to positive uplifting stories, but they know that NEGATIVE "stories" sell. They are much more captivating. This is JUST LIKE THE EGO, and they tend to go to the extremes, don't they?!! Extremes catch our attention...extremes SELL. Once we are drawn in, well, it's game over...hooked, just like a big bass on a really enticing worm. Gotcha!!! Hook line and sinker, freedom...from a mind perspective, is GONE. We got caught, reeled in and fileted. SUCKER! Instead of having a nice dinner and a good time, we were dinner. That's no joke...it's very real when we judge, compare, or condemn. OK, then how can we do better without being critical, measuring and judging and picking sides?

First, take a step back and a BIG breath, a really deep one. Let it go, nice and slow. Close your eyes and do this again, clear your head. We must be balanced with a high-level view here. In order to see the truth, let's keep our composure and truly assess this from the faith and belief factor in a healthy way, in and from an unemotional, rational, and balanced state of mind. There can be no attachments or any level of emotion kicking up the gearing internally. We need to squelch the storylines and all of that stuff that is contained in that personalized drama bucket for a minute in order to really grasp this perspective. Leave any and all animosity, jealousy, or whatever emotion / attachment out of it for the time being. If we let our "selves" go back there later then we have probably missed the point anyway, right? Taking a higher stance, let's not succumb to the blame game and start pointing fingers here, that's certainly not the intent of this discussion. If you find your mind trying to go down that road, pay attention, and snap out of that "want" for a moment while we get through this together. This is empowering and educational and looking at it from a different angle truly paints a different picture. This is important, and powerful, so stay with me here, this is BIG!

This EXACT situation is in the BIBLE, of all places. In fact, it can be seen in many biblical statements, in different ways, depending on bible version...but I don't think that this is understood the way it needs to be understood. It needs to be internalized to really EMPOWER us the way that it should if it is to be an experiential understanding. The one Biblical statement that immediately comes to mind is this one, below. The general perspective is that we get what we think / believe. They say it this way: To those that have, more shall be given...and to those that have not, they will lose what little they have.

Mathew 13:12 says it this way:

> **"For whoever has, to him more will be given, and he will have abundance; but whoever does not have, even what he has will be taken away from him."[18]**

Well SH**! That's enough to piss us off right there...and launch all kinds of stories, if we let it. Deep breath, please, breathe. Yes, indeed, the ego will step right into this TRAP DOOR in all kinds of life situations and particularly with headlines and news stories. Social media is also loaded with click bait to lure us in. CLICK! Then off we go, the ego will flare up, self-justify all manner of emotional rationalizations relative to anything near and dear to one's life, or someone else close to them with a relative storyline...clicked and "ticked". I should say we clicked and got even more ticked off or it engendered some level of emotional kickback. That's the beginning of a dark cloud. Then the ego will defend the "selves" within, loved ones, friends, associated groups, or any other situational developments that leads to, or exacerbates some level of victimhood / blame. That's the isolated dark cloud developing into an internal storm where it is bumping into another cloud called LIFE externally. The CLASH of emotion is an opportunity...but we miss it because we go unconscious and get emotional. That's what the ego does, and then it is LOST in thought, "self-pity" or some other justified emotion. BTW, don't get sucked in to someone else's "Misery loves company" storyline either, other than with enough situational awareness to help them out of it. Don't be fooled, don't take the bait and the following detour through hell, no matter how momentary it may be in your own mind, someone else's drama, the news media, or situationally. Those "heated" detours through hell are typically lower "self" generated, or at a minimum "allowed" one way or another. So, take a long deep breath instead and stay with me, nice clear fresh spring air...suck it in and enjoy that peaceful easy feeling. Watch the "selves" internally and be entertained. It's kind of fun if you let it be. So, "LET IT BE"! The Beetles had a song long ago that had some similar advice.

By the way, this is NOT to say that showing people empathy and love is not warranted or needed. IT IS! Please understand that is NOT the point of this particular discussion. Just try to keep this in context relative to money, and things, and "stuff" so that this can be understood conceptually. Compassion, empathy, and love are absolutely 100% needed. So, please don't read into this and get the wrong message here. The point in this dialogue is to SEE SOMETHING within these mindsets, the things that push and pull us towards these edges, and away from them for that matter. We need to pay attention, particularly when we are at these edges within, whether that be a comfort zone, a wall, or a personalized limit / ceiling. It is about these thresholds in the mind that we create haphazardly, and then when we reach them, or MEET THEM in or just prior to a moment, they don't flip our switches, trigger our triggers and take us out of the moment. With awareness we can stand tall and OBSERVE our potential reactions so that they DON'T become reactions, and instead we can become NEW! Fight or flight mode did not kick in. Resistance nor avoidance took us over, and steadfast; we remained PRESENT to ACT!

So, as an example, once animosity or some other emotion engages the mind, the ego can go into DEFENSE mode in a manner of "self" protection. For that reason, this RICH / POOR dilemma can be problematic for a lot of people. Not only do we defend our "selves", but we tend to defend the people close to us as well. It is mainly because it is not understood though...and sometimes because there is a bit of jealousy, bitterness, or other emotions get involved. Relative to the world, and situational dynamics, many things can affect this. For whatever reason, maybe it hits just a little bit too close to home. I always want things to be fair for people, and that doesn't seem fair. I have seen both sides of this in my life, so I can relate to both extremes. Even the "middle class" is just a concept, label or tag that is used as a way to measure people, put them in a bucket with a certain "identity". How does that feel? There were times when I had my back to the wall with little to no money, and then others when I had a good amount or money was plentiful. Thankfully, I learned a bunch of lessons through the school of hard knocks, and the lord knows a huge amount of errors. Ultimately and fortunately, I have had a good amount of success when it comes to money as a result. I am very blessed to have had good people, parents, coaches and a stick to it attitude / persistence on my side, but it's a bit of a sore spot for me too. Why? Because I have been through the struggles. It's NOT FUN! I totally get it because I experienced it and got through it. I had to go through HELL for a number of years. It was extremely difficult. The good news is that I did make it through to the other side. Being able to see both sides is truly enlightening, because now I can explain it in DETAIL. I felt the pain, and I wouldn't wish that on ANYONE! I can't stand to see people in pain, and I truly want the best for people, ALL PEOPLE, not just some, or the select few. So, WHY is this dichotomy true?

It's complicated and simple at the same time. A lot of people seem to think, well, if I am "GOOD" I should get rewarded...like MORE, not less. But it doesn't seem to work that way, does it? Sometimes, yes, but other times, not so much...so there must be a caveat, right? So, let's talk about that. If you don't get it from the above, it has to do with faith, but in a slightly different context. The basic answer is that it isn't necessarily based on "merit", per se, but it CAN BE, so yes, caveat indeed. In this case it is based on our BELIEF in merit, which is what? In a different frame of reference, it is essentially what we are having faith in, what we are believing we are entitled to, or "deserve", at a deeper level. It is a certain "worthiness", or lack of it. A deep embedded unconscious belief, OR karma if looking at it from a different spiritual philosophy. So, let's dissect it. It's not that we are not using faith, we are. The reason it is problematic is that we are using it incorrectly, or unconsciously. We haven't fully digested how to use it more productively and consistently in our lives by focusing on what we WANT and then being PRESENT to make powerful decisions in the moment that will move us in the right direction in order to get what we want. AIM! Taking aim before shooting our proverbial bullets is important. We want to be able to take our shots in life, obviously that makes a huge difference. In battle terminology, rather than spraying bullets all over the place hoping to hit something, there are better options. That is a vast waste of resources exhausts our supply of bullets, and our energy is depleted as well. We need to focus and PICK OUR BATTLES! This facilitates our use of FAITH, focusing on what we want vs what we don't want. Taking aim matters. That means understanding where faith is AIMED in any given moment, as well as if we are having faith at all.

By understanding both sides of the same coin,
We get past the philosophical stumbling blocks!
This eliminates problematic thinking!

Please believe me when I tell you that I was on the other side of this equation, both sides, multiple times in fact. I began by getting it right, but I didn't know or understand why I was getting it right because I was UNCONSCIOUS! Then I began to get it wrong, because I was doing it wrong, focusing wrong, didn't understand the issue that changed my results, because I was UNCONSCIOUS! With a tremendous amount of self-study, along with failing repeatedly, the light bulbs turned on quite suddenly because of a fairly dramatic sequence of events and ultimately a more pronounced and literally ANNOUNCED state of readiness on my part. That is when I BECAME CONSCIOUS! I woke the hell up and started paying closer attention. As a student, I was ready to learn when that revelation hit home with such an astounding impact and potency. It was dramatic, eye opening, and it was a major turning point for me. It was then that things began to click again. This time though, I knew why, mainly as a hypothetical. Because it was only understood as "book knowledge" or seen in its potentiality in my mind, it needed to become experiential. So, over the course of 12 long years, that "SELF-STUDY" continued, in trial-and-error mode. I continued to see poor results intermixed with good results as I was being watchful with the eyes that can see, ears that can hear, and feelings that were dialed in to the whole charade. The realization had come to me was that "I" was the problem. So, "I" began to be more open, less rigid, and that openness and observation mode offered me opportunities to be the solution instead. As the lower "selves", I got out of my own way more often than not. The higher "SELF" began to see these lower "selves" and started to override their "impulses" and the emotional components were processed and understood more fully as a result. I was constantly testing myself. I failed a LOT. ☹

This was the beginning of what I am now explaining to you. Seeing, truly is believing. That's what makes it experiential. Belief actually comes first, not second though, as you can see. In my case, that had to develop because the pain of failure left scars that needed to be worked through. I knew success and failure at that point and was able to discern some dramatic and impactful lessons from it. Faith did not immediately convert to trust though for me, but it did give me the impetus to take the next step. That process took a long time though, it could have been accomplished in a fraction of that time had I more fully trusted the "process" and the insights I received along the way. This is explained more fully in my book "Be the Instrument", but ultimately it is landing on these pages as well. Since that made all the difference for me, I wanted to teach it, show what I learned to prevent the "pain" approach and eliminate a lot of suffering for other people that may be hitting the same roadblocks or similar ones. It is super powerful, and I wanted to explain it so that there isn't any question as to whether this is a me vs you, or me vs anything, or YOU vs anything for that matter. In reality, it is the higher "SELF" vs the lower "self". There is no one upping, bragging, or elemental measurement going on. This is about knowing we can all be on both sides, in any given moment, and KNOWING when so that we can step up and make a difference, CHANGE! BEHAVE! Funny, actually, but did you even realize that behave is spelled be-"HAVE"? Kind of a fun way to look at the word...

BE HAVE!

Have some fun with that one (Be "HAVE" vs being "HAVE NOT")

INTRO: When we are in a particular state of mind, we are "LACK" oriented. Flip the coin, mentally, change the momentary point of focus and from a better emotional & energetic frame of mind we can be more balanced and / or optimistic, per se. We can all be "haves" and "have nots". The key is recognizing when we are in these states. Abundance vs scarcity mentality would be another way to look at it.

So, let's start with the "selves" and others that are showing up to life with a "have not" mentality. That would mean that we are MIS-be-"HAVING", right? Haha, LOOK WITHIN. Watch those thoughts.

HAVE NOTs: A "have not" mental state has patterned beliefs that are programmed, and within, just like the "haves". We are all essentially the same, are we not? Some folks, unfortunately, are just not conscious, not present, not awake, and NOT aware more of the time so they are more susceptible to the "selves" and the internal programming that goes along with that lack of presence, and it becomes an issue as a result. Trust me, I really do know, because I did it. In fact, did it A LOT! It was a pattern that I truly needed to overcome. I had to break free, that's why I am explaining it in such detail, so that you can understand what is required, and how to accomplish it. So, if we are locked inside a pattern, whatever that pattern may be, then, what are we when that happens? <u>Unconscious</u>! So, when we are consistently unconscious, or asleep at the wheel, remember that our core beliefs are driving what occurs in our life, NOT ME! Certainly not the highest and BEST, PRESENT ME! The "I" in that case is unconscious, (not in the moment.) When we are unconscious, our CORE beliefs are driving our behaviors and decisions. These are generated from the database or projections, and aligned with the little ego "selves". So, it is the past and future "illusion" on the mind screen which is driving their attachments, and THEIR STORIES. It is THEIR will, not our will as the higher "Overseer", PRESENT & FREE SELF! We have no power if the lower "selves" are in control of the mind. Their patterns become us in the moment when we are unconscious, they are making the decisions "unconsciously". Another way of saying that is that what we think are our moments are actually theirs, they are in control. Our lower "self" nature is determining our life... FOR US! (NOT us as the highest "SELF")

Unfortunately, if we are unconscious, they (as us) will step into every situation and respond to that situation as if it was that past or future as the ego "selves" relative to their attachments, storylines and illusions. (Their stories = little "me" / the ego) Therefore, that "have not" personality or "self" is programmed to, believes in, and has FAITH in "have not" at a core level. When a situation presents itself, as it will, and since the higher "SELF" is unconscious, we RE-act from the programmed lower selves (vs. the REAL SELF...the NEW ME, higher "ME"). As a result, the programmed RE-action is going be aligned with "have not" and so what little we have shall be taken from us... until we make a decision to WAKE UP and stay conscious to make different choices. Unconsciousness does NOT become anything NEW; it stays the same and can often get worse without intervention. Taking different actions would change our world but we are / were unconscious, asleep at the wheel, so nothing changes. This is why paying attention to our "egoic" / automated responses and their associated results is so important and beneficial. It helps us put the pieces together relative to cause and effect as well as our current level of "control" / awareness. Unconsciousness needs to become CONSCIOUS! We do that with awareness, paying attention to DETAILS! Life happens FOR US; we need to be paying attention to understand what is being provided.

Without waking up, we are on autopilot, nothing can change. Consciousness is REQUIRED! We can wake up with SKILL when we change our state, energize, empower our highest "SELF" and somehow some way muster the strength, and where-with-all to ARRIVE in the moment with focus, awareness, faith, trust, and PRESENCE to see, hear, and even FEEL all the information being provided in the moment. We are missing a massive amount of information and details by being unconscious, triggered, or emotionally occupied and mentally absent. With awareness and presence, everything changes. That is where a NEW choice is available to the HIGHER "SELF" within us, the one that is NOT aligned with LACK, or "have not". This NEW "I", with awareness and presence can CHOOSE abundance, and make abundance-oriented choices. As an example, we can also CHOOSE to "feel deserving" if we align with or believe in a more merit-based system. In that world, we will have moved from "not worthy", to "WORTHY" from a mind and belief / faith perspective. Semantics, really. The point is, with presence, CHOICE is available, and we can CHOOSE a better thought which affects our state, our magnetism and our results. Law of attraction, what we focus on expands, right? We are CONCIOUSLY CHOOSING what to focus on. Abundance vs scarcity, as an example. It took me through my own personalized version of HELL and back to truly understand this powerful mind toggle. I almost had NO MONEY. I was essentially broke, so I get it, truly I do, from first hand experience. I have been in this boat, with the water flowing forcefully through the hull. Thankfully I learned the lessons, but it took a bunch of years to plug the holes. I missed the mark a lot, even poked new holes...there was a lot of pain and suffering. I wanted to save people from having to go through that, so that's why this book exists.

We see every level of have and have not in society and the world at large. We can also see these within our "selves". The ego and the news media tend to take things to the max to the extent that they can get away with it. Measuring & comparing things and EXTREMES with dramatic images and storylines that SELL because they capture our attention. It is really just sales and advertising, propaganda. They bring in emotions with theatrics and SPIN in order to JUSTIFY their position and sell it to the mind. Whether we "BUY IN", well...I guess that depends on our "sucker" status at that moment (our awareness / vulnerability.). The same goes for the ego vs higher SELF. Depending on our state, or vulnerability and the level of energy & consciousness we may or may not be aligned with LACK vs ABUNDANCE! We may be feeling worthy or unworthy. We need to know which it is moment by moment and we do this with our conscious awareness: PRESENCE! We literally see the have and the have nots internally by looking within, wide awake. The potential is there, although maybe latent, for either of these to emerge at any given moment.

Relative to feeling "worthy", and to appreciate their purpose. Aren't the 10 commandments designed to make us feel more worthy? It's like a top ten list. Do all that, and we should, at a minimum, feel a little better about our "self". Wouldn't that be in essence, treating others as we expect and want to be treated? Do we not feel a little bit more deserving? We feel a little bit better, have a little more self-esteem. Not that it puts a chip on our shoulder or anything, we can simply value our "selves" and feel good. That is the religious version of a merit-based system. Integrity, morality, all that "stuff" contributes to that feeling of and belief in worthiness. That is of course assuming we are conscious enough to HAVE CHOICE and make the right ones. That is the difference between having beliefs and being able to honor them, it means waking up, being in the NOW to make conscious choices that are in alignment with our core values. Consciousness & PRESENCE matter if we intend to take the high road. If we are NOT conscious to make "good" choices and are therefore unable to follow the commandments for example, then where does that put us? What happens if we lie, cheat, steal, etc.? Remorse, regret, guilt = no fun. All the negative emotions come into play. Do we feel good about ourselves in these examples? Worthy? In addition, WHERE / WHEN are these emotional attachments? IN THE PAST! It amplifies our unconsciousness and then we miss the next moment too, because we are looking back to the past, and again we miss the moment / lessons...which compounds it. It cycles on and on until we wake up. Until we wake up, the negative cycles just repeat. This is what happens when we allow our programming to respond to life in any manner of unconscious-ness. Programs tend to repeat until they are RE-programmed. That doesn't happen if we are asleep at the wheel. Consciousness is required to reprogram or UN-program the program, but we are UN-conscious, so we stay the same.

Programs "answer" the way that they are programmed to respond. The "selves" are programmed and unconscious. So, in essence that means that the lower "have not" selves, in the merit-based system, due to programming are getting what they believe they deserve...at their CORE! Why though? It simply comes back to the fact that they are unconscious. Unconscious responses and the RE-actions are going to be aligned with our core beliefs if we are in a state of unconsciousness. In this case, our core beliefs are NOT WORTHY, the belief is in "have not"! So, is that fair? It could be argued that it is. Of course, whether we see it that way or not is up to us, but first we must see it in time to be able to make NEW choices. Did karma come back and bite us or did we simply get what we <u>believe</u> we deserved, and/or what we had faith in? Arguably, we got what we had faith in unconsciously. With a higher-level view, we can see that faith is being used either way. By being watchful as we proceed through life, as the overseer of it, real time, play by play, tick by tick, wide awake and aware we can see where faith is being used in the positive, and when it is being used in the negative. FAITH works. It isn't that it's not being used, it is. Unfortunately, it is just being used backwards in this case. We just need to RE-program the program, ME with a new approach, new program. The interesting thing about the new program is that it is programmed to: NOT BE PROGRAMMED! To do that we need to wake up. Consciousness and presence are the "cure"...HAVE FAITH!

So, this example amplifies the importance of paying attention to our internals within at a very detailed level because it happens fast. Our internals drive our state, our state determines our magnetism, and our magnetism is highly influential relative to our results. The whole progression happens in a flash. It can also change in a blink. The realization comes that we can change it, it can be directed. The law of attraction, highly simplified is the NET total "ALL" of our internals. Without an overarching awareness, our programming determines this, to a very high degree. So, what does this do as we are seeing it from the overseer / awareness perspective? It shows us where, when, how, and how much faith we are bringing into each moment as well as what we are having faith in, as the "selves", as they are RE-acting to life. OMG! It literally shows us which way we are headed, up or down by the MILLISECOND as the ego changes US, WITHIN, and our balance / "NET" is affected and adjusts to life's inputs! As our internal "shock" absorbers are "impacted" it kicks up the emotions, our "internals" are activated, attention & focus adjust and as a result, our magnetism changes, INSTANTLY! Our RE-actions to life happen ridiculously fast. That is why it is hardly noticeable. We need a more advanced level of awareness and some separation in order to see it. We see it by watching our internal programs RUN. Our internal programs are driven by THOUGHTS, and thought patterns, storylines, emotion, etc. which generate our RE-actions to life. From above, with awareness and separation, we see ALL! As a result, we can CHANGE!

PRESENCE ALLOWS CHANGE!

So, let's look at the other side of the equation, haves. Again, please remember that it isn't "THEM" vs "US". We all have BOTH of these traits, mentalities or tendencies within us. In any given moment, we can be a have or a have not, we must be paying attention all the "TIME" to know which that is. So, in essence, it is US vs us, ME vs me…higher SELF vs lower self. Just keep that in mind. Be watchful and BE-HAVE! LOL. Seriously though, Have fun with this. It's a comedy show, once seen.

HAVEs: To those that "HAVE" more shall be given. Yes, indeed, we see it all the time. Let's be honest, some people just seem lucky right? Stuff just falls in their lap and tends to go their way one thing after another. I get it, really, I do…did you ever wonder though, WHY? I mean, seriously, why is that? Is there any jealousy or animosity here? Can you say "trigger", uh oh, time to do some digging. Ok, so either way, let's dissect this too. Please understand that "haves" are also programmed, and have beliefs, we all do, right? We are human. But, contrary to the previous example, now those CORE beliefs are in "having". Their ego "selves" within them believe in the abundance idea, and they are aligned with "MORE" internally. The interesting thing is that even though they, as ego, can often be asleep at the wheel, their programmed responses can still be reasonably successful. (In the eyes of the world and relative to money, things, etc.) The fact is that they TRUST in abundance, they have "FAITH" in having...and so their "default" choices are going to be biased and aligned with more because at their core, they believe in it...and so they are given more. EVEN if unconscious. Makes perfect sense, right? They are also getting what they have faith in. Their internal magnetism is "geared" towards MORE! That's what they have faith in. So, they get more. They are really good at having faith in MORE! Mentally, they are "entitled" to it.

Put another way, those that have not are programmed and their software is geared to have not. It is possible that they are fearful, or don't feel worthy for whatever reason, and that could be due to any number of negative patterns. Moses gave us 10 of them! Regardless, their beliefs are aligned with NOT having. Their true faith is in not having. Where attention goes, energy flows right? If we are not paying attention, energy will flow to our pre-programmed beliefs. Have not's have beliefs that allow them to have not. For whatever reason they are not entitled to _____! Fill in the blank. "it", "anything", "much", "abundance", "Happiness", or whatever else. In this case we are talking about money, but it can be applied to everything. Mentally speaking, haves have pre-programmed beliefs that allow them to HAVE. In some cases, haves are thankful and appreciative for what they have, that attitude of gratitude amplifies it. This is nothing more than an EGO / programmed response to having, and so it is expected. If it is expected, it is more apt to come even if we are asleep at the wheel and unconscious re-acting as an EGO. Belief and faith build on one another and they are only DELIVERING what is believed in, and what the ego has faith in. Said another way...if we think we can or we think we can't, we are right. Fact is, we are delivered, every moment of every day...EXACTLY what we believe in at a core level. As shown above, that can go both ways, North or South.

What do you believe you deserve?

REALLY?

At a core level, does your life match up with this stated belief? Are you in alignment? BE HONEST! Ask your highest SELF where it might be able to challenge the beliefs that are generating your current life. This is an opportunity for a new beginning, creation begins NOW!

Are you conscious enough moment to moment to see, hear, and feel what you are truly believing in? Do you believe in your "SELF"? Do you exhibit that level of belief some of the time, or ALL OF THE TIME? It changes in degrees and is dependent on a lot of things, doesn't it? Our state of mind and beliefs drive the equation moment to moment, and they can change very quickly. In a fast-paced world, that's milliseconds. If we want to change our life, we must WAKE UP, hop in the driver's seat, focus, and take hold of the wheel CONSCIOUSLY, attentively. We must be watchful and realize what or WHO is making the decisions in our life, NOW! These former "selves", their programming, and their choices might not be aligned with our glorious imagery of the future. When we see this consistently, over and over again, we begin to override the pre-programmed responses in favor of our higher "SELF" and higher guidance. In doing so we can override the negative cycles, the recurring patterns, and ALLOW a different ME to bring different results by making new and better decisions / taking new actions in the moment. This is because we are INTENTIONALLY redirecting our focus IN THE MOMENT to have faith in something different, our TRUST is INTENTIONALLY placed in our NEW version of "SELF" in this moment, and our ability to ACT from the guidance we receive. We have great power within INTENT, but it needs to be intent that is unattached...untainted, that is a part of the skill. We CAN arrive to NOW with intent that is untarnished, we really can. But we must wake up and stay conscious. Presence is key. That highest version of ME can have faith and trust in the higher "SELF", "GOD" or the "Universe" and arrive in the moment to receive the guidance to ACT in the moment. Do this and we will know the TRUTH and our actions will be according to TRUTH...and we will be AMAZED at life and what it can deliver. Our entire state and magnetism changes. The law of attraction works, and we are the magnet...we just need to see what we are magnetizing / attracting so that we can redirect the magnet at the "times" when it is necessary. (That's NOW!)

Abundance vs scarcity thinking is very real, and that storyline or pattern of thought reflects very heavily on our results in life. Our state of mind is imperative and seeing it with awareness as life unfolds is key. We can see it happen as it happens with awareness. Intent, carrying baggage within such as a fear of failure, guilt, remorse, regret will fail. Even though we may visualize a wonderful outcome, our intent is tarnished by an attachment (negative association, negative charge, FEAR) and that attachment will drive the "me" or "I" that is "attached" into the current moment when it is captivated by that past / future. As a result of this captivation, the lower "self" now has control of the mind. That "core" lower self will make the decision in the moment (Instead of the real higher SELF as the NEW "I") and the decision will be driven by where our "core" attention and beliefs are. That also determines our magnetism. In this case since we are driven by fear, the fear is going to drive us to WHAT IS FEARED, and we will get our feared result rather than what we "wanted". Wanting something while fearing the alternative doesn't work to get us what we want, it works to get us what we DON'T WANT because that is what we have faith in, by default. We are focused there. In the merit-based system that is what we believe we deserve. When the fear of the alternative is greater than the faith in the desired, fear wins. The observation, recognition, and "understanding" changes with awareness of the underlying theme, or what lies underneath the emotions. It shows us the actual program which reveals the BELIEF. Our attention, our focus, our "core" vantage point must change. So, it goes back to consciousness. Are you conscious of these core vantage points and are you willing to challenge your beliefs? In order to do so, awareness and presence need to become a priority. These are key skills that help us to observe EXACTLY what we are having faith in moment to moment, if we are having faith in anything.

We must break the cycle of fear in our life and the only way to do that is by understanding the selves that drive that fear, their attachments, as well as the other emotions that come to the surface as a result. We do that by being present to our "selves" and watching them as they show up within and react for us over and over again in situation after situation PRESENTLY, NOW. As we do this, and as we start to understand the old versions of "me" that need updated software, the opportunity will present itself for us to release these patterns...by CHOICE. We can see these fear vs desire-based patterns. Fear drives us towards what we don't want, and desire drives us towards what we do want. When either one of these is HEAVILY weighted, it pushes us into more of an emotionalized state which tends to tip the scales sending us into unconsciousness. As "wants" escalate into more of a NEEDY state, it "becomes us" and the emotions that drive it are "attached" to that NEED. That's not a balanced approach to life and it translates into unconsciousness and missed opportunities. The result is that we get more of the same instead of what we may have wanted. The selves that took us over get more of what they are accustomed to. If we are in a state of "don't want", or a negative attractor factor, we get what we don't want rather than what we DO WANT. Our PATTERNS become more of the same "core" PATTERNS. That's HABITUAL! So, we stay the same, get the same, or even less of what we want. As we release more and more of these "old me" patterns, we release more and more of these little "selves", we "empty our cup". Our cup is full of LIMITS, and they are "self" imposed. We need to UN-limit these "selves". HOW?

EMPTY THE LIMITATION CUP!

The answer is in the details. If we see the moment as it unfolds then we can see the trigger. The trigger is that thing that captivated us. Whatever THAT was that grabbed our attention in that millisecond is the key to see. It shows us the "program" and the associated "attachment". So, as the program attempts to RUN in the mind, and take us over, we see it ahead of the takeover. AHEAD OF **TIME**! With awareness, and SPEED, the higher "SELF" averts the mutiny, and that captivation doesn't happen. This process, as it happens faster and faster, generates learning and growth in rapid succession. At times, it happens so fast that we need to stop and truly digest the amazing lessons that have been revealed. The result is an increase in our overall level of consciousness which enhances awareness. From that moment on, we see life from a whole new level with a deeper understanding of these underlying themes that drive us to do the things we do. It is "peeling back the onion" and seeing the layers upon layers of layers of "affection". Everything has an AFFECT on everything else. Once seen, it can't be UNSEEN! Eyes wide open is a real thing. It changes us. Everything affects everything and we see it happen right before our own very observant eyes. As we release these patterns with observation and understanding, we empty our cup. RELEASE and LET GO! For some patterns and programs this is a whole lot easier than others. That is for sure. Some linger, mainly because we just don't want to let go. Nevertheless, we can see that it is holding up progress and so eventually we do move on, sometimes begrudgingly. LOL The good news is that once we do, we can take that next step UP.

As we empty our cup of the baggage, we simply allow FAITH to fill it up.

As more programming is released, more faith enters, as more faith enters, more TRUST arrives, as more trust is allowed in, better decisions are possible because they are no longer being blocked or filtered out by the ego. In fact, the highest answer can arrive...LOVE! Love is the answer, right? Yes, and LOVE can arrive in each moment, as "needed". As we begin to HEAR and SEE with clarity, even more faith comes. As even more faith comes, better decisions result, LOVE grows...as better decisions result from our ability to see and hear the real-time guidance available in the moment, more faith grows. And to those that have...more shall be given. FAITH: to those that have... more shall be given. FAITH! Faith literally builds on itself like a snowball rolling downhill which builds up the trust factor. It feeds on itself, gains strength, and gives us the intestinal fortitude to take that next step because we believe in it. As our consciousness grows, we are able to see very clearly as we enter each moment how faith is activated within us and how quickly it can CHANGE! By amping up and directing our focus, we can pay even closer attention in order to see which direction it is AIMED! Quite honestly, it is almost as if we are seeing the future...and as such, we can RE-AIM before taking action. With a refocus, and some retargeting we can "clear the programs" that may have just been activated within us, refocus, re aim and then with a balanced and PRESENT internal "system" we can take more appropriate actions IN THE MOMENT from a mindset that has been optimized and maximized just a millisecond prior. That happens with PRESENCE! We get faithomized...although I think I just made that word up. LOL

GET FAITHOMIZED!

Faithomized: Knowing and consciously directing the mind moment to moment, IN THE MOMENT, to live faithfully. HAVE FAITH! Focus and really drill down on it, pay attention, and SEE it as often as you can muster the energy...faith, faith, faith, faith! I cannot say this with any more emphasis or any more emphatically, but I'd like to, so in ultra-BOLD, please hear this:

FAITH DELIVERS!

**Whatever I am focused on IS what I am telling my mind
to have faith in and deliver!
That means consciously or UN-consciously...YOU CHOOSE!
(Assuming you are awake and aware.)
So, what happens next is that since I AM having faith IN it,
good or bad...**

THAT IS WHAT IS DELIVERED!

We need to pay attention to our IN-tensions, WITHIN! Where is the focus? Where is the tension? Where is the friction? What is the mind doing with it? Whatever it is "attending to" or drilled in on and focused intently towards, THAT is what will expand. After all, at our core...that is what we believe in and it is revealed in our results, moment by moment. Focus in on and drill down on anything related to LACK, small, depleted, scarcity, limitation, then LACK will expand which means LESS not more. The alternative, of course, is to focus on ABUNDANCE, UN-limited, inexhaustible, un-bound, FREE, expansive, immeasurable and these type thoughts being expansive magnetize ABUNDANCE,

MORE and so it expands. This is determining our magnetism. We get what we are. What we are we will magnetize to ourselves. Consider it this way: I AM the MAGNET! What is inside of us magnetizes whatever it is to itself. So, if what I am is full of LACK thoughts and LACK stories, what am I magnetizing? Lack & LESS! So, just by the nature of my internals I am basically creating a life of depletion / negativity. That is enough to make us want to assess what is in our cup, right? What am I filling it up with? What kind of thoughts are in there? Mind FULL is the problem if it is FULL of negativities & lack oriented thoughts. EMPTY THAT CUP right away. Take a dump, fast.

If we don't focus on anything at all, well then flip a coin. If we are unconscious though and allowing the ego to respond to life for us, just know that the probabilities will favor our core patterns and overall magnetism. That is determined by the content in our cup. Our cup is our mind, which is full of THOUGHTS! The progression is that our thoughts become us, and it happens really fast. When our thoughts become us, that's our "house". The odds favor the house, so if our house is filled with core beliefs that are all negative, we need to find the door, or clean out our house / closets, else we will attract more of that. Sorry, that's just the reality of it.

Thanks to AI-Eli Art on Facebook who created this image!

The odds favor the house![19]

The law of attraction is attracting what is inside of us, our MAGNETISM, look within. The law magnetizes to us what we are, and in that moment, what we are determines what we see, in our life...we are the MAGNET! What we BE, we SEE! What we ARE goes FAR! This is relevant to everything we do, in all areas of our life. We don't have true maximizing and expansive, growth-oriented choice until we arrive IN THE MOMENT to CHOOSE for our "SELF"! We need to take care of our highest "SELF" and choose wisely. The door is right after yesterday, and right before tomorrow. Right after the past, and before the future. This is where, when, and how we can choose for our higher "SELF" which is FREE from the lower "selves". We must have FAITH in this new SELF that we have never seen or been before because we are over-riding core patterns. By OVER-seeing them faster and faster, growth happens faster and faster. The required ACTION to reprogram can only happen in the moment of NOW, with presence. So, our focus MUST drill down on that ever so small TIME SLOT called now...PRESENCE and awareness are the keys that can unlock that door and get us there...into the moment.

With faith we can get there, trust opens the door, presence walks through, there we have CHOICE. NOW!

What we need to realize and see is that life moves fast. While we all know this, DECISIONS and OPPORTUNITIES are won and lost in minute fractions of a second. As life begins to speed up, along with growth, our speed needs to keep up the pace. Our ACTION vs RE-action time can be the determining factor between success and failure. What that boils down to is that our level of conscious focus can CHANGE in an instant, which breaks down to milliseconds. These can be make or break moments. Once seen in this way, awareness moment to moment becomes a MAJOR priority. Massive present awareness is the key of keys; integral to maintaining a laser sharp mind that can fully incorporate situational context. We cannot be asleep at the wheel in life's vast playground, particularly at critical junctures. A lazy mind is a hazy mind, and that's just not acceptable in situations where momentary consciousness and focus can determine the trajectory of the rest of our lives. The way I look at it is that _EVERY_ moment does that. Every single second dictates the trajectory of the rest of our lives in one way or another. Once realized that every second counts, we decide to make them count. We stop wasting time by sleepwalking through life and we live out each moment as if it were our last. Creation starts NOW. YOLO (You only live once) should be expanded to state that YOLOMAAT! You only live one moment at a TIME! That time slot is called NOW!

MAKE BETTER CHOICES, live in the NOW!

One way we can "GET MORE" assuming we want more in our life, is to find a way to FEEL more deserving, and worthy. It totally builds on itself. HAVE FAITH! Wide awake, aware, focused and present...make choices that are aligned with MORE of what you want. Of course, that is assuming you want more. That may be more peace, happiness, love. We all have our priorities, of course. These are choices, as are money and things. Maybe we can have it all?! We live in a more, more, more society. Why not pay attention to what we want more of instead of living by default? (or focusing on what we don't want.)

We live in an abundant universe. KNOW THIS, THINK THIS, LIVE THIS...it takes practice, and conscious aware PRESENCE. What we have had faith in, up to this moment, IS being demonstrated in our life right now. If we think we deserve better, then we need to BELIEVE we deserve better. We need to ACT like it, THINK like it, and DECIDE like it. We need to make the choices that are aligned with it. If that means doing good deeds to "earn it", then we need to do good deeds. One way or another we MUST have FAITH, TRUST and BELIEVE! With presence we can CHOOSE worthiness, BE WORTHY! Once we become worthy, which we some "times" need to teach our "selves" to do, at a CORE LEVEL, then THAT becomes our magnet.

Let me pause here to suggest that the most powerful form of prayer is to believe in something BEFORE IT HAPPENS, AS IF it has already happened. That is 100% faith. At a core level, that becomes our MAGNET. Magnets ATTRACT! This is the law of attraction working, in all its glory. Act as if it is true already and BELIEVE it is true for you in the present / past. If you really want to cement it in place, then you must become it in your mind. Make it as real as possible, with energy and then add some emotion to it. That means that once this is true as a visualization / prayer in your mind, BE THANKFUL as if it has already been delivered. Gratitude is the faith cement that makes it stick. This is the virtual "answered prayer" in advance. This is HOW TO PRAY, in real-time.

KEY OBSERVATION: Observe prayer positioning relative to TIME.

The time element matters, <u>BIG TIME!</u>

Praying for some hypothetical FUTURE is where in time? IN THE FUTURE! This is what <u>keeps it there</u>. There are many reasons why it might stay there, vs becoming true in our reality right now, one of the reasons is because we are planting it in there, IN THE FUTURE ...by constantly visualizing it there...in the future. Our mind puts it there all the "TIME", as a picture or short "clip" and the clip, mentally as a visual, is IN THE FUTURE! In the mind this is problematic because it sees that it is NOT TRUE NOW because we are still WANTING IT, that's a "self" that is LACKING IT. It's a LACK mentality! That lack mentality carries the weight of 1000 words, because it is being seen in the mindscape, and WE DID IT! So, that means that we are not BELIEVING it is true now, which it isn't...so the answer to this dilemma requires a bit of a mind trick. The ego wants to play games, play games...trick it. FLIP IT AROUND, make it look at it as if it has already happened and already exists in your life. This can be difficult to do if we don't feel entitled to such a thing, or we aren't able to make it feel real, which is absolutely critical. One reason that may be true is that we are NOT worthy enough to have it NOW, or at least we don't FEEL that way. Not yet anyway...otherwise we would have it, be it and believe it. So, the answer is that the belief comes FIRST, not second. We flip the "prayer" by flipping the thought, We can do that by making it true NOW in the mind, by sticking it in the past mentally as if it has already happened. By taking that hypothetical future, putting it in the past, within the mind, it makes it REAL to the ego mind. What is in the past is true...it already happened.

If we go a little further and be super thankful for it...and take a moment to truly enjoy it, feel the feelings that we would feel as if it were true NOW, then it is REALLY real. That's belief. In the mind, it has already happened, it is already true...that is WITHIN, it has become our core for that moment which is a true and POWERFUL PRAYER / THOUGHT! What does our magnet magnetize? What we are. So, in this moment our core magnetism just changed. Pray without ceasing is the recommendation, now we know HOW. This is SUPER POWERFUL, if we do it. That is a really powerful visualization. Pay attention to detail though, timewise. HAVING, by the nature of the tense, is BELIEVING. Having believes it is true now because it IS TRUE. All we are doing is tricking the mind... Now, look at it from the other vantage point. WANTING, by the nature of the tense is NOT having, and therefore: NOT BELIEVING! Wanting actually believes 100% that is does not "HAVE". It's NOT TRUE now, in fact it is so NOT TRUE that we are getting frustrated and angry that it is NOT TRUE. That's the problem, we keep reinforcing the belief. How often do we "WANT", and how often do we do that wanting with some level of emphasis, or an ANCHOR!?! The anchors are crying, asking why? Why? Why? Complaining about it, getting frustrated, etc. These emotional anchors PROVE to the mind that it is NOT TRUE NOW! It is proven that it doesn't exist in this reality now with EMPHASIS! As if that's not bad enough, even worse is that it is this anchoring process that kicks it further out into the future. More emphasis, more delays. I will explain this further in the upcoming chapter on wanting. The moral of the story though is QUIT COMPLANING! Stop with the emotional outbursts, gossip, chatter about it, MOVE ON, LET IT GO! Get back to NOW!

To be TIME-WISE, we need to pay attention to TIME as it relates to the images in our head. Where we are in TIME relative to our visualization is really important. Let's say hypothetically that we go a little overboard with this "habit" and we are consistently visualizing our amazing future, adding emphasis, adding emotion and anchoring it but we keep picturing and visualizing it IN THE FUTURE. In our mind, we are placing it in our future because we see this amazing possibility and we get excited about it. Understandable. We all want what we want. So, in our mind it is basically a hypothetical, and we are truly happy to see it as a "potential". In this ERROR in execution, we are "doing it" but we are doing it with a methodology that is flawed. I would refer to that as kind of over-faithomizing, meaning we got too excited about that hypothetical future and forgot how to visualize properly. All that excitement is counterproductive... but why? What we are doing is taking a very productive idea, but we are using it ineffectively. In fact, the error in execution pushes that amazing future FURTHER OUT into the future to the extent that we emphasize and emotionalize it. We are still wanting by the nature of the visualization occurring in the mindscape when we are wanting, even if we are not deliberately visualizing, the MIND IS. We must see this. We may even get frustrated by the fact that it hasn't happened and then that energy is continually used to "WANT IT" more, which further emphasizes the fact that we don't HAVE IT! So, let's back up and do it RIGHT. To test this in your own "projections" and visualizations, please consider where in "TIME" your "visualizations" are. Questions to ask are as follows:

1. Are you a believer, and confident that you have a bright future and spend a lot of time visualizing? Maybe you even created a dream board, or a power point presentation detailing your amazing future, save glorious images of things you want, and places you'll visit on some of these new social media platforms? That's WONDERFUL! Good stuff, really...but ask a more pointed question, #2

2. When you visualize these things, situations, goals, desires, wants, needs...where are you mentally putting them in TIME? Is it in the future, mentally, as a projection? Well, if that's the case, that's just fine, if you want it to stay in the future...you are just pushing it out further into the future every time you emphatically do it! You do that by anchoring it with excitement, frustration, and all the other emotions you are emotionalizing WHILE you are visualizing that future

IN the future. In essence, if you are taking the positive approach, you are STAMPING IT with your positive APPROVAL that it is in your future. The stamp is the emotion, which cements it in the future in the mindscape. If you are taking the negative approach and getting angry, frustrated, stressed, or whatever else, then the STAMP is the disapproval. That emotionalized content validates to the mind that it is STILL in the future! "I WANT" as an attitude is fueled by one of two vantage points, positive or negative. Whether we use frustration or excitement, anger or joy about that hypothetical future really doesn't matter because either way it is telling the MIND that we don't have it NOW and then with a heightened EMOTION, PROVING that we don't have it NOW! The emotion is what makes the mind BELIEVE that it is NOT TRUE NOW! It's like a backfiring strategy in disguise...it's counterproductive. We don't see it because the mind is so busy WANTING! The "wanting" with emphasis is THE PROBLEM when the mind sees that it is not HAVING it NOW! Not only does it NOT get you what you want, it pushes it further out into the future...like dangling a carrot and the carrot just keeps getting further and further way, and WE ARE DOING IT TO OURSELVES! We are fueling LACK because we are trying SOOOOOO hard, we are WANTING it sooo badly! Meanwhile, our internal "saboteur" is continuously and energetically spinning its wheels and "self" defeating its "SELF". The lower "selves" are defeating our higher "SELF" with this non-sensical behavior. BAD AIM, Bad energy, bad pattern, bad HABIT! "WANTING" doesn't work! Actually, if no one ever told you how to do it effectively, that's not your fault. Now you are wise to it

See the point? The bottom line is that:

WANTING = VISUALIZING
VISUALIZING IN THE FUTURE DOESN'T WORK to have it
NOW!
Visualizing in the future works to have it in the future, which
NEVER COMES!
IT KEEPS IT IN THE FUTURE!
WHY? Because we keep planting it there with our beliefs in NOT
HAVING!

Pay very close attention to where the imagery is in the mind when you are planting it in the mindscape. The "proper" way to do it in my best effort to explain it is to REACH INTO that "DREAM" where you "HAVE IT ALL" and take that whole clip or image out of the future, plant it in the PAST, in the mindscape, and then BE THANKFUL AS HECK ABOUT IT, NOW...as if it is already true. Thank God or whatever, whomever you pray to for delivering this amazing "stuff" in your life. NOW that you absolutely 100% BELIEVE in that truth, it's time to LET IT GO, get back to NOW and make it happen. Expect the best, believe the best, and BE THE BEST SELF you can muster...the one that "WAS" in that dream in that future, BUT do it NOW! ACT AS IF...is a very powerful methodology So, once your amazing future is visualized, LET IT GO! STOP with the wanting and START with the HAVING! Belief comes FIRST. The seed is planted, now let it go and let it GROW. In order to make it happen, we must be in the moment to make it happen, so let faith do its work...get the MIND out of the future and into the PRESENT MOMENT, NOW. We must come back to reality full of faith to make it happen. NO DOUBT! Allowing doubt / worry / fear creep into the mindscape is basically faith wavering, so be watchful. Note that all of these are the mind "projecting" a potential future. GET BACK TO NOW!

OK, so, back to worthiness. If our "core" is NOT worthy, not believing, then our faith will deliver results that are NOT WORTHY! It's easy to see that, right? We are living in a lack mentality. What we lack is refined and directed BELIEF! Therefore, we must "self" correct. If we truly believe that we are not worthy, then we will be fighting an uphill battle. We need to lose the guilt, remorse, regret, or whatever the negativity is. Drop the story, let it go. Please, please, please under-stand this, the stories are in the past, process it. Whatever it was, understand that it was a former self that made that decision, basically a former life before waking up. Back then whenever that was, we were not consciously creating our lives...that could be 2 seconds ago, or 20 years ago. LET IT GO! Even when we are making our best efforts, we still have momentary lapses, particularly when we are not fully energized, tired, or run down...for whatever reason. The fact of the matter is that bad choices are made unconsciously, while a lower version of "self" is unaware... FORGIVE IT! One way or another, we have to let it go, MOVE ON, and just do our absolute best to be present next time so it doesn't happen again. New starts begin right NOW, this millisecond. Not letting it go is no good, in fact, very BAD! It's like holding on to a bad attitude. Let's say guilt, as an example. It causes all kinds of negativity inside of us, in the mind AND body, simply by holding onto it. It is like subscribing to a mind program that states very specifically "PUNISH ME!" As a result, it is the equivalent of subconscious POISON to the mind and body. We must GET conscious in order to LET IT GO! Holding onto negativity magnetizes more negativity, emotionally, energetically and physically. There are some incredible books that demonstrate and explain the linkages between the mind & body. John E. Sarno, "The Mindbody Prescription" is a great book.

Louise Hay, is another great resource!

"You can heal your life".[20]

At a minimum, please understand this: our core, internals, body, mind and health, as well as our spiritual availability will ALL be better if we can RELEASE THE PAST!! After letting go, the next step is to WAKE UP and STAY AWAKE to new levels of consciousness each and every moment. Focus on awareness and being present in the moment. Do whatever it takes to energize systemically to mentally, physically, physiologically, magnetically, and from a higher level of awareness perspective...just STAY AWAKE! This means conscious awake, aware and present...not to stay awake physically for days on end. We do need sleep in order to replenish and restore, else our health and wellbeing suffer as a result, as well as our ability to remain focused and aware. A tired mind is a shape shifter, it's all over the place mentally. JUST STAY PRESENT! Once we release the past, then our mind requires FAITH so that the future mindsets don't reach in and grab our attention. If that happens then we are captivated all over again. It's just we went from a prisoner of the past to a prisoner of the future, mindset wise... Neither is FREE!

So, to accomplish this higher conscious awareness presently, with some consistency, we need to stay energized so that as this higher "SELF" we can be watchful of our thoughts, body language, demeanors, expressions, feelings, tone, etc. Once we are WIDE AWAKE, aware, and fully conscious, with massive, concentrated focus presently , we can make the internal changes, or add the midnight oil necessary to shed light on whatever unconsciousness still exists in the mind in order to wake up and receive life from a different state of mind. It is this NEW state of readiness, or receptivity that opens us up to bigger and better possibilities for our more current and present higher "SELF". This translates to opportunities to be new and create NEWNESS in our lives instead of the same ole same ole. Where once there were weeds, we start to see flowers emerging and so we fertilize them with our attention instead. What we focus on expands.

One option, as we step forward and are NEW NOW, is to arrive in the moment being mentally worthy enough to BELIEVE and have faith by CHOICE which creates a major shift internally. That internal adjustment produces a different magnetism and that shows up in our present thoughts & actions. It must be with a really high degree of focus & confidence to MAKE IT HAPPEN! Change requires re-programming, that means dealing with the "selves". Life delivers as we are delivered from our "selves". That's why trust & faith are the key of all keys. They help us to remain present, awake, aware and consciously directing our mental energies appropriately. We need to empty our cup first, and then we can fill it up with FAITH and NEWNESS. The faith state drives our results. That's why I say to get "faithomized". This is something we do for our highest SELF as our highest SELF, moment by moment as we achieve presence and master the "selves". This allows us to maintain our focus in the moment vs going into a different state...such as "wanting" or "NOT wanting". Desire, fear, and other heightened emotions can toggle us to both extremes. As a result, our mental state changes along with our magnetism. It brings on a state of unconsciousness. The two biggies, desire and fear, are BOTH anchored in the FUTURE when we are projecting on the mind screens. Not present NOW = Not FREE NOW!

As we arrive to the moment, we need to step up in a way that truly maximizes our potentiality. Our MAGNET needs to be re-magnetized and we need to be FREE to make effective choices. There are very real ways we can do this, and we need to figure out the personalized settings & ways that work for us as individuals, moment to moment in all types of situations. As we implement these internal strategies, we get charged up, fired up and READY! It needs to be enough to move the needle on the faith gauge though! That's where the magic happens, but it isn't magic, it is our personalized, optimized and maximized, highly influential internal settings that influence our magnetism. With presence, we have choice, we have the "controls". We know our own personalized and internalized settings that "DELIVER US" to the moment in order to have more faith in the moment. Some "times" we just need a reminder. Some level of emotion kicking up a notch is often a good hint to refocus and as a part of that mental shift / awakening, we tell our "selves" to have faith, think faith, live faithfully. Faith demonstrates what was believed in a moment ago. That is our current life. Think about that. Now, we are using that newly introduced ENERGY to change our faith state which changes our life.

EMOTION = ENERGY
ENERGY IS FOR USE!
We must recognize, interpret, and use it productively!

If we don't like our current life, we can't focus on it longer than it takes to realize we need to think a new thought that has the potential to generate something new.

This means interjecting rather than focusing on the negative emotion which is TIME related (past / future)! If we can muster the where with all to START A NEW stream of thought that is "AIMED" in a little different direction, we change the "FLOW" of our life stream. Going with the flow isn't the answer if the river of thought is headed in the wrong direction. Now we know how to change it, consciously, by redirecting our thought themes and thought streams. Every moment is a new beginning, we start where we are. We must be present to CHANGE OUR MIND! That's where it all starts, in the mind. The mind generates our faith state with THOUGHTS! Emotionalized thoughts are typically emotional about something they are attached to in the past / future, they are time-locked out of the moment...so by waking up to that consciously, we can snap our "selves" back to NOW, get present and think a new thought. We are no longer at the mercy of that lower attached self (in time), we can be new, NOW!

So, literally right this second, we can start believing in something different. That means starting a new stream of thought. If we don't know what to believe in, or where to start, then we must start by clearing our head. If nothing else, it is a fresh start, a blank slate from which to make new and better decisions. Our lives can be new each moment and by changing our thoughts we change our lives, moment by moment. Some moments are obviously much more influential than others because we are receiving bigger lessons, changing the direction of bigger thought themes, and waves of thoughts, larger mental "HABITS"! The only opportunity to steer is THIS MOMENT, right NOW! Change your thoughts, change your internals, change your magnetism = change your life. This progression happens lightning fast though so we must "catch the wave".

If surfer language, we must see it forming and be ready as that mental wave is approaching. Mental thought waves can be "caught" very early in the creation stages. We see that happen by watching it and overseeing our internals moment to moment consciously with awareness. We must KNOW what we are believing in, having faith in...which is INSIDE the thought waves. So instead of being reactive as waves are hitting us in life and trying to keep our mental boat afloat, we are literally changing and upgrading the wave. From this new masterful and commanding presence, we are one with the waves. In fact, we are the waves, it's just now we are aware and consciously directing the internals of those waves. That VOLUME, or the content of the "thought waves" has massive power to MOVE US as well as everything in its path. Once organized, understood, combined and redirected, that water volume can form a TIDAL wave of thoughts which can push a LOT of water. As we stay in tune and consciously create our thought waves, we can truly focus on making bigger, more powerful waves. Once that mass of water volume is moving in the same direction, we can break out our surf boards and ride these waves for an incredibly enjoyable experience. What FUN! This is NOT hypothetical; it is very real!

CHANGE YOUR THOUGHTS = CHANGE YOUR LIFE!
GO MAKE SOME WAVES!

You can play small, making some ripples in a pond, or you can THINK BIG! Thinking BIG makes bigger waves. Just be sure they are POINTED intentionally towards the shoreline you want because once that water starts rolling it can be quite a ride and hard to stop. We create, have faith, and ride the tide. That is the difference between a reactive life and constant creation.

Shrink and hide vs CREATE AND RIDE!

Which sounds like more fun? THINK BIG, and then go ride some BIG WAVES! At a base level, our internals drive thoughts and thought waves. The swells, or waves of waves are driven by larger patterns of thoughts, our habitual nature. That is the water in the waves. The water in the waves is moving because of the lower "selves" within an unconscious mind. They move us with emotions and thoughts which move the water. This can cause CHOP, and we go nowhere, or they can be organized and move us in a particular direction. That can happen consciously, or unconsciously. Once these thoughts of LIKE KIND produce a wave, it starts moving in a particular direction, towards a VERY SPECIFIC shoreline. Once it is moving, it's moving. We just need to understand that we create the waves. We need to back up some "times" to see the powerful waves we have generated in the past to understand how we ended up on this particular shoreline. That's our life right now. We can "SELF" generate and ride new waves, but we must be conscious enough to DO IT. In addition, it requires a certain level of BELIEF in our higher "SELF" and the ability to control, as well as ride the thought waves These thought waves are FULL OF FAITH, we need to look inside the water though, so that we can see where this water is headed. In some cases, we are forced to ride out some fairly negative thought waves that we created via unconsciousness as we wake up to this new way of living. As we start to create new waves, our lives can change quite dramatically, but waves are waves, and they can carry a lot of water. If we created some bigger waves that might be headed in the wrong direction, we need to hop off, grab a different wave or create a new one. Sometimes that is easier than others, particularly if we are on a larger wave and it is curling over headed towards shore and we are in the tunnel where there is only one way out. In that case, so we don't get completely pummeled with water, we need to ride it out a bit before we can catch a new one...hopefully that makes sense. Our surfing skills get better OVER "time".

Taking that same wave of thought and relating it to the bible: Jesus calmed the sea, right Impressive. WE CAN TOO mentally with the right tools. If you are a believer, why did Jesus die for our sins? The simple answer is explained in the above paragraph. It is to empty our cup if it is full of negativity, clean the slate in order to enable / forgive / make a "sinner" FEEL WORTHY again. The negative "waves" were neutralized "forgiven". It eliminated the requirement for us to "ride out" the waves. In addition, it eliminated the necessity for "suffering" before we could hop on a new wave and change course, "right the ship". It is similar to being let out of the penalty box, or prison for that matter. It can be difficult if not almost impossible for people that have done really bad things to forgive themselves. (Their former past "selves"). Sometimes, carrying that forward is almost unbearable and the mental RUT, and possibly physical ailments that can follow as a result have the potential to make life extremely difficult. The fact is, if that is what we believe we deserve, we punish ourselves semi-consciously, and unconsciously so we keep getting pummeled by the same type waves of thoughts, much of which is unconscious. We essentially create our own prison cell and punishments because of the things that we have done in order to carry out our own sentencing (Karma). With understanding, it is FORGIVEN, no matter what. Jesus basically cleaned the slate, for lack of a better way to put it. No longer is it up to us to do it. He said, I did it FOR YOU. We must believe IT IS DONE, because it is. He even said so. This is also how "SELF-LOVE" works. We forgive our lower "selves" that messed up, because quite honestly, they didn't know any better. It seemed like a good idea at the "TIME". We have to let it go and GROW through the experience. Say: NEXT. Because we have learned and internalized that lesson, we can wholeheartedly step up with faith and take another shot at life with a much more favorable attitude as well. Probabilities for a favorable outcome are a lot higher.

"GO; it shall be done for you as you have believed" -Mathew 8:13[21]

Now, with a massive amount of awareness, SEE WITHIN! Ask questions like this:

Did I truly let it go, or do I need some more punishment? This is obviously sarcasm, but it can be very real. Bottom line is the internal assessment with oversight: Do "I" truly believe I AM deserving? Am I SHOWING IT, FEELING

IT? Is that reflecting in my attitude / magnetism? Or: am "I" going to need to convert this internal state, and preferably NOT punish my lower "self" some more? So, seriously consider the overall state of the internals. Wake up, assess. Unconsciousness bleeds into more punishment which shows up in our lives and our bodies. We need to see that kind of stuff. Be watchful! What signs am I seeing in my life, body, or within my mind, thoughts? Do I see freedom or limitation / pessimism? What do I FEEL physiologically in my body, is it confirming or denying this mental belief? Am I demonstrating optimism, potentiality, belief, trust, FAITH or the opposite? What signals can I observe internally that would confirm or deny this WITHIN myself? Does my body physiology align with what I THINK I am thinking or is it telling a different story? Why, what's the story? Is my mindset in alignment with my facial expression and confirming my supposed "optimism"? Am I relaxed and focused? Is the side of my mouth facing up or down? (smiling or not?) These are all indicators of our overall STATUS, or state of mind / body. This determines our magnetism and shows us signs of what we believe and trust in. Sometimes we really need to pause and assess this. Our state is critical...it determines our outcomes. We are producing this state over and over again, moment by moment. It is constantly changing, ever evolving, QUICKLY! We need to monitor these internal fluxes by stepping up and observing our state with a highly attentive overseeing awareness. This will allow us to optimize and maximize our highest and best SELF geared towards its highest and best outcomes. It is NOT by controlling outcomes themselves, it is by controlling the internals that generate those outcomes as we are meeting the moment. As a reminder, some self-love and / or self-forgiveness may be a requirement to move up the proverbial ladder in some cases. That would be to promote a better "FEELING", to be more optimistic, to feel more deserving, and worthy IN OUR OWN VERY JUDGEMENTAL and critical EYES! We need to FREE our "selves". We do all that by letting go of the "self" that wants to blame, or feel bad, get in negative mindsets, and maybe even feel unworthy for whatever reason. Get the lesson, learn, grow and let it go. Move on!

As the higher SELF, I am being watchful and aware, ASKING: What am I as the lower "selves" within my mind habitually believing in and focused on? What am I focusing on right now, or lately? Am I holding onto anything, looking back in TIME? What have I been focused on lately that has brought me to this moment? Has that produced the life I want? If we don't like it and / or we don't want it to continue as it is, we have to CHANGE IT! Not the result, that ship has sailed so to speak. That outcome is DONE, in the PAST! We need to learn the lesson and change the thoughts that created that result, not repeat them, so we don't continue to produce what those thoughts produced. We are living right

now in a NEW MOMENT and can show up as a NEW SELF, thinking a NEW
THOUGHT! In our lives going forward, that means that the next time we
don't re-create the same thing. We must think different thoughts & take different
actions to get different results. We have to kind of back up and see it so we can be
better the next time but with a really good spirit of learning mindset. We need to
SEE it to BE IT!

Do IT AGEEEEEEEN, one of our coaches used to say, with EMPHASIS added!
That was his highly energized way of saying "Do it again!" because someone
did it wrong. So, do it again... Just, this time, do it differently. Maybe correctly,
BETTER with more energy and maybe a better state of mind / magnetism!
Whatever it is that I have been doing and thinking has created this life that I am
living RIGHT NOW! That understanding creates the impetus to assess these
thoughts moment to moment so that we can make real time adjustments, as
needed! As we do this and see the various changes unfold in our lives we get
better at it and the process develops faster internally. So, the result of that faster
progression is that our life has the potential to change a lot faster as well! Growth
SPURTS do happen, and then we reach a digestion phase. Very REAL! Plateaus
do occur because we need time and energy to digest what we have learned in order
to implement it going forward. Then we can grow / amplify / focus and expand
some more because we have the capacity and more energy to do so!

In order to DEMONSTRATE a new pattern, for example, in someone's life,
what must happen? Faith and belief in something different must happen. Right?
Where does this start? WITHIN! **Faith is WITHIN!** Faith is demonstrated
by the ACTION we just took, by the choice we just made. We can recognize
when the ACTION we just took was a new ACTION, or a RE-action: a NEW
choice or a something that resembles a more habitual response. It was generated
from within, either way, we must see this. WE MUST arrive IN the moment
to **REPRESENT** as our "SELF", higher SELF that is! If we allow the former
"selves" to run our life, what change is possible? What do the former selves believe
in? We must look at our life and realize that our life right now is what they believed
in, up to today's date, a moment ago. Acknowledging that fact is where we step in,
step up and deliberately start to believe in something different consciously, with
massive awareness and a very deliberate focus.

Are you ready to believe in something different? Maybe have faith in something
different? How? You know the answer already, NOW! So, **don't project "wanting" into the future in the mindscape.** We must BELIEVE, and that's actually
NOT BELIEF! Putting it in the future actually does the opposite, it makes it
UNTRUE NOW! "Believing" by projecting it into the future is not a belief

in having, it is a belief in NOT HAVING! It's a fool's paradise. What we are wanting will never happen, or at a minimum, it will push it further out on the timeline because it is actually believing in the lack of having it already. We must believe it is TRUE NOW! So, what that means is that "WANTING" is a disguised "LACK" mentality. Wanting something really badly is even worse then, right? So, we must watch for this, as it is happening, so that it can be redirected, energy-wise. The emotion is the clue where we can see our "selves" WANTING! Frustration, anger, and the heavier emotions fuel it by projecting the mind and whatever we are WANTING into the future as we are striving for it, trying to GET IT. The emotion is the cement that keeps it there... Don't do that. Catch the emotion. As the frustration is building, we must **catch our "selves" doing the wanting...and start the faithing instead**! It's all about faith and belief, but the mind gets hung up and CAUGHT IN TIME by the emotion of NOT HAVING! The emotion of "NOT HAVING" is disguised as innocent and perfectly normal "wanting". The result is that we don't recognize it as a "LACK" mentality. Thoughts are very powerful. This is a case where we are not being watchful of the impact they are having on our lives.

Catch the "selves" WANTING!

Wanting is a lack of belief or essentially having faith in LACK, belief in the negative, belief in the opposite of what we want. Having faith in what we don't want gives us what we don't want. It amplifies, and even perpetuates the LACK OF IT! Sometimes that can simply mean we don't have faith in what we DO WANT! It boils down to a belief in lack. We must restructure the thoughts that are RE-generating this "lack" in our lives. We do that by BELIEVING something NEW is true now, which is a mind hack, mind trick. The most powerful form of prayer is believing in something BEFORE it happens, and what is that called? FAITH! So, what are you believing in when you are "wanting"? (The answer is the negative of what you want.) Flip the thought around. START BELIEVING IN SOMETHING NEW! By seeing this in retrospect, we can see that our prayers (thoughts) are being answered every moment of every day? Our thoughts generate and perpetuate, BE WATCHFUL!

<u>NOW</u> is where and when FAITH is implemented.

NOW = HOW we FAITHOMIZE our "selves"!

So, now we have a thorough understanding of how faith works to get us one of two things:

1. What we want.

2. What we don't want.

We now have the recipe. We are the "haves" and we are the "have nots", ALL THE TIME! We just need to know which one is showing up to the moment. We spend a lot of "TIME" flip flopping back and forth. FOCUS! Be diligent, highly AWARE and watchful. It is based on where we are focused, and what we are paying attention to, as well as where we are in TIME! THOUGHTS MATTER! This is driven by our core beliefs. The moment we CHANGE our focus, stand firm with PRESENCE, and change our state of mind / being in the NOW moment, we enable a pattern recognizing level of awareness that sees these behaviors, programs, thoughts and patterns for what they are: patterns of beliefs, rules, and LIMITS! Making it a game, it can be looked at as FORMER little me vs potential NEW higher ME / NOW ME! HIGHER "SELF" vs lower "selves". These new eyes and new ears see and hear differently as we look within and optimize in order to MAXIMIZE. This is where change occurs, WITHIN! We see the patterns that produce inferior results, and we CHANGE the program, or erase it. THINK NEW THOUGHTS, while being aware of the old ones that no longer serve us. This promotes learning and growth. Over-riding poor programs is an ongoing self enhancement feature that is ever expanding as long as it is attentive, focused, aware and PRESENT! It is in an ever-ready stance of BECOMING NEW and ACTING as this NEW SELF! We can literally be running A / B scenarios in real time with this level of IN-sight and OVER-sight running in tandem. This is hugely powerful and lightning fast.

The vantage point that I think is most productive in this regard is from above and slightly behind the mind AND inside it. From this vantage point we can see with a broader more all-inclusive contextual viewpoint externally & internally, as well as being drilled down and focused on the content with a heightened level of concentration. It's kind of like your mental coach running alongside you, always able to keep up and instruct because they are seeing what we are doing as we do it, IN THE MOMENT! We often don't see things in ourselves that we need to see, we are too close to it. That's where this oversight comes into play. It sees everything we do, how we do it, why we do it as well as where and when we TEND to do it the most. It is more of a detached and elevated perspective that we can stay on top of our "selves" and look within our "selves" from this more expanded, all-encompassing viewpoint as the "Overseer" of the mind. We enable this expanded omni-vision so that we can be the overseer of all of the context and yet be extremely dialed in to the details at the same time. As things play out on the life stage, the overseer of the mind can see thoughts without being attached to them from the "field" perspective and the DOER within can execute with skill and precision, in the moment, like a surgeon. Let's explore this overseer perspective in some additional ways from different angles and vantage points, I think it will help because this shows us when we are in these states.

From this perspective we can see WANTING / NOT WANTING, HAVE / HAVE NOT mentalities. These are mental core states that DRIVE our results. Now we can see the positive and negative associations being made in the mind as well as where they are in "time". We see the emotions STAMPING them with our approval or disapproval. These are the problematic mindsets that are keeping them in the future. We can do better, so let's explore some more.

9

THE OVER-SOUL
Overseer: Higher "SELF" Knowledge

W E HAVE DEFINITELY DISCUSSED this concept, quite extensively. Sometimes it is healthy to hear it in different words though because words mean different things to us. We translate them differently, they paint different pictures within us and as a result of that imagery, they tell different "stories". A picture is worth 1000 words, right? From some other perspectives, this will paint the picture in a different way, and of course, I will explain the similarities along the way so that this is really cemented in the mind and readily usable.

The following is from **Ralph Waldo Emerson** in his essay **"The Over-Soul"**[22]. **Emerson** says we don't even represent ourselves. What a bold statement...consider this from the perspective of the lower selves, vs higher "SELF", and who is representing as "I" / ME in the moment. If we are unconscious, it is the lower "selves" that represent us.

*"A man is the facade of a temple wherein all wisdom and all good abide. What we commonly call man, the eating, drinking, planting, counting **man, does not, as we know him, represent himself**, but **misrepresents himself**. Him we do not respect, but the soul, whose organ he is, **would he let it appear through his action**, would make our knees bend. When it breathes through his intellect, **it is genius**; when it breathes through his will, **it is virtue**; **when it flows** through his affection, **it is love**."*[23]

To expand on that, he says:

*"Ineffable is the union of man and God in every **act** of the soul. The simplest person, who in his integrity worships God, becomes God; yet for ever and ever the influx of <u>this better and universal self is **new and unsearchable**</u>. It inspires awe and astonishment. How dear, how soothing to man, arises the idea of God, peopling the lonely place, effacing the scars of our mistakes and disappointments! When we have broken our god of tradition, and ceased from our god of rhetoric, then **may God fire the heart with his <u>presence</u>**. It is the doubling of the heart itself, nay, **the <u>infinite enlargement of the heart</u>** with a **power of growth to a new infinity on every side**. <u>**It inspires in man an infallible trust**</u>. He has not the conviction, but the sight, that the best is the true, and may in that thought easily dismiss all particular uncertainties and fears, and adjourn to the sure revelation of time, the solution of his private riddles. He is sure that his welfare is dear to the heart of being. **In the <u>presence</u>** of law to his mind, he is overflowed with a <u>**reliance**</u> so universal, that it sweeps away all cherished hopes and the most stable projects of mortal condition in its flood. <u>**He believes**</u> that he cannot escape from his good. The things that are really for thee gravitate to thee."*[24]

New and unsearchable, in my opinion, is not in the past or knowledge. In other words, as discussed previously, the mind isn't going to find it in the "TIME" database in the past. No matter how hard it tries to search for the answer, it is only available in the NOW, and it is NEW! It is available by stepping into the UNKNOWN, FREE from the past "selves" and knowledge that it arrives in the moment. What is required for this to happen? Letting go of the PAST, and the "selves" that are attached to it. It is at that exact moment when FAITH must be engaged to keep us focused and to maintain the PRESENCE we just earned by letting go of the past. That presence is "at risk" though if we are not paying attention because the future can be very alluring. Since we just released the past, we are momentarily FREE, but we are "tempted" to go forward and lose that freedom very quickly as the mind tries to project out what's next, coming soon, in anticipation, excited, or fearful. Faith is required at this juncture so that the mind does not wander into these "potential" FUTURES locked up and captivated by an illusion. It is by use of faith that we maintain that freedom, or regain it. Faith allows us to become UNATTACHED and STAY unattached to the outcomes we like to "WANT", dream up, get excited about, or become fearful of, stress about, etc. What does that sound like? TRUST, right? An infallible trust = FAITH, in my opinion. Like as in error free, unfailing, faultless, PERFECT! How perfect can it be, maybe infinitely perfect? It explains how we are to be the "watcher", and how that allows us to "see and hear" (in the moment) and also the nature of the relationship with GOD. Quite cool really, take the time to understand it. Emerson really helped me grasp this idea, and this understanding. Faith becomes that "infallible trust" he speaks of, and from that STATE which enables presence, we ACT new, untainted, un-biased, un-affected, un-influenced, or otherwise known as FREE. We are FREE from our ties to the "selves" that would be attached to the future, once again... captivated in "TIME" "WANTING" or "NOT WANTING", in resistance or avoidance modes. Visualizing <u>LIMITED</u> futures in the mindscape via the internal "PROJECTOR" selves! This translates to an ability to take NEW ACTIONS in the present moment because we are not all caught up in that "illusory" projection, good or bad, responding to a mirage. So, these are NOT ego generated RE-actions that are based on a false data set, it is the higher "SELF" taking ACTION based on REAL-TIME data, NOW! That is how we BECOME new. Wide awake and aware with an infallible trust & presence, NOW! As this internal state is stabilized and maximized, we are guided, and we can become new, UN-limited by our past / future oriented lower selves. We are FREE to BECOME whatever is necessary and are highly adaptable to the moment and it's needs vs being attached and susceptible to the uncompromising needs of the lower "selves" which tend to be more rigid, unbending and BIASED!! That is probably why they call it "self" ish...it is very much like the little self I was a minute ago. <u>LIMITED</u>!

HERE, **EMERSON** guides us to a state of freedom, INNOCENT and PURE, like a dove: NEW! He even shows us again that words are LIMITED! This is how we remove the limits, OURS! Check this out:

*"Of this pure nature every man is at some time sensible. Language cannot paint it with his colors. It is too subtle. It is undefinable, unmeasurable, but we know that it pervades and contains us. We know that all spiritual being is in man. A wise old proverb says, "**God comes to see us without bell**"; that is, as **there is no screen or ceiling between our heads and the infinite heavens**, so is there no bar or wall in the soul where man, the effect, ceases, and God, the cause, begins. <u>The walls are taken away</u>. We lie open on one side to the deeps of spiritual nature, to the attributes of God. Justice we see and know, Love, Freedom, Power. These natures no man ever got above, but they tower over us, and most **in the moment** when **our interests tempt us** to wound them."*[25]

Who holds our interests? THE EGO! That's our baggage. In other words, we are tempted to RE-act <u>AS</u> the ego. That means from the little "selves", and their illusory perspectives. The unconscious selves, they are "attached" to something. What is it that they are attached to? That is the question. So, we need to be watchful of our perceptions/biases because **"our interests tempt us"**. Is this not a specific instruction to look WITHIN? Within what? **Within Temptation**! More specifically we are to look within the temptation we are shown WITHIN to RE-act from the "selves" and as the "selves" instead of BEING NEW and UN-limited! We must SEE these self-created walls, limitations...and take them DOWN, UN-LIMIT them! This is HOW we do it. IN THE MOMENT with oversight and IN-sight. We need to challenge our limits...they are lower "self" IMPOSED.

We must become this pure nature that Emerson speaks of. Untainted, untarnished, unbiased and UN-LIMITED! (Undefinable / unmeasurable). We like to use words to define things, don't we? That is the problem. When we use them, the definitions we use are constantly setting LIMITS! They can weigh us down and bring us down if we are not careful with how we are using them. We could SOAR, but WORDS create limits, walls, and ceilings. We need to take the top off these self-created boxes. We create them our "selves", we need to see it happen and stop doing it, unbox the box, open it up.

WORDS ARE LIMITED!
We tend to use them to DEFINE our "selves"!

This is why we need to be so diligent with watching our thoughts, because we are constantly using words that define us. The lower "selves" being unconscious, don't see the problem: WORDS LIMIT! Then what happens is we unconsciously combine them with other words and create stories with lots of words, and we forget that we are further defining stuff and our life. We are literally creating more limits with our stories, but we don't see it because there are too many words flying around. These word stories are created so quickly that we don't even see it happen before reacting. WATCH THE WORDS, as the MIND creates the stories. In other words, we need to watch our thoughts as well as the pictures and images these thoughts create in our mindscape. Our words within the thoughts being produced by an unattended mind can create walls and ceilings we didn't even realize we were installing IN MILLISECONDS. By removing the thoughts, or maybe even just tweaking them just a hair, we can change how we define our life, circumstances, our past, present and future. Our words and stories "tempt us" as we use them to subscribe to, justify, explain, and create the "WHY'S" of our lives. We are "tempted" to label our "selves", our lives, and the MOMENT as we arrive IN IT and exit from it. Words and stories create and DEFINE our LIMITS as we explain and justify our "selves" to our "selves" and others. As we see this and free our "selves" from this tyranny of "self" limitation, we ACT NEW in the face of that attempted hijacking. Temptation is real, within temptation is the CURE...if we can see it, we can be that, or we can BECOME NEW!! Be the answer, be the cure, be the instrument of change and BE NEW!

WITHIN TEMPTATION is also the name of the band I reference so much, coincidence? I think not. Within our temptations to react in the same old "self" defeating ways is where the lessons are. That's where the growth opportunities are. We can be tempted by the lower "selves", and then we don't RE-act from the "selves" perspectives. Instead, we choose newness, and we DO ACT from the higher "SELF" with CLEAR VISION, NOW which equates to new actions. With conscious awareness and presence, new choices are available. Each time we do this, we UN-limit the selves just a little bit more by seeing them and their "interests" / LIMITS (wants/attachments) and then we have choice to do more and better...or in the case of something bad, once seen, we can choose to do less of it or NONE of it. We do not NEED to be defined by the "selves" or ego, good or bad. In the moment of awareness, NOW, we have a choice. UN-LIMIT the "selves"! First, with awareness, we need to SEE IT, where these little ego "selves" are creating these imaginary walls, ceilings, and limits. As they are being drawn, we see the words within thoughts, we see the stories they create, and we see the labels the ego label maker is making. We can, in that moment, watch what this label maker is labeling and drop the label maker. STOP JUDGING! Sound familiar? Once accomplished, the label is NOT created, and therefore, we are not defined by it. These are the limits, CAUGHT IN THE ACT of "judgement"! They are recognized as labels, and the imaginary lines in the sand and sky disappear. LIMITS BE GONE!

Words judge, measure, and define...but we are told: DON'T JUDGE! (In the Bible!) In order to communicate internally and externally we use words constantly though, so just by the nature of thinking in words, we are defining, labeling, and limiting. Are we not? Uh Oh! So, we just need to be more conscious and aware of how we are using the words and the thoughts. Words LABEL, Words DEFINE...so what does that mean?

LABELS = LIMITS

NO LABELS = NO LIMITS

The ego loves to define, measure, weigh, compare, and LIMIT with words...RE-LEASE THEM! Let them go, put the label maker on the floor and walk away, lol

Kind of funny, but not really a joke because the label maker (the ego) is a judgement machine. That's what it does. It is constantly spitting out all kinds of words, stories, and labels...THAT JUDGE! We use words all the time, for everything, internally and externally. WORDS JUDGE, words LIMIT by that judgment. We do it all the "TIME". So, here we are face first into TIME again. First, we set limits, and then by the nature of the way that the ego operates, the ego selves get time blocked out of the moment and we can't change the limits. When we are unconscious, THAT'S US, we are STUCK, dumb and BLIND. Because the ego is perpetually focused in the past or future, the higher "SELF" is locked out of the moment by time, essentially useless. Change only happens now, so things tend to stay the same when we are unconscious like this. We set and define limits with words and stories and then we lock ourselves out. DANG! The truth is, we did it to ourselves, unconsciously.

I know, if it were easy to transcend the ego, everyone would do it. Seriously though, once we see this progression and how it happens so quickly, it makes us SPEED UP! If we let go of the label maker sooner in the progression which is creating the limits, we would have no limits. The ego is the label maker, the judger, the resister, measurer, avoider, etc. Drop the ego related stories and the ceilings disappear. These personas WITHIN create the stories. Seeing this is how we can BREAK FREE! Freedom is the answer, and this is a recipe for our true independence from any and all self-limitations. CHANGE happens NOW: Free from the past, free from the future, and free from the ego "selves". All of their worldly limits are left behind, transcended, and they disappear. This whole progression can be seen. The ego label maker, as an internal dynamic, and the label maker identities are isolated, highlighted, and brought out into the light of day. The ego and its incessant need to label is WATCHED, seen, and the associated limitations are plucked out by the root. As awareness sheds light on these internal processor errors, the ego labeling and attaching to those labels by the "selves" is released, along with their limits.

FREEDOM = NO LIMITS!

The answer to ceilings is to step out of the self-created box into the light of day with awareness where there are no ceilings. That's FREEDOM!

Freedom is UN-limited

YAY

At a minimum, be watchful and selective with the words you use! SEE the limits they create as they are defining! Furthermore, and to amplify that point, **EMERSON** states:

"***The sovereignty of this nature*** *whereof we speak* ***is made known by its*** ***independency of those limitations*** *which circumscribe us on every hand. The soul circumscribes all things. As I have said,* ***it contradicts all experience.*** *In like manner* ***it abolishes time and space. The influence of the senses has, in most*** ***men, overpowered the mind*** *to that degree, that the walls of time and space have come to look real and insurmountable; and to speak with levity of these limits is, in the world, the sign of insanity. Yet time and space are but inverse measures of the force of the soul. The spirit sports with time*"

"*Can crowd eternity into an hour or stretch an hour to eternity.*"[26]

Sovereignty is what? FREEDOM / Dominion... SUPREME POWER! It also seems to imply that maybe we should look at time with a little different lens. When we do, we can see that we essentially get locked out of the moment BY TIME! Mentally, we get stuck in the past, or momentarily visualizing the future. With awareness, we can see it happen faster, like real time, as-in... NOW! We must increase our awareness to the point where we can see it happen. Seeing it happen is the key, the eye opener. Seeing from above the mind, and above thought as the overseer allows us to see where we can get locked into these past / future stories, visualizations, dreams, remembrances, etc. Desire and fear are fueled by wanting and not wanting, the push and pull of these ego selves. Resistance and avoidance, or wanting and needing can put pressure on the mind toggles that are fired up by the emotions and then as the pressure escalates or is triggered suddenly, they can flip our switches one way or the other. By staying with it mentally focused, and consciously drilled down on the moment as the moment unfolds, we can see the exact moment where we get taken out, and miss the lesson due to some attachment, emotion, blink, or what have you.

Lots of things take us out of the moment...but what we must see is that it is our reactions TO those things, people, situations, words, and thoughts that do it TO US instead of FOR US! That's our ego RE-actions to the events in our lives, the words that are spoken to us, as well as the words we hear internally which can be different. Our reactions are the result of our own personalized interpretations and definitions of these events, words, thoughts, etc. Why? Because we just labeled it. Once we label it, then the words and images start a whole new progression and off we go mentally into that new abyss called the mindscape. That affects everything we do. Everything affects everything and so all of these words flying around impact us in ways that we fail to observe. Mainly this is because it happens so fast. Nevertheless, they all influence us and the things we WANT, the futures we are imagining. We imagine our "selves" as the "haver" or the "have notter", having or not having at some "time" in the future. That projection inspires the emotions, which are self-generated based on that illusion, so we go "Oh Noooooh", or "Oh, YEAHHHHH", excited or fearful. These are BOTH in the future as far as the mindset goes. We become attached AS we defined it, which is much earlier in the progression. That is actually why we miss it. The reaction happens so far down this timeline that we would need to backtrack to see it.

So, we need to see them FIRST, that means BEFORE the RE-action takes place. It is a progression though, so as we gain some speed in this skill, we get better at it. First, we must catch the ego mind after it takes us over, we see that it happened. Then, the next time, as we grow better and faster, we catch it as it is trying to take us over, as it is doing so...but we are still too slow to make a new decision. After some mental adjustments, learning opportunities and more mistakes / missed opportunities, we see some pretty remarkable changes. With some major progress and advancements in SELF MASTERY we get faster and faster to the moment. As a result, with some elevation and oversight, we can interject before the lower "selves" take us over and ACTUALIZE our own NEWNESS! We must interject BEFORE RE-acting so that we can take a new action, make a new choice, do something new / different. That means presence to do so...the little past and future selves can't take us over in the mindscape and STEAL the moment.

So, moving on... Emerson then points out WHERE the lesson is, in <u>OBSERVA-TION MODE, WITHIN</u>! We just need to get out of our own way. This is from a different essay: **Emerson "Spiritual Laws"** In this Essay, he says:

*"**<u>The lesson</u>** is forcibly taught by these observations, that our life might be much easier and simpler than we make it; that the world might be a happier place than it is; that there is no need of struggles, convulsions, and despairs, of the wringing of the hands and the gnashing of the teeth; that we miscreate our own evils. We interfere with the optimism of nature; for, **<u>whenever we get this vantage-ground of the past, or of a wiser mind in the present, we are able to discern that we are begirt with laws which execute themselves</u>**."*[27]

That is basically the "selves" "RE" acting unconsciously. So, we just need to get out of our own way. Tell me that's not easy. Why not just let life flow, why are we always getting in its way? These are the "LAWS" I am speaking of...and explaining. We are interfering with optimism. Once we UN-limit the "selves", that no longer happens. The instructions are written a little differently by **Emerson**, how cool right? **Emerson** goes on to say a lot more so let's break some of it down. He says that with PRESENCE, things can go a lot better, we can be a lot stronger and WISER by lowly listening.

*"...A little consideration of what takes place around us every day would show us, that a higher law than that of our will regulates events; that our painful labors are unnecessary, and fruitless; that **only in our easy, simple, spontaneous action are we strong**, and by contenting ourselves with obedience we become divine. **Belief and love**, -- a believing love will relieve us of a vast load of care. O my brothers, **God exists**. There is a soul at the centre of nature, and over the will of every man, so that none of us can wrong the universe. It has so infused its strong enchantment into nature, that we prosper when we accept its advice, and when we struggle to wound its creatures, our hands are glued to our sides, or they beat our own breasts. **The whole course of things goes to teach us faith**. We need only obey. **There is guidance for each of us**, and **by lowly listening we shall hear the right word**."*[28]

GUIDANCE IS AVAILABLE!
WE MUST LISTEN, HEAR, SEE and FEEL when answers are being provided!
That's called "TUNED IN", being in the ZONE!

GOOD NEWS: With presence, we SEE and HEAR the right words, with NEW eyes and NEW ears. The right words are only available to us in the NOW, the moment, and we finally learned how to get there to TUNE IN! The moment is infinite, eternal...the future and the past do not exist. NOW is always HOW! In addition, it is undefined, LIMITLESS! We just got done UN-limiting the "selves" that were producing the limits. WE ARE FREE! NOW truly is how, and it is UNLIMITED!

Spiritually speaking, my perspective is that with presence, heaven is at hand, it is NOW. GOD exists NOW! The more appropriate question is where are we? An even better question is WHEN are we? If we can BE present...we can experience GOD in his UN-LIMITED fashion, we can get the guidance, with faith and trust. The ceilings are removed revealing the "infinite heavens". UN-limited = infinite right? If we can only move from the past to the future, we are defining and setting our "selves" up for their preferred LIMITATIONS by allowing them access to the moment and in doing so, we are skipping over our presents (presence), locked out by "time". FAITH is not something to be believed in, as if some future result, some future outcome, some future thing...**FAITH is a SKILL**, an ability...and it only comes with practice and effort... NOW! Faith & trust are two of the keys that open the lock box to that elusive time slot called NOW! WE ENTER vs allowing the "selves" access to the now in order to ACT for our higher "SELVES" as our highest and BEST SELF! With a completely clean slate, and a fresh new moment, crystal clear instructions, we act on the advice given in the moment, and we are able and willing to hear the right word. Once we do, it is in our simple, easy, and spontaneous ACTION that we are strong. Spontaneous is WHEN? NOW, right? With awareness of this, as it happens, by paying very close attention from this elevated position, this "overseer" TEACHES us where, when, how, and how much faith is working in our lives...we need only pay attention as it works in our lives to produce what it is producing, OUR LIFE.

This reinforces the lessons we have been working so hard to internalize, so let's continue with this, from **Emerson**. This is from the essay **"Self Reliance"** and relative to the moment, divine wisdom & TIME:

"*The relations of the soul to the divine spirit are so pure, that it is profane to seek to interpose helps. It must be that when* **God speaketh** *he should communicate, not one thing, but all things; should fill the world with his voice; should scatter forth light, nature, time, souls,* **from the centre of the present thought***; and new date and new create the whole.* **Whenever a mind is simple, and receives a divine wisdom**, *old things pass away, -- means, teachers, texts, temples fall;* **it lives now, and absorbs past and future into the present hour***. All things are made sacred by relation to it, -- one as much as another. All things are dissolved to their centre by their cause, and, in the universal miracle, petty and particular miracles disappear. If, therefore, a man claims to know and speak of God, and carries you backward to the phraseology of some old mouldered nation in another country, in another world, believe him not. Is the acorn better than the oak which is its fulness and completion? Is the parent better than the child into whom he has cast his ripened being? Whence, then, this worship of the past? The centuries are conspirators against the sanity and authority of the soul.* **Time and space are but physiological colors which the eye makes,** *but* **the soul is light; where it is, is day; where it was, is night; and** **history is an impertinence and an injury, if it be anything more than a cheerful apologue or parable of my being and becoming**."[29]

In the instance where we can gain the lesson, history is a parable, my history...when I use it PROPERLY, to look back quickly to a moment ago, just long enough to get the lesson, grow, and then BECOME NEW...so that the next time, I SEE IT! I AM BECOMING NEW, that is a cheerful way to look at the past vs BLAME or any of the negative emotions, don't you think? A little more productive? It even explains that if we use it for more than that it is inappropriate, and it INJURES US! We are to use it for BEING and BECOMING! It is a LESSON, nothing more, please get the lesson and BE NEW! This is where and when that pause to rewind and replay the previous moment real quick can be incredibly beneficial. In fact, our ability to dial it in and facilitate this momentary replay mechanism can truly make or break our ability to grasp a lesson because it is still fresh in our head. If not now, it isn't happening, because we are on to the next thing...out of sight, out of mind. So, by refreshing it in a lightning-fast manner, we reproduce the lesson as it just happened in a flash before moving on...all the better for the lesson learned instead of bypassed in unconsciousness. Awareness caught it, saw it again, highlighted it for us, and we grew better as a result. The whole progression only took a fraction of a second.

It sure seems as if Emerson is saying the same thing here, in different words. I love that it reinforces the lessons we have been looking at so thoroughly. No blame, no animosity, no frustration...just growth compounding at a faster and faster pace. That would imply forgiveness as a necessity. Lessons come with mistakes...failures. Failure, in order to recontextualize and move forward quickly, requires forgiveness. That's how "all things" are forgiven which enhances and speeds up growth. They are basically dissolved because once seen and understood, the lesson is learned whole HEARTEDLY and almost instantly. We are "healed", our hearts and souls move on, no baggage.

We learn and grow and LET IT GO!

Forgiveness gives us the freedom we need to enter the next moment without the baggage, FREE to ACT / PERFORM BETTER after having received a lesson. Learning and growth happen as we accept these lessons and BECOME NEW! That happens NOW, or it doesn't happen at all. The future is an ILLUSION, so once we free our "selves" from the past we must maintain our PRESENCE, NOW! As Emerson states below: "above time". That is where faith must step in to help us maintain our presence ability vs getting drawn very quickly into the future in the mindscape. That can happen in a flash as we exit the past and since time is moving so quickly we are drawn into some very enticing or very scary futures, as the pictures and clips in the mind shift towards what is coming soon...so it is that very moment that we go from a momentary "FREE" state (from the past), to a NOT FREE state, because the future grabbed us, lured us in, and captivated us by envisioning some WANT/NEED or NOT wanting it's opposite in the future. The emotions relative to desire and /or fear are the triggers and so we go off and running again mentally into some future mindscape. The mind toggles are based on the ego wants and "needs" we are projecting and protecting.

The "selves" are wanting this, wanting that, resisting this, or avoiding that. On and on it goes. What we don't see, because we are not present to do so, is that these are all projections IN THE FUTURE! That future oriented illusion is NOT PRESENT, and NOT FREE! The temptation to go there is real. The bait is our attachment to outcomes, the things we WANT / NEED! If we succumb to the temptation, then the mind goes there. Once the mind goes there, we are no longer free. As a mindset goes, we are captivated by that illusory future.

"Man is timid and apologetic; he is no longer upright; he dares not say 'I think,' 'I am,' but quotes some saint or sage. He is ashamed before the blade of grass or the blowing rose. These roses under my window make no reference to former roses or to better ones; **they are for what they are; they exist with God to-day.** **There is no time to them.** *There is simply the rose; it is perfect in every moment of its existence. Before a leaf-bud has burst, its whole life acts; in the full-blown flower there is no more; in the leafless root there is no less. Its nature is satisfied, and it satisfies nature, in all moments alike.* **But man postpones or remembers; he does not live in the present, but with reverted eye laments the past, or, heedless of the riches that surround him, stands on tiptoe to foresee the future. He cannot be happy and strong until he too lives with nature in the present, above time.**"[30]

It is also above words, above stories, above judgement, measurement, comparing, etc. Living in the NOW, appreciating life. Loving life. No Labels, NO LIMITS! Now, that's living. This quote below comes in one paragraph later, again **EMERSON**:

"And now at last the highest truth on this subject remains unsaid; probably cannot be said; for all that we say is the far-off remembering of the intuition. That thought, by what I can now nearest approach to say it, is this. When good is near you, when you have life in yourself, it is not by any known or accustomed way; you shall not discern the foot-prints of any other; you shall not see the face of man; you shall not hear any name; -- **the way, the thought, the good, shall be wholly strange and new. It shall exclude example and experience**. *You take the way from man, not to man. All persons that ever existed are its forgotten ministers.* **Fear and hope are alike beneath it**. *There is somewhat low even in hope. In the hour of vision, there is nothing that can be called gratitude, nor properly joy.* **The soul raised over passion beholds identity and eternal causation, perceives the self-existence of Truth and Right, and calms itself with knowing that all things go well.**"[31]

THAT IS FAITH! Faith raises us up OVER our passions, which is that state of "WANTING"! That shows us how we are to get out of our own way. Step into the unknown, with FAITH. – THE WAY excludes the known, in other words, we cannot rely on the past. In addition, we are raised up OVER our passions towards the future, "wanting" is seen from above, as the overseer...SEES. More specifically, that is the lower selves visualizing our future: our wants, needs, biases, stories, definitions, LABELS, etc. From this vantage point the higher "SELF" can see more clearly, UN-attached, and UN-limited, what is true and right in this moment, NOW! With intense awareness, focus, and perception of what is "TRUE and RIGHT", this enables us in that moment to become THAT...what is needed. We are, of course, FREE to choose it. That brings us to FREEDOM. We must be free to choose, being FREE is KEY!

BEING FREE IS KEY!

BE FREE AND SEE!

10

FREEDOM

Putting The Pieces Together

F REEDOM CAN BE LOOKED at in a lot of ways. For this discussion, I am speaking very specifically about THE MIND and freedom to THINK as our higher "SELF" in order to make effective and life altering decisions. Specifically, to be clear, that means arriving to the moment and being IN the moment:

    1. FREE from the past

    2. FREE from the future

    3. FREE from the ego & lower "selves"

    4. 100% awake and aware: PRESENCE.

As a reminder, The TRINITY of F's can be an AMAZING guide.

Forgiveness

+

Faith

=

Freedom!

Conceptually, as a schematic, forgiveness, and faith allow us a manner of protection from both sides of the moment looking at time from a sequential perspective to isolate the time slot of "NOW"! This can be watched / seen with awareness from above and a heightened focus within as the mind is processing. Forgiveness is a tool that allows us to LET GO, and so it frees and guards us from the PAST "selves" and their mindsets. Faith allows us to LET GO of the future "selves" and their "projections", isolated within the moment with awareness and a commanding level of PRESENCE! So, faith acts as a buffer that untethers, frees and guards us from the future "illusion" on the mind screen allowing us to become more TRUSTING in the moment of NOW, PRESENTLY. The "attachment" or DRAW to the past and / or future has been overcome, over-ridden, transmuted, and we are transformed as a result. We have, in a sequence of extremely rapid time slots, overcome our past & future "selves", and transcended the ego. These are the ones that either had, or still have the potential to captivate with some level of "attachment" to the past or future and that emotional attachment is what draws the mind there. That also means rather than BECOMING new in the PRESENT, we are stuck / a prisoner of the past, or captivated by some fearful or glorious future in the mindscape. That's what the ego does, however, in this moment we transcended it. With massive awareness, forgiveness and faith are like the guard rails against the "gutter ball" (bowling reference), keeping us in our lane, and out of the gutter, so to speak. Our "lane" is that time slot called now, aka: PRESENCE. With awareness, forgiveness and faith are the "Letting GO" tools that are kicking us back into our lane (the moment) constantly. Wide awake and aware, we maintain our PRESENCE, NOW! No more falling down into life's gutters. No more falling out of the moment ...we maintain our presence with forgiveness and faith very consistently. Our triggers don't trigger. We are FREE, from the past, and we are free from the future. Since the "selves" are the ones that put us there, we are free from them as well.

The result is an extremely fast "SELF" transformation, and unwavering presence. VICTORY! With awareness from above, the higher "SELF" saw the whole thing happen so this evolution of the moment becomes experiential. As a result, GROWTH speeds up. Once "known" it is amplified "WITHIN", and stands out, so it just happens faster. We evolve faster as moments unfold right before our very observant and perceptive eyes. So, growth compounds...FASTER! Faith and TRUST build...FASTER! In the extreme positive, faith practiced can become more trusting and LOVE has the capacity to emerge as a result, but we have to let it through us as the answer (We become LOVE). At a minimum, we are now free in the moment to choose. Love is but one of the many choices available as options.

LOVE CHOOSES WELL!
LOVE also chooses FAST!

The SPEED OF LOVE is extremely fast! This can be seen from above with awareness, "above time" as documented in the previous chapter. This is a progression. As we become more awake & aware, we show up to life as a better version of our highest "SELF". Once seen, because the choice is available, love CAN come through the US, and we must LET IT come through. It is a choice. Love comes through us as we BECOME IT. Unconditional love exemplifies God as our "highest and best use" in the human realm. THAT = GOD! GOD is in the present moment eternally to GUIDE US, although many people refer to it as different things, names, etc. That's how heaven and earth MEET, in the moment. Heaven is NOW as we merge. In a manner of speaking, we are letting GOD have his way with us by becoming his "instrument". The truth is not static, it is fluid...ever changing, adapting, becoming "AS NEEDED". Therefore, His wish is my command, to the highest "SELF". This is where the term "CO-creator" comes from, conceptually. We must perceive that command in order to become it NOW, with presence. NOW is timeless, eternal. With courage, trust and persistence, we can arrive there with GOD in the moment...but only with FAITH! GOD is timeless... GOD is NOW! (OMNIPRESENT).

They call this "Oneness". All-ness vs nothingness. Allness = limitless. This progression happens extremely fast and to be blunt, we fail a lot. The MIND / EGO is what gets in the way and that is why it must be transcended. Understanding changes things, and our approach changes as a result which changes everything. Remember, everything affects everything. This realization can be a little mentally burdensome if we let it be. That can also bog us down. Just be the best SELF you can be right now. We must stop limiting the UN-limited. The minute we put a label on anything, good or bad, we draw LIMITS. What we end up seeing is that we (as our ego self) are trying to do this in advance by projecting what will be needed in the next moment. So, what we do mentally is create and "project" a hypothetical "answer". That's what plays out on the mind screens in our unconsciousness as we are temporarily locked in "time", namely the future. So, before the moment arrives, we mentally get detoured "time" wise, instead of being wide awake, aware, and present. Since we are time locked out of the moment in these cases, we are unable to BECOME what is needed since we are responding to an illusion and unconscious. The alternative, of course, is presence: to remain conscious, adaptable, fluid, changeable, receptive and responsive in the moment. As CHOICE becomes available with presence, we CAN let love choose. Love is FAST at becoming, we must trust that. The only way to do that is by becoming it, and loving it experientially. As we become it with practice over time, we get better at it in more difficult situations. It builds on itself as we achieve the "becoming". As a result, faith becomes trust, and trust becomes more trusting. More trusting converts to MORE SPEED! If anyone knows me, they know I like speed. LOL. More speed ultimately lands us in the moment or keeps us in the moment perpetually. PRESENCE is attained and maintained this way.

Omnipresent means present everywhere, at **all** times = ALLNESS! If that's true, that would include everything, which includes us, as in for-"ever" correct? Think hard on that...please understand the implications of this revelation. If everything affects everything, at ALL TIMES and we are a part of that everything...then we affect EVERYTHING! So, we are to become the answer to EVERYTHING! MIND boggling. In fact, we ARE the center of our universe, and the ripples go far and wide. Every moment matters, huge ramifications. At a minimum, even if we want to start small, we have to realize that we have much more power and influence than we had previously imagined. We need to see where we are drawing LIMITS for our "selves". Heck, it seems to me that with this as a backdrop we are barely tapping into this vast resource, our POTENTIAL! There seems to be an unwritten OBLIGATION to have faith as a matter of practice in order to TRUST, and break through these limits that really should not be there. OMG, how exciting! We are simply putting up with our "selves" and their limiting limits out of habit which is primarily driven by unconsciousness / unawareness. The possibilities are staggering. That's what I mean when I say that we need to UN-limit our "selves". The selves are creating our ceilings, we need to see them, and break through the ceiling. QUIT THE HABIT. The ceiling is a mirage, and we are trained to see it. That's just bad training and we need to UN train the mind and the trains of thought in order to prevent the train wrecks we see in our lives. That would be the result of the negative thought patterns playing out...our bad thought habits generate bad results. Some "times" that is a result of seeing a ceiling that isn't really a ceiling at all. As a result, we slow down, moderate or completely turn around... because of a mirage. That is us getting in our own way due to some level of unconsciousness that is due to a lower self that is seeing an illusion in the mindscape. We created that illusion as the lower "self". We just need to wake up to SEE with new eyes. The illusion disappears and the limit is UN-limited which means we are FREE from it.

To me, this is an ever-present challenge because as humans, the mind gets in the way, A LOT! The ego is a specialist in this regard. Unfortunately, and fortunately, we have it. In fact, we NEED IT, it is highly useful, it just needs some direction, and guidance. It can be used to accomplish AMAZING things; however, it also has its limitations. We need to be able to recognize where these edges, walls and ceilings are in order to SEE where we are NOT FREE so that we can raise our "selves" up to BE FREE! We must see our way THROUGH these self-created obstacles and limitations. It is my opinion that with enough awareness we can get the clues that are given as to when the ego is trying to overtake us but that requires us to be awake, aware and 100% present to do so. We need to be tuned in, tapped in and turned on so to speak. That means when we try to revert to the past, and / or disconnect / project an illusionary hypothetical future, we get an alert / jolt. The jolt must grab our attention, snap us OUT OF THE ILLUSION with some kind of a signal such as a virtual tap on the shoulder, a hint to WAKE UP and see these attempted mind hacks & projections as they are about to be inserted into the mind which is what is creating the illusionary limitations to begin with. Come back to reality, NOW! NOW = FREE!

That crisis can be averted if we see the virtual indicator light flashing internally beforehand. That equates to a lot more green lights and a lot less yellow and RED ones What does that mean? SPEED! Yellow and red lights slow us down mentally, we need to pause, and then regain our focus. SECONDS MATTER! So, what happens is that we see these in "TIME". We get the yellow indicator light and so we have to slow down and be watchful, carefully, we learn our lessons, and transition through these "delays". The difference is that each time we do it, the transition happens just a little bit faster. We get back to fully 100% PRESENT, and we do it FASTER! With a high degree of presence and oversight, we are pretty much already there, so it is like we never lost it, a BLINK of an eye, like milliseconds. BLIP, and green again. Off we go...

So, in the detailed analysis, what happened? As far as the indicators go, that yellow or red indicator "flashes", twinges, or is heard. So, whether it be an audible, sight, or intuitive feeling, it then alerts us with the clues we need to GET PRESENT, dial it in. It could be an emotion kicks up, something feels "off", fear, worry, or whatever else. Who / what did that? What's the story, what's the label, what is the definition, or limit? Where is the edge, where did we internally draw that line? The same applies to the past and the future. It's one thing to see that we have just revisited the past...that is fairly easy to see. We must also see when we get our "selves" all fired up, or feared up, towards some "projected" future. If we are getting emotional about it the mind doesn't snap back as easily. That is why it is said that we are "captivated". We basically got stuck at a mental "red light" but everything else keeps going. Reality doesn't stop. So, we need an alert system to tell us when we are doing this. That's what awareness does. It is constantly on alert, as long as it is powered up, WATCHING. So, as we dream up some amazing future, in the same manner, we get a signal, a twinge, a snap of the fingers so to speak to get back to NOW! REALITY! The NOW, with presence is where choices need to be made to "make it happen". That future we are dreaming up can't happen if we don't make the choices in the NOW to get us there. Wake up, get the guidance...it is invaluable. It also shows us where / when we are dreaming up some horrific future, something bad, or negative with worry, doubt, or FEAR!! This way we can SNAP out of it, get present, change our focus and redirect. As a result, we free our "selves" of that fear by becoming PRESENT. The fear is in the future projection, so gaining presence offers us the freedom and opportunity to become something new, WITHOUT THE FEAR! It is a choice in what we are attached or relating to in the moment. Sure, we can certainly become FEAR by allowing it to take us over and by completely identifying with the projection. We must see that the FEAR is being fearful of the projection, like watching a movie. It's NOT REAL! It's a projection, Turn off the projector. Notice the virtual "red light" mentally and change the mind to GREEN! The projector is the fearful lower self that is projecting what it is fearful of. THAT IS THE TEMPTATION and the OPPORTUNITY. Go right ahead and succumb to the fear (sarcasm), "SIN"...listen to the fear. Stay at the red light...NO! That would mean one of two things.

Option one; you are losing time and stuck at the light.

Option two; you ignore the red light and proceed anyway, deliberately, semi-consciously or unconsciously. IGNORE means that no lesson is learned. (Ignorance is NOT BLISS! Lol)

BETTER to choose neither of those options, which brings us to option 3. See the red light, understand that it is an illusion in "time", and come back to NOW, mentally. That's when you can ATTRACT what you WANT vs whatever it is that you are fearful of because presence shuts off the projector, NO MORE FEAR! No projector projecting = nothing to be fearful of. With presence, we can see our way through very clearly without the illusion on the mind screen.

FEAR = a MAGNET

When that is where our attention is being placed, FEAR WINS! OR. The opportunity, with presence as an alternative, is to Be NEW! Be mentally in an illusion in the future, or unplug / disconnect, or "detach" the projector which is projecting our "attachment" and BE NEW NOW! It is your choice. This is how we see these limits we are drawing for our "selves" and we UN-LIMIT them. We realize that the lower "self" is NOT ME, I don't have to succumb to the fear, I don't have to stay at the red light or "identify" with the illusion. Once seen, the "time-lock" is released, presence is regained, and fear disappears. POOF, GONE! The projector "self" is shut down. The light turns GREEN. The movie we were briefly playing via the projector self at the red light is OVER, projector stopped, so now we can proceed. Since it is over, we walk out of the theatre, and it is as if we walked right through fear. Fact is, the process just described ELIMINATES fear, it just goes away, we can walk right through it because there isn't anything left of it to walk through. It was just an illusion on the mind screen. The light turned green and we are off and running again.

With presence, we are not "locked in" to the illusion, and we are NOT "locked out" by TIME. Therefore, we can CHOOSE to have faith in something else. There is an alternative, and there is a choice being made. That something else is called FREEDOM. Freedom from the last thought, the patterned thought, the behavior, the limited hypothetical future, and the lower limited "selves". Freedom is a choice. Relative to fear and the associated emotions, it is an opportunity that must be taken whereby we choose to DELIBERATELY release the "attachment" that is causing the fear. (This applies to other emotions too; I am just using fear as an example here). The pattern is seen, understood, and interrupted, ultimately LET GO. That's not to say that there won't be any trepidation. Fear is directed towards a negative imagination and aimed towards something in the future. If that is an ugly future being pictured, then YES, by all means, it may very well be scary. What if we paint a different picture, or simply stop the projector that is projecting the illusion, then what happens? The mind was creating a mind movie via the ego, and we were watching it, becoming fearful. If the mind movie is no longer playing on the mind screen with us IN THE MOVIE, in that hypothetical future...then where is the fear? It doesn't exist because it was based on an illusion and the illusion is GONE! That illusory future that was being visualized was being broadcast on the mind screen, however, with PRESENCE it is no longer being broadcast or seen, the illusion disappears and along with it so does the fear. FEAR can disappear in favor of faith and trust, but it has to be CHOSEN, prioritized. Presence is chosen, with enough awareness to choose. With a heavy dose of fear, this is no small task. In fact, this is a MAJOR accomplishment, once seen in this way and experienced.

We MUST maintain our presence and FAITH is a key tool that will help us to choose it and use it more wisely and effectively. It acts as a buffer to maintain that non-attachment stance relative to the future we have become so attached to or fearful of. That includes fear of the "unknown". The way it unfolds in the mind is quite incredulous though when dealing with fear. The mind doesn't let go easily, fear can be "gripping" and compelling as these stories the mind tells are quite convincing. What we need to realize is that it is being fearful of something that hasn't happened yet, and probably won't. When dealing with illusory fear that is a future oriented projection. Once we realize that it is ME as one of the "attached selves" doing the projecting, we also realize that we can stop the projector, or project something else if we wish to. We catch the mind as if it was in that illusory future and bring it BACK to NOW. It is a fine line, but for some reason the mind keeps getting caught on the other side, IN THE FEAR, in the future in the illusion. As the higher SELF we are literally demanding presence instead, overseeing and overriding these lower "selves" by choice. These are the fearful "selves" that are insisting and persisting to tell their stories. They keep plugging the projector back in so that we see their bad mind movies. It is a major unyielding commitment to focus, determined to stay present in the now moment where & when we are FREE from that consternation which frees us from the fear that is associated with the mind movie. We must let go of the "illusion" that the lower "self" is broadcasting on the mind screens. FAITH is the tool we use to do so.

We must begin to TRUST in something other than what the fear is projecting on the mind screen and that begins with attaining presence via awareness to UN-attach from the attachment. The attachment must be seen, but it is UN-DERNEATH the fear / emotion. It's "behind the scenes", that's why we don't see it. We don't look hard enough; we don't dig under the surface emotions. We turn too soon, we react too soon, we get taken over by the "selves" too soon. With awareness everything can change, we just need to be faster. We must wake up and get present BEFORE the "selves" get captivated by the illusion and caught up in TIME which is where the fear is...attached to that imagery in the future. That's how we get taken over, the "selves" get caught up in the emotion and off we go...trapped in the illusion, and TIME. Fear, worry, bad mental mind movies in the theatre of ME. My mind was HACKED, and I did it to myself.

Freedom is a choice; FORGIVENESS, FAITH and TRUST are the tools we use to BREAK FREE! It is TIME that we free our "selves", by choice. We can be bound by the limitation of the past and / or future, TIME-WISE, by our subscription to it consciously or unconsciously. If we relate to the ego and stay on the opposing side of that fine line we tend to draw in the mind, we are NOT "time-wise", we are presently being FOOLISH because we are unconscious. The "selves" did it. The "selves" are the ones that keep us in "TIME", in this case, the future time slot, wherever and whenever that might be. Watch the mind, it could be a moment ahead or ten seconds or minutes ahead or even ten years ahead... Any of these could cause some apprehension, that's for sure. The alternative is that we can be NEW, and FREE from those limited versions of our future "selves" with presence. Freedom opens up the mind space to make NEW choices, as the higher SELF in the NOW, where and when we are detached and free from that illusory or uncertain future and the attachment to it. It is our choice, and once we are capable of arriving to the moment, in the moment with enough energy directed in the right WAY, we can break the pattern of fear in our lives and as a result, we effectively UN-limit that version of self. There are times when this might take some intestinal fortitude, and we MUST push through this at some point in order to BREAK FREE from these personal LIMITATIONS! Bondage is "self" given and ego driven; freedom is higher "SELF" / GOD given when we have faith and TRUST that it is available, NOW! With this overarching awareness, we can see where and when these lower ego selves try to draw ceilings, walls, and limits. In that moment, we UN-limit them, as the higher SELF with awareness & PRESENCE. FREEDOM is attained and maintained with presence. Walls and ceilings disappear as we turn off and / or "detach" the projector self, so bad can be better, and good can be gooder. (better)! LOL WE CAN BE GREAT!!!! The limits to greatness were just removed. NOW is how we do it.

As we are doing this, it may require us to push through some physical & mental barriers, edges, and being extremely uncomfortable. That's why it can require some intestinal fortitude. The heart may race, the hands may sweat, the stomach may turn, and these "demons" may threaten our presence in the mindscape. Demons = emotional attachments or physical "symptoms". The threat, in this case, is an illusion. This is where / when we must wake up to SEE. As the moment is unfolding, ask and be conscious of where and WHEN the mind is. IS IT PRESENT? What is it projecting on the mind screen? When is the projection? Is it in the future, the past, or are we in the present moment, the one called reality, right NOW? This can change in a flash, we must be vigilant, highly aware and observe the slightest maneuverings of the unconscious ego mind and its habitual nature to interrupt the tendencies it has to automatically subscribe to fear and other emotions relative to future "self" projections. Once the mind gets engaged by a fearful storyline (a mind movie), it must be deliberately over-ridden and drawn back into the moment with our awareness. This is a higher SELF vs lower self scenario in which we must understand and learn a key lesson, interrupt a mental / behavioral pattern. We must STOP the mind movie (The "self-projector") and ultimately gain a huge victory in higher SELF discipline, higher SELF management. As this pattern is seen, we can interrupt the pattern earlier and earlier in the progression. As we get better at it, we can overcome these ego related illusions because we see that they are illusions, we can walk right through them, PRESENTLY! We can't do that in some fearful next moment, it must be done now. We can certainly imagine our "selves" doing it, but again, that's simply a hypothetical. When we snap back to NOW, it's real. Now is the time that it must become REAL, WE MUST DO IT for REAL! Choices are never made down the road; they are made NOW! With presence, that illusory future disappears. It is no longer being broadcast on the mind screens. We interrupt this program...and by doing so we don't have to watch it play out. Poof, fear is GONE! The illusion is GONE...we can BECOME, as needed.

As a reminder, this technique can also be used when we see a pattern of OVER excited relative to the future because that can be equally dis-empowering as it takes us out of the moment. NO presence = NO CHOICE! Excitement is also an emotional RE-action. That also paints pictures & storylines on the mind screens. If the mindscape is captivated in some illusionary future, positive or negative, the mind is NOT PRESENT NOW! Over-excited self-projections are just as blinding. We are still in a movie theatre called the mind "projecting" some illusory future. In this case, it is good, and we need to snap back to reality just the same to MAKE IT HAPPEN for real. We do that NOW, and NOW, and NOW!

WITH FAITH &TRUST, we can arrive IN the moment and STAY in the moment!
The MOMENT is when CHOICE is available.
PRESENCE = The ability / SKILL to stay in the NOW!

This all circles back to FAITH which is the requirement to STAY PRESENT vs allowing the ego "selves" to draw us into some imaginary future, good or bad. Getting into the nitty gritty details...the ego or the "selves" basically steal our freedom by diverting us or distracting us with emotionally driven words, stories, imagery and tricks. This important attractor factor draws us in and attaches us to it via some storyline / propaganda that takes us on various "time-detours" into the past / future relative to time and NOW! We need to be more alert to see these attempted ego / mind hacks so that we can keep our attention and focus on what we NEED TO SEE in the moment, such as critical, life changing data, NOW with presence. These ego "selves" basically "hack" into the exposed mindscape via unconsciousness and/or a lack of presence interjecting them "selves" into these short periods of time where / when we were "bleeped out". They are the BLEEPERS, pushing our bleeping buttons where and when we are bleeped. ("Bleep" = triggered) Hopefully this makes sense, it is similar to a curse word in the movies that is bleeped out so that a younger audience does not hear an offensive word. That's how the ego stays the ego. It is unseen and unheard. In a similar way, our EGO bleeps us out of the moment because IT is in "self-protect" mode, it doesn't want us to see something or it is so engaged / enraged about something, that is all it sees. AKA: It is BLIND. Basically, IT either prioritized something else, or it wants to stay the same. Since we were bleeped out by that ego element, fear or desire, our PRESENCE was DIS-connected and when we were not present, we were bleeped out. So, in that moment, we were unconscious for that millisecond or longer. As a result, for that particular time slot where we were in a state of unconsciousness, we really don't know what was said or done during the bleepage without a higher level of awareness. (BLEEPAGE= a momentary presence outage). Since this isn't actually a word, I had to create it and define it. LOL) So, now that we are alert to it, and the various ways it can happen, we are one step ahead of the lower selves that drive these devilish characters that are stealing our moments and our lives. We can be watchful and know all its various shenanigans and maneuverings, so this should help us get better at being FREE vs letting that bleepage happen to us. We do that from above, with awareness.

NO MORE BLEEPAGES!

At first, when we begin this process, there are so many bleeps that it is nearly impossible to decipher what is actually going on since we are almost entirely bleeped. Pretty much unconscious much of the time. As we become more aware, it is as if the bleepages are more intermittent. Over time, with practice, the bleeps really stand out as more isolated, we notice them much more readily. Eventually, with higher "Self" consciousness, there aren't many bleepages at all. At this stage, we are moving towards what I refer to as an unwavering PRESENCE.

Understanding is a very powerful tool to have on our side...and it allows us to see the many ways that we allow "the takeover" (bleepage) to happen. To refresh that conceptually, this is where the ego selves take us over and act as us for us in the moment. When we are unaware / unconscious they're basically hacking into our MIND and taking us over since the space between our ears is unoccupied. Our self-protect awareness & presence virus protection was disabled and freedom was stolen. Without presence, we let our faith / forgiveness guard down and we are basically incapacitated from a present mindset perspective and therefore, our highest and best SELF is unable to take new actions because it was bleeped out. Bleeped out is the equivalent of unconsciousness, not awake, not aware, and NOT FREE! Another way to look at it is that the higher SELF was on vacation momentarily. Since we were bleeped out, that is when our ego patterns and programming respond to life AS US, FOR US instead of higher ME having a choice. Change cannot happen in these moments, so we stay the same. If we can step back and look at this unfoldment relative to the finest and most intricate detail, we can see that these are the "TIME SLOTS" that we are essentially MIA! (Missing in action). The "selves" or ego elements WITHIN us become us in these time slots in the moments where we as the higher "SELF" are unconscious. These are fractions of seconds, in some cases...soooooooo fast that we often don't even take notice. We take a lot of mental vacations. What we don't see though is that they often happen in these ridiculously short little blips...of TIME! Like milliseconds. It happens so fast that we don't consciously even realize we were gone for a BLINK of an eye as far as the time bleepage goes.

Taking this one step further, we can oversee these isolated milliseconds where we are getting in our own way via the lower nature responding to life via habit / programming vs arriving with PRESENCE as the higher SELF to take a NEW action. As an example: If a "self" is momentarily captivated by being attached to a FEAR relative to some future "outcome" being visualized on the mind screen, then it cannot be present NOW to make a new choice. FREEDOM is accomplished via PRESENCE vs being held captive by that future "outcome" in fear or excitement via desire. **FAITH is the freeing element** that is activated within to release the ties that bind us to that particular future outcome which opens us up to something NEW. We can see also that if we do stay attached to the fear and the future outcome that WE DO NOT WANT, that we are magnetizing our "selves" to that undesirable result. With freedom, which occurs by stepping THROUGH that emotional attachment, into the NEW MOMENT, free from the GRIP of that fearful ILLUSIONARY future. It is THEN that we have choice. We see that it was just an image on the mind screen, and we can walk right through it, because it is a mirage. It was simply a mind projection; it doesn't even exist in reality...IT IS NOT REAL! Not yet anyway...like the monster in the closet as a kid, we needed to be shown that it wasn't even there, we had to wake up, open our eyes, open the doorway to the "darkness" in the closet in order to see that it was all a dream, an illusion. What "exposed" the darkness was turning the light on. In this case that means the light of awareness. Once seen in this way, these momentary bleepages can be prevented because by opening our eyes, we see the doorway to NOW being closed via the TIME-LOCK. Prevention is not by resistance or avoidance though and that is key to see. It is via awareness, presence, and a lesson OVER time, not locked up in it. That is how freedom occurs, which is a huge difference maker. The result of watching as we proceed to step BACK into the moment FREE, while watching as the "selves" get out of the way and ALLOWING presence is a huge wake up scenario and this translates to many lessons because we STOP DOING the bleepages. We stop taking these time detours because it is seen in this manner going forward. KNOWING how the takeover happens is the road less traveled because we purposefully travel it LESS with this new higher level of awareness. Awareness sees ALL once it is really enabled and empowered. We tend to project our "selves" into the future because we want certain things, or want to experience something specific, and then we get all caught up in that future illusion because we are excited about it, or afraid of the alternatives.

Sometimes we want something so badly that it drives us BONKERS. It is so real to us that we can almost taste it. This is a really key time to be watchful because it is these times that what we want is VERY CLOSE, yet for some reason, it doesn't happen. The reason it doesn't happen is because we keep pushing it away, so I want to explain that concept. It has to do with "WANTING". So, let's discuss that in more detail.

A Chance To Explore Your Limitless Potential With Doug Giesler

South Carolina, USA
From the desk of Doug Giesler

Dear Friend,

I hope that by this point in the book, I CAN call you a friend *(just one I haven't met yet or maybe I have)*.

If you're reading this, I believe you're someone who's ready to break free from self-imposed limitations and step into a life of boundless possibility.

Congratulations on taking the first step towards unlimiting your mind!

How would you like to explore what your "Limitless Potential" could truly be? That's right, even if you're already achieving great things, there's an even more extraordinary version of you waiting to emerge.

I invite a select group of individuals each month to join me on The UNLimit Breakthrough Call. This is your chance to look beyond the horizon and discover what life has in store for you when you remove the barriers holding you back.

Space is limited, so please visit the link below and enter your contact information to reserve your spot:

TheFWordFaith.com/breakthrough

Don't worry if you don't get invited this month. You can enter your name every month for a chance to participate. (Only ONE entry per month will be registered, and slots reset on the 1st)

For approximately 1 hour, you'll have the opportunity to work with me on:

★ *Identifying and challenging your self-imposed limits*
★ *Developing a heightened state of presence and awareness*
★ *Learning to make conscious choices that propel you towards your goals*
★ *Mastering the art of learning from mistakes without emotional attachment*
★ *Balancing your past, present, and future perspectives for optimal growth*
★ *Creating a personal blueprint for unlimiting your mind or whatever is personally imporant to you right now...*

This isn't just another call — it's going to be a true breakthrough for your personal evolution. Together, we'll explore the edges of your comfort zone and discover the extraordinary potential that lies just beyond.

Are you ready to unleash your limitless self? Join me on The UNLimit Breakthrough Call and let's break through those barriers together!

TheFWordFaith.com/breakthrough

Remember, the only true limits are the ones we choose to believe in. What limit will you shatter today?

Warmly,
Doug Giesler

P.S. *Don't let another day slip by trapped in your own limitations. The clock is ticking, and every moment you hesitate is another moment lost to mediocrity. Claim your spot on The UNLimit Launchpad Call now and start your journey to unlimited success!*

11

WANTING

Wanting is a covert "LACK" mentality. It is the epitome of "self-sabotage" because it is so innocent. We can see it when we want something, but it falls apart at the last minute. Something happens "out of the blue", or we get in our own way, and the result or whatever it is that we wanted so badly gets erased, doesn't happen, or gets postponed indefinitely. Our self-saboteurs are fast, I mean SUPER FAST. It can happen in a flash and is hardly noticeable, but we do it ALL THE TIME! That's why it goes unnoticed, we were not taught to see things this way. One of the things that can do this is "The bleepage". Because we want it soooooo bad, two things happen:

1. WANTING happens in an ongoing persistent like manner, relentlessly. It is an intense kind of wanting though = RAGING DESIRE. I must have this is the attitude.

2. FEAR of the alternative happens as we become overwhelmed with the thoughts like "what if?"...and the mind races to conclusions based on fairy tales that shows us all the various possible outcomes in which we don't get what we want.

You would think that "Wanting it BAD", or creating a mindset that has a feverish pitched desire to GET IT is good right? I mean, it is taking the extreme positive approach, that's what we are supposed to do, or at least that's what we are told. WANTING anything is a future projection in the positive form, I mean, we have it in the future imagery. So that's a positive visualization, right? NOT SO FAST THERE, PAL! Pay very close attention because this is where it gets really interesting. The degree of that desire can be intense, or mild. It doesn't change the fact that the projection is a projection. It is an illusion, a visualization in a future imaginary scene. We are imagining a scenario where and when we HAVE what we want. Because it is soooooo positive, and we are envisioning it, we are taught that this is a GOOD strategy. Get jacked, GO FOR IT! Make it happen! Meanwhile we imagine this amazing thing in the future. This is BAD, not good. Here's why:

1. **Problem #1: WANTING** something intensely with any level of excitement has a tendency to take us OUT OF THE MOMENT. That's the time-lock we have already discovered. We cannot accomplish anything, no less what we need to accomplish NOW if the mindset, time wise, is in the future. GET BACK TO NOW! The temptation to "project" potential futures MUST be caught, so that we don't spend our "TIME" mentally captivated in that future. Once we are drawn into it, snapping back to now can be more difficult, and of course, that takes TIME. While that may mean fractions of seconds, it is imperative that this is seen because life moves fast. This can be impactful in certain situations when impeccable timing is required.

2. **Problem #2: WANTING** is particularly bad as a visualization because it is ADMITTING to the mind that it is NOT real now. It is not true, doesn't exist, not mine, hasn't happened. Think about this in detail. This mind pattern 100% BELIEVES in the OPPOSITE of what we want. (NOT HAVING!) We believe, within that fraction of a second that we just took to go see that projection of what we want in the future, that it is IN THE FUTURE! That means that what we WANT, we don't HAVE right now. That is a PROBLEM! That is faith, but it is using it BACKWARDS! By the nature of "wanting" we are defeating ourselves over and over again by believing in what we don't want, don't have, haven't produced, isn't real NOW! The thought habit, or "programming" responsible for this "LACK" mentality is called "WANTING"! Wanting something PROVES that we don't already HAVE IT! We "LACK" it. That's not belief in having it is belief in NOT HAVING!

3. **Problem #3: NOT WANTING** is the focus on the negative. This is the same concept, but fear is the captivator vs desire. This is resistance or avoidance mode. Seeing on the mind screens of where we don't want to go, don't have, where we don't want to be...NOT HAVING! Mindset wise, this is a negative bleepage. The ego selves want something so badly that it becomes FEARFUL of its opposite, or FOMO kicks in. Fear of missing out. It is projecting all the fearful scenarios where we don't get what we wanted. When, mindset wise, is "not having"? It's

in the future. Our own self-projector is projecting us as wanting but not HAVING. So once again, we have defeated ourselves by visualizing and BELIEVING in NOT HAVING. We are seeing that very fact on our own mind screen, only we don't see that it is an illusion. Nor do we see it as a "lack" mentality. We have proven to the mind that we do not HAVE what we want NOW. Our nervous energy is nervous because the imagination is imagining us WITHOUT IT and continuing to be WITHOUT IT...which means that in this imaginary scene, we don't have it now and for some reason we can't get it. CAVEAT *** Sometimes we actually do have something, but we are afraid we will LOSE IT, which is also a "LACK" mentality. This is a little different in that it believes in "LACK" in a different way, in other words, there isn't enough to go around which produces less, not more.

Either way, we need to step back in time, get our "selves" out of that "virtual" FUTURE which is an illusionary timeslot and as our higher "SELF", we re-establish presence by arriving back INTO the NOW time-slot, REALITY...presently. PRESENCE IS KEY! If you really think about that sequentially, we have delivered our "selves" from that future illusionary imagery, and as the higher "SELF", we are "delivered" back into the moment, REALITY! With oversight, this entire shift can be seen, as lower is transcended to HIGHER... So, we ultimately see within that transition that:

WANTING IS THE ISSUE
NOT WANTING IS THE ISSUE!
TIME IS THE ISSUE!

One is triggered by desire; the other is triggered by fear. We are either picturing something we want or picturing the alternative in resistance or avoidance mode. Not only do they both take us out of the NOW, within the context of this mindset, but BOTH of these scenarios are PROVING to the mind, WITH EMPHASIS, that we do not have what we want right now. That is 100% BELIEF in the OPPOSITE of what we want. That's using faith alright, but unfortunately, we are trusting and believing in what we don't have. This mindset produces more of the same, it expands on what we are focused on, which is LACK! So, we get LESS, not more. What we WANT eludes us, gets kicked down the road, doesn't happen, gets stolen, disappears, gets smaller. What we don't want PERSISTS because what we resist stays in our life much longer than we would like. We are either missing, resisting or avoiding the lessons. This is WHY that is so. What we ARE in this moment GOES FAR because we failed to grow out of our "selves".

What we are filled with is a LACK mentality, so lack persists and we continue to LACK what we want. In reality, we get even less of it...until we consciously decide to grow out of it. WE NEED TO GROW!

What we need to see in these momentary bleepages is that we are LACKING. We are operating from a LACK focus, LACK consciousness, or UN-consciousness really which produces more of the same in our lives. In this case that means we continue to NOT HAVE. If we add more and more emphasis, with frustration, anger and the like, we just extend that even FURTHER OUT in the future. When we add emotion to things in the mind it is as if we are adding exclamation points to it, it makes it "TRUER", and CEMENTS it in place.

WANT = Overwhelming desire "PROJECTING" a good future.

DON'T WANT = Overwhelming fear, "PROJECTING" a bad future.

Both of these put us mentally in the future, which means that we are WITHOUT what we want NOW. That's what we believe. We believe that we don't have it now, and so by the nature of thought, it's TRUE in our MIND that we don't have it. We just proved it to ourselves with this fairly innocent thought process. Looking at it in detail though, we can gain some valuable IN-sights. TIME and how we relate to it has PROFOUND consequences relative to BELIEF! Putting it in the future keeps it there. We prolong the agony and the "WANTNG" continues. Crying, complaining, fretting over it, and whatever else we do only amplify the beliefs that we don't have it. We do these things habitually; they are TIME related. Be watchful, SEE when your thoughts are "projections" relative to TIME! Catch the thoughts and correct them. GET BACK TO NOW! Be persistent and determined to catch the "NOT NOW" thoughts.

Narrow is the gate, right? The way I see it, there is a gate BEFORE and AFTER the moment, looking at time in a unique way. They can BOTH lock us out of the moment when we go unconscious. That's the time-lock. What we don't see when we are unaware is that WE HAVE THE KEY! Awareness and forgiveness are the keys that open the door TO the moment by releasing us from the past. The implementation and skill of its use is the key that allows us access to the moment in time, as a progression. Awareness and FAITH team up and are the keys that open the door to a NEW FUTURE, one that is not pre-determined by our past programming and habitual responses (wanting and / or not wanting). It does this in another way too, in that it's use allows us to STAY PRESENT, once we get present. We don't get bleeped out via the "wanting" or "NOT wanting". Being awake and aware with faith is the key to PRESENCE which enables our ability to have choices and to make them with wisdom. So, faith, in a manner of speaking, RELEASES the future opening the virtual door to the moment. It is kind of like a back door conceptually. It allows us to LET GO of our attachments to outcomes, which are all in the future, in TIME. This is effectively releasing our LIMITED and DEFINED illusory future, the one we just created in the mindscape. With FAITH, we shut off the "projector". If the projector isn't projecting, the bleepage doesn't happen. Maintaining our presence is driven by our effective use of the F-words and disconnecting from the "self" that is projecting or remembering. Projecting is done by the future selves, remembering is done by the past selves. Either way it is an illusion on the mind screen, and the "selves" are doing it. Forgiveness and Faith help us to achieve this miraculous milestone called PRESENCE where we can BECOME our highest and BEST SELF NOW. That's done via awareness and DE-tachment...or in movie land, that means turning off the self-projector. Obtaining and maintaining presence is the key to the freedom we need to become our UN-limited highest and best "SELF".

KEY NOTE:

Past "selves" watch the "remember" projector.

Future "selves" watch the "projecting" projector.

Pay attention within contextually in very particular fashion as to what they actually have faith in. Sometimes that will mean that we need to pay closer attention to what they emphatically DON'T have faith in by the nature of its time relativity and how that is being broadcast on the mind screen. (a future scene, a present scene, or a past scene) As shown previously this can make all the difference when it comes to the BELIEF in whether we have it now, or we don't. BELIEF MATTERS! When we are in the time-lock, what the selves SEE, HEAR, and FEEL is based on a projection, or an ILLUSION. It's not real, but where that is in TIME makes a big difference in terms of what that means they have or don't have faith in. Please pay close attention by watching your thoughts in real time, the stories on the mind screens, and their time relativity. This particular elemental factor can have ENORMOUS ramifications relative to belief, which will affect your results.

BELIEFS MATTER!

What we see on our mind screens, the emphasis we add, and the way that we imagine it in the mindscape is pretty cut and dried. It determines whether or not we BELIEVE it is true. TIME has a lot to do with this.

Having said that, let's talk about how to convince the mind in a positive and proactive way TO BELIEVE, using some visualization techniques.

12

FAITH EXPOSED
Real Visualization That Works

S INCE LOTS OF FOLKS like to visualize AMAZING futures, this may present somewhat of a dilemma because we want what we want, and visualizing is wanting, right? At a minimum, it poses some questions relative to THINKING in general, because we are doing this quite literally, ALL THE TIME! Everything we do is geared towards getting what we want in the near or far future. Funny thing is, we are never really taught how to think, we just do it and assume we are doing it right. There we go assuming again. LOL. The fact is, everything we do is really geared towards getting what we want, and it requires thought. We can't get around that. We are also taught that we MUST BELIEVE! However, if you really break down visualization, it isn't actually believing if it isn't done right.

If we investigate the content and context aspects of visualizing relative to TIME, we can assess the overall technique and its potency relative to belief, thereby challenging the efficacy of the methodology. At the surface level, visualizing is more or less just an elevated, more focused and intentional version of "WANTING". Take that to the next level though. If we are simply amplifying that "wanting" thought pattern by projecting that "DESIRE" into the future, in the mindscape, then where / when is that imagery? It's in the future. So, if that's the case, then what have we done? The simple answer is that we have proved, without a shadow of a doubt <u>TO THE MIND</u>, that we do NOT have it now. All we did was amplify the wanting! That's problematic, because belief matters, BIG TIME! We have essentially done the OPPOSITE of what we want. While all of our efforts are geared towards getting something, whatever it is, the mind technique we just used is making it more difficult by putting up a big old mind roadblock!

It is taking us on detours, and maybe even postponing it indefinitely by the way it is thinking about It relative to TIME. Why? Because the mind doesn't BELIEVE IT is true NOW. By projecting that imagery in the future, and literally PLANTING it in the mindscape there, the mind believes that it is in that future we just imagined, which makes it NOT TRUE NOW! Uh-oh, that's kind of a bummer of a realization. You mean, all this time, I have been doing it WRONG? That means that I am thinking WRONG. On top of that, I do this ALL THE TIME! Yikes. So, when I am doing it intentionally in the same exact manner, with emphasis, I am making it worse, not better. CRAP!

So, how are we supposed to be "thinking" when we visualize or "WANT"? GREAT QUESTION! Visualizing is easy, the "wanting" is much more complex because this is a ridiculously bad habit that takes massive focus to unwind in the mind relative to how it thinks. The reason is because the habit is intertwined so deeply with how we live our lives, how we relate to time, and that needs to be dissected, SEEN, and then deliberately unwound. We need to be watchful of how it happens, and also how fast it happens. It is actually really important, but no one ever really considers or explains it to us as a "strategy" relative to THINKING. I mean, seriously, who thinks about thinking, or wanting for that matter, we just do it. We can't even fathom the possibility that we are doing it in suboptimal ways, no less flat out wrong. The truth of the matter is that we need to unlearn this bad habit because we are probably NOT going to stop wanting things, stuff, situations, etc.!

So, let's start from scratch with visualizing, having a dream, and picturing that situation, thing, relationship, or whatever it is in the mind's eye. We are taking a deliberate time out to do it PURPOSEFULLY, with a goal of some kind in mind. Creating, exploring new ideas, imagining our potential futures is supposed to be JOYFUL, idealistically. That is true, for most people. It can be FUN, but now let's make it productive! This is where it gets interesting, so pay close attention IN DETAIL, particularly relative to the time element. If the visualization is NOT done properly within the right context (time wise) it can be counterproductive, for sure. At a minimum, we would be cancelling out our own best efforts. Worse yet, an error in execution here could be doing the opposite of what we intend. The effect would be the cancellation or postponement of what we want.

Visualizing can be VERY productive, and as always, DETAILS MATTER! Technique, energy, content, context, time and the level of emotion one can generate relative to the goal can all affect the minds' ability to BELIEVE! So, be sure to have a plan, be ready to energize it, stage it, add some drama, and make it believable to the mind. A playful and electrified imagination helps. This needs to be the best sales pitch you have ever made in order to CONVINCE the mind, beyond a shadow of a doubt, that whatever it is that you are visualizing is TRUE! YOU KNOW your own BS, your mind knows your own BS, now is when and where this will be tested. A half-assed effort isn't going to get it done, nor is a moderate effort with a level of Indifference. Ideally, it has to be IMPORTANT and carry some weight with it, preferably HUGE MEANING! If it isn't a major priority, then the delivery will be with more of an apathetic tone, and it just won't be convincing. Indifference just isn't going to "get it done"! Once accomplished, a level of satisfaction, joy and climactic delight are the preferred result of the visualization, so let's get to the theatrics! CARE MORE is the attitude, not careless! "Care-less", is just a lazy mind, or one that is somewhat impartial. "Whatever" can't be the attitude! When we don't care then the attainment of that something we are supposed to be striving for is obviously not going to feel like a huge accomplishment. There needs to be a driver, a significant one that is being satisfied. There has to be some passion behind it, like a more intense motivation, and the result of that "why" has been realized in this fantasy that has just come true!

While we are visualizing, let's also consider that perspective in a more spiritual context. Since we know that it can be self-defeating when done incorrectly, let's pay attention to details relative to religiosity, contemplation, and prayer. Is this type of thinking not considered "praying"? Think hard on that, particularly if you are a believer. Jesus basically taught that **WE MUST BELIEVE!** Nothing will be impossible for us. All we need is faith: FAITH the size of a mustard seed. So, if that's true, which it is, then there is a right way and a wrong way to visualize. The more spiritual version of "visualize" is to "pray", mainly because we are setting aside time to "ASK" so that we "RECEIVE"...very deliberately, and purposefully!

Granted, there are many ways to "PRAY" and that is not always asking for something. The prayers that I am speaking of here are the POINTED variety. We either WANT something really bad, or want to ELIMINATE IT, intensely. In fact, we want it OR don't want it so bad that we are taking EXTRA time and effort to ask in a more emphatic fashion with some direction and hopefully some really good choreography! Visualizing is essentially asking for something in advance, before it happens...basically prayer, assuming people do it in the same traditional ways.

So, rather than assume we know how to do it, we need to think about how we visualize! Let's back up and dissect the way we do it and how that "delivers" things in our lives. Not only when we are "goal setting", visualizing, or praying, but ALL THE TIME! That's kind of important, especially if we are to "move mountains". Change requires new ways of looking at things. By doing so, it generates NEW THOUGHTS that are formed differently, contextually, and time WISE. Thoughts MATTER, they are the building blocks of our lives, and we are constantly BUILDING with them. It starts with a foundation and in order to see the progression, we need to back up and rebuild it as a compilation of thoughts.

The life we have built is the result of everything we have thought and BELIEVED up until today's date. What we are experiencing TODAY, right NOW is the result of all that thought, all that prayer, and all that visualizing. Whether we did it with some level of intentionality or not, here we are! After all that, we can see that these are just a congregation of thoughts. Some are just more impactful than others. That being the case, everything we have thought previously has made its contribution, and translated into some kind of action. Some of these were lazy, or haphazard, others were more directed and energized. The grand sum and accumulation of that progression has resulted in our present life. Again, sometimes, we make them a priority, other times, not so much. The bottom-line translation to that is: THIS EXACT LIFE is what we had faith in, and DE-MANDED be true, by our own thoughts right up to a millisecond ago. Yes, we are responsible...at a very minimum, to a "degree". Whether that is 100% or not, subjective. Oh boy, smirk...I think you see where I am going with this, right? We need to back up and dissect FAITH and THOUGHT relative to TIME which takes us back to more than just a few seconds ago.

What is faith in this very specific context? Believing in something before it happens. Faith, interpreted in a more traditional way is PROJECTING a potential FUTURE and the possibility, hope, or expectation that this PROJECTION is a possible REALITY, when? IN THE FUTURE...so what is that? It is "WANT-ING", disguised. From the spiritual side of things, it is the things we might pray for. "Coming soon" type things, which again, is "WANTING". So, if we pray or visualize and we project that imagination into the future when we are doing it, then our faith is being misplaced. We don't believe it is TRUE, NOW! That simply means we have a methodology issue.

BELIEF MATTERS—BIG TIME!

The plain and simple truth is this: We are back to square one of the building blocks because the mind doesn't believe, YET! So, we haven't built anything. WANTING is NOT BELIEVING! Well, let me correct myself for your benefit. Wanting IS believing in the lack of what we WANT in the present, because we are projecting it into the future. Please try to contemplate this for a bit. It is like a tongue twister...in a way. The same is true for prayer and visualizing. If we are praying for something we don't have and visualizing it in the future, then what are we doing? If we are visualizing something we don't have, why are we doing this visualization? TO HAVE IT, right? But we are doing it wrong because faith requires trust and BELIEF. What we just did is NOT trusting, and NOT believing. It is actually a lot like HOPING. No matter how hopped up on "hopium" you get, hope is not a strategy. Planting a future building block in the future doesn't build a foundation TODAY, NOW!

Spelled out, that means WANTING does NOT equal HAVING. So, in terms of the level of belief goes, this is the equivalent of 100% BELIEF that we do NOT have what we want now. That is a HUGE problem. Not only is it a huge problem in the land of manifesting, but it is also even more of a problem when we add emphasis to that "wanting". We do that by adding emotion to it, such as: anger, frustration, blame, finger pointing, huffing, and puffing, cold shoulders, guilt trips, complaining to other people or internally, explaining all the details of whatever shenanigans prevented the desired outcome, or tirelessly reliving what we just went through to NOT GET what we wanted, etc. These are all POINTED! In a lot of cases these are pointed outwardly, or externally onto others, people, places, things, situations, etc. Also problematic is when we point them INTERNALLY, towards the "selves" that are to blame, guilty, made a mistake, failed, went the wrong way, etc. Adding emotion to these "wanting" scenarios is just proving with a lot more emphasis that what we WANT, we don't HAVE! Increased awareness will see this going forward. Pay attention! We must stop this self-defeating behavior. We absolutely MUST BELIEVE, and this is not believing!

What did Jesus instruct relative to BELIEF? My summarized version is that what we BELIEVE is TRUE for us "WILL BE DELIVERED" to us...and it IS. It's so consistent that it is PREDICTABLE. We can SEE IT COMING. That's how well FAITH WORKS! The problem, in these cases, is we are using it backwards. We have to dissect it to see the real backwardation of it...so let me explain this in more detail.

If the mind is PROVING, TO ITSELF, that it doesn't have something, what happens? It will continue to NOT HAVE IT. Why? Because it doesn't believe it's TRUE! It's a hypothetical, imaginary, and the mind keeps imagining it, as imaginary...IN THE FUTURE. If it were true NOW, well, then we would trust in it and know it existed already. If we believed it was already true then we would NOT BE WANTING it right now, we would HAVE IT ALREADY! In that case, we would be on to the next thing in reality, but what if we took a moment to APPRECIATE the having of it? What would that do in the mindscape? In the mind, that illusion, or "projection" would become real, it would be true, because we already have it...hypothetically, as a visualization!

What we are doing when we are "wanting" is using faith backwards and proving to the mind that we do not have something already. If this skill is being used backwards, then what happens? We get what we DON'T WANT rather than what we DO WANT or we continue to kick it further out into the future we just imagined it in. That will of course depend on how much emphasis we put into our thoughts. Thoughts energized with emotion will have an effect on the timeline. Things like frustration, desire, excitement, and even the milder tones in between. Lack of emphasis matters too! It's like a gauge, and the mind definitely weighs it! We can pour a little gas on it, or a lot. By doing so, we are feeding the flames of desire, anger, and the other emotions by the thoughts we think because they are thoughts that DON'T BELIEVE! It all comes back to faith and belief! That cycle feeds itself! We can see it happen with oversight as we light an internal fire only to throw water on it immediately! (by accident of course at first!) By accident means that we did it without awareness, which means we don't know why we are failing to produce what we want! Without an enlightening awareness intervention, it inevitably continues to happen which is what causes the frustration to begin with. We keep postponing it with misplaced belief. Then, by the nature of the wanting, which is now elevated to a frustrated level of wanting, we kick it even FURTHER out into the future...because we are EMPHASIZING to the universe that we still do NOT HAVE IT. We still WANT IT, and now we want it BAD, even more than before! This is BELIEF, but we must really look at what is believed. What is believed is that we do not have. So, we have defeated our "selves" by faithing WRONG. That's why we ask the question, "WTF"? What the faith am I believing in? Is that BELIEF pointed in the right direction? If that faith / belief is framed as a "WANT" then we are essentially believing in what we don't HAVE! The proverbial light bulb hasn't turned on yet, we are still in the dark!

Taking this to the next level, when we add emphasis, which we do over time, it amplifies the belief that we don't HAVE! So, the belief in having wavers, disappears, and we begin to question if we will ever have it. The bottom line is that these things we want keep running away from us, until we BELIEVE they are true. SO, that begs the question, if we do not have it now, how are we supposed to GET IT?

ACT AS IF!
Pray without ceasing. (PROPERLY!)

Give thanks, in ALL CIRCUMSTANCES.
REJOICE, ALWAYS!
Have an "Attitude of Gratitude"!

These are the instructions we've been given. They are the same thing, ALL OF THEM. These all begin with faith and belief. Believe = BUILD! Belief is the building block, the seed we plant. It is the way we start our foundation, build our house, plant our tree so that it grows roots. Unfortunately, this is not what is traditionally taught and done. That's not how we THINK. Particularly if we are WANTING. What we actually do can be quite different. When we are "wanting", we are "projecting" some imaginary thing, situation, or whatever else into the future on the mind screens. NO! STOP!

Here is what TO DO: You take that future "illusion", you do that same thing in your imagination playing it out on the mind screens. You do all the things you were doing. Picture it in the mindscape, visualize it, feel it, taste it, touch it, play with it, enjoy it, be thankful for it, appreciate it to the ends of the earth. DO ONE THING DIFFERENT though. That one thing is that instead of planting it in the future in this imaginary scene, plant it in the PAST, as if it is already true for you. Not the seed, but the fully grown tree. Not the first brick, but see, feel, taste, and imagine touching the completed house, walking through the front door, etc.! Literally breathe it in and feel what it feels like in the mind. To make this true in the mind, we need to ADD ALL THE EMOTIONS, imagery, scenes, people, accolades, or whatever else you can dream up and then fully immerse yourself in the experience of HAVING it with ENERGY! Again, mindset wise, we need to "FRAME THIS" as a retrospective, time wise. Don't get bogged down in the figuring it all out part, like as in HOW it happened, but enjoy the fact that it is ALREADY TRUE! In fact, amplify it, experience the truth of it, go into exceptional detail about all the particulars that appeal to you. Have a blast with this, take in all the satisfaction. The "Why" has been completely fulfilled. The satisfaction and climax of all this built-up expectation, and for the finality of it coming to fruition as the result of all your effort and persistence paying off. Finally, after all this time, YOU HAVE IT! It is TRUE, you attained it, you bought it, you lived it, you are experiencing it. Whether you imagine it was difficult, or easy...just make sure that the mind BELIEVES it is true and BE THANKFUL! This is adding the exclamation points to the fact that this is 100% TRUE already. In the mind, it has become real, NO DOUBT remains if it is already true! THAT is a powerful visualization because the mind BELIEVES it is TRUE, NOW!

13

FAITH EXPOSED II
Real Visualization That Works

B Y THE WAY, THE more often this is done the better. I recommend that at a minimum, this should be the last thing that gets done before going to sleep at night, and the first thing done on awakening. Do your prayers. Now that you know a powerful visualizing type prayer, do it the way you know you need to do it to cement it in the mind. Your mind can then have fun with it all night long, and once it wakes up, it is reminded again with more visualizing and appreciation before stepping out of the bed. Remember to stay away from "projecting". True prayer is "HAVING" and being thankful in advance. BELIEVING and APPRE-CIATING are the key to seeing and hearing the answers to those prayers as a reality in your life. So, start each day reinforcing good mental habits! Exercise these inner muscles as often as possible!

Now the hard part, that was EASY, right? ...and hopefully it was FUN! If it wasn't fun then you didn't live it, or put enough energy into it, so it wasn't real and probably a waste of time. Do it again, until you feel it as so real that the tears of joy are literally running down your face! That's BELIEF! If that's not possible with what you just imagined, then imagine something that would generate tears of joy! Something you would be thrilled with! THINK BIGGER!

Now, wipe the appreciation tears from your eyes and pay very close attention because this is extremely important. You just did a really good and powerful visualization, or in religiosity / spirituality, I would call it a prayer. Doesn't matter, semantics, really... the effectiveness is going to be more relative to the level of BELIEF you can muster than the label you put on it. You planted it in the mind, and the mind now believes it. Inevitably, we must come back to REALITY, right? This is where the mind goes whah whah whah whahh, crap, now I need to go make it happen because while that was fun, it isn't real yet, so we go right back to WANTING IT, and projecting it in the future again. NOOOOOOOH! With all the good stuff you just did, this cancels out all that BELIEF! If we go on pouting, or right back into frustration, complaining, feeling empty, or defeated... that isn't going to help us. We just lit a candle and at this stage the smallest tear, or even a puff of frustration can put out that delicate new flame. The mind needs to continue believing and faithing, so we need to be gentle with our "selves" and guard the presence with all of our fire-starting fervor! And no, I am NOT saying to live in the fairy tale either, except when doing the visualization purposefully. Watch the mind wanting to "WANT". Don't let it go there, this is where FAITH and awareness MUST STEP IN to BE WATCHFUL. Presence must be maintained. Be on the lookout for the "wanting" lower "self" that will WANT to continue WANTING! Don't allow it. We MUST disconnect from that future "self" and that future TIME – SLOT while we build a raging FIRE with this little candle! Faith is the tool we use. I call it a buffering mechanism in this application because it gives us a very particular functionality. It's almost like our eyes are twitching (not literally) because we are seeing reality and the illusion intermittently until the buffer is fully implemented and integrated! At that point, the faith buffer is fully installed and can be counted on to eliminate the "attachment" to the future while we enjoy the NOW and the journey we are experiencing while we are getting to that future!

There will be some cognitive dissonance going on which is what we need to see because the mind is going to want to go right back into the "wanting" states we are quite accustomed to producing when we WANT. Our mind is a machine, it is accustomed to "behaving" in a particular way unless it is reprogrammed. It's actually misbehaving if you really want something badly. So, AWARENESS needs to be dialed up and drilled in on this tendency within the mind to do this particular behavior. So, every time we find ourselves in that state of WANTING, we catch ourselves, and come back to NOW! LIVE IN THE NOW! In the now, we cannot be "projecting", that will no longer be allowed within our newly optimized mindsets. After all, it is the projecting and WANTING that is convincing the mind that it isn't already true. We can see this as self-defeating now because if we did allow that to happen, we would be overwriting our own scripts and cancelling out our new "BELIEFS". Setting goals and then going after them presently is a whole lot different than a mindset that is relentlessly "WANTING"! That's where and when FAITH must act as the buffer with unwavering commitment.

The time-thief must be caught in the act with persistence so that presence can be solidified and maintained!

Consider it like this. This is a software upgrade that needs to be integrated and the more we visualize and practice the feelings and satisfaction of this new truth for our "selves" the faster it will happen. It is very similar to planting a seed and fertilizing it or filling the pot and putting it on the stove. The watched pot never boils, and the seed never sprouts when we are watching. That is why we must TRUST that it will, so we LET IT GO! How? With FAITH! Let it go, GET PRESENT! Once the seed is planted, we have to leave it alone and LET IT GROW! We let it grow by letting it go. Leave the future alone and keep the mind present!

"Letting go" is not just for the past, it is for the future as well, so that we can faithfully cultivate our garden WITHIN, presently, as in, NOW! We are providing the optimal inner garden conditions to faithfully operate the MACHINES. The machines that cultivate this garden are our thoughts. That can't be done if we are NOT IN THE GARDEN! Faith keeps us PRESENT, IN THE GARDEN. We can work these thoughts, fertilize them, and PLUCK the weeds, with presence. Without it, we are on the other side of the fence. That's why our thoughts need the light vs darkness, so they grow. The light of awareness is that light. It shows us which thoughts we are fertilizing, and which ones are IN THE DARK. What that comes down to is super simple, the ones that are holding our attention are getting fertilized. The others are in the dark. No light, no fertile soil, NO GROWTH. That might equate to slower growth, but that we can also see. Slow growth just means that we are not amplifying or concentrating THOUGHT in the right ways. When we visualize, we can add emphasis, emotion, appreciation, which adds to the belief factor. The alternative is also true though, frustration, anger, and other heightened emotions suck the moisture and fertilizer out of that soil as the MIND GOES UNCONSCIOUS. What happens next? Our garden is IN THE DARK again, we don't know what's going on in there. The weeds can flourish in the darkness. The longer we stay unconscious, the longer they have to "TAKE OVER". Doesn't it seem like these weeds just pop up overnight?! WTF! (What the faith?!)

To summarize, we plant the seeds very effectively with our visualizations and prayers. We add emotion, satisfaction, and truly enjoy the "HAVING" of it, whatever that might be. When done with massive appreciation, the mind so believes it to be true, and is so happy about it that tears of JOY will stream down the face. Once this is done, the seed is planted. Tears of joy and gratitude = PROOF that the mind believes. It is DONE! Close the virtual gate (to the future),

GET BACK TO NOW, and make it happen. Use FAITH to keep the door safely closed, maintain that presence, and let awareness GUIDE, while being watchful of any seed killing "thoughts" or behaviors. Faith gets us in the moment and keeps us in the moment. Awareness oversees the faithing!

This gives us a whole new perspective on faith. Faithing, assuming that is the "use of" faith as a skill, is something we can use as a tool in the land of manifesting. That is assuming the WANTING is still not a HAVING. This is "manifesting", using visualization and our mind tools. Faith is a key skill in making things happen. It is an essential ingredient to co-creation, because it starts with 100% BELIEF / TRUST. By letting go with complete TRUST, it is very impactful to the mind. That action states very powerfully, that there is no longer any DOUBT. We have already planted the seed and seen the fully grown tree in our mind's eye with the time element behind us. We have seen it in all its glory, felt the truth of it, and are extremely thankful for it. That is 100% BELIEF! Being thankful in advance is the emotional cement that makes it TRUE. Now, is where faith comes in. We must let it GROW by LETTING GO. Keep on believing, and stop worrying, fretting and doubting. TRUST and BELIEVE!

We must stop going into the future all the time to check on everything. It is growing roots and "wanting" is a BELIEF KILLER. Belief killers kill roots and destroy foundations. Specifically, they tear down the foundational building blocks of our amazing visualizations. Thoughts build, and thoughts destroy...BE WATCHFUL!

The bottom line and easiest way to say it is this: WANTING is not belief in what we want it is belief in what we don't want or don't have. So, we need to stop with the wanting and start with the having and appreciating what we do have. That is 100% belief already, that's where we start. Then what happens is automatic, what we do have EXPANDS and the visualizations, backed by belief, fertilized with generative thought make it happen ABUNDANTLY! Fact is, these are abundance geared thoughts, so LACK is relieved of its duties. Do not succumb to the lack attack, watch those thoughts, and tend to that garden WITHIN. Use faith to stay in the garden. The mind is a powerful machine. We must be IN IT presently to cultivate the thoughts in our head.

BELIEF KILLERS: Fear, worry, doubt, resistance, avoidance, complaining, frustration, unworthy thoughts, and WANTING!

Let's review, because this is truly impactful. If we are focused on what we don't have, then what expands? What we don't have expands and that means we get

LESS OF IT or we don't get any of it at all. So, in looking at the details, WANT-ING is a LACK mentality. What does a lack mentality produce? LACK... LESS. What we have is taken away from us, JUST LIKE IN THE BIBLE! So, STOP the mental pattern of "WANTING", and start with the habit of "HAVING". Having means BELIEF that not only do we have enough, we ARE enough, produce enough and have so much that we are not WANTING! What we are GOES FAR! We must believe it though, so we have to practice that. We are obviously not accustomed to doing this, otherwise it would have already produced what we "WANT" in our life. Basically, we have to play the part, and act as if we have already produced it. The "wanting" has been overwhelmingly satisfied. THAT is a belief in having. Since the mind always wants to be doing something, give it something productive to do, an alternative: APPRECIATION and GRATITUDE! BE THANKFUL for what you have and it will expand.

Appreciation and gratitude help build STRONG FOUNDATIONS!

Once dissected, we can see that if we need to be believing, that means we must turn our thoughts around. ACT AS IF what we are "wanting" to be true, is already true...because then it isn't wanting anymore, it is HAVING. Once we already HAVE, conceptually, then we need to focus on appreciating what we have and plant new seeds in the mind as well...but not in the future, IN THE PAST! It is a bit of a mind trick, and it works. Here is the way to handle this little ego mind trickery. MAKE IT REAL, with every fiber of your heart and soul, IMAGINE IT! While we are "playing", we must be the actors and / or actresses in the scene to provide the mind with the visuals and sensory validations it needs to "BELIEVE" it is true, NOW. Here's how:

Do whatever it takes to mentally go back in time, just for a moment, and go back as far as it takes to justify this virtual reality. See that these seeds were planted previously and are already flourishing. Mentally, this is convincing the mind via BELIEF by using TIME as our accomplice and our imagination to reinforce this fake "truth". This is a deliberate mental mind maneuvering that is geared towards assuring the mind that what we want, we already HAVE. This will not only fertilize the existing garden, but it will help these new "thought seeds" germinate. With this mental manipulation, it will help them come to life, grow, survive and thrive with the light of awareness as we picture this and LIVE IT, in the mindscape. As we fertilize them with our attention, energy, focus and appreciation, they grow deep emotional roots in TIME which anchors them in this new fertile mind soil. Acknowledging this "truth" by treasuring it, and sharing it with intention, JOY and an ongoing commitment to proactively be THANKFUL provides BELIEF that we already have enough. The fruit that our garden has produced and is currently producing is overwhelming, so much so that we have to give some away. We are satisfied, thankful, and HAPPY as it feeds our every need, and that of others around us as well. That is ABUNDANCE MENTALITY!

By fertilizing our internal mental gardenscape in the mind, and spending "TIME" in it, everything in our current life garden will grow to produce even more because what we focus on EXPANDS. We MUST tend to our current inner garden. That means PRESENCE, in the moment. Our mental garden cannot be left unattended, we must maintain our presence IN IT. Time is darkness, presence is LIGHT! Our garden cannot grow if it is in darkness all the "TIME". Once we step outside that garden fence in time, WANTING in the future, all bets are off. It is as if we say to the universe, *"we don't have enough, we are starving over here, begging for what little can be mustered"* NO, that's lack again, we must do exactly the opposite. That "begging" would negate all of this BELIEF and our seeds would perish. We must be SATISFIED, satiated, not thirsty. We are completely delighted with all that we have to the extent that every last need, seed and "want" has already been met, fed, delivered and PRESENT in this reality. Victory is at hand, and we stand tall, triumphant, looking and feeling 110% fulfilled. Our proverbial bellies are full, and our thirst has been quenched. Our garden is LUSH, and we are flourishing in every way. Life is good, we are flowering in all our glory in this sun filled light of our PRESENT awareness.

Please play with this and be watchful during your day, moment-to-moment. Try to catch these "wanting" type thoughts and notice where they are in TIME. Correct them, OFTEN. Think abundance-oriented thoughts, know that WANTING doesn't work, HAVING DOES. Appreciation, gratitude, joy, happiness, putting a smile on your face. Associated actions also contribute. They tell a story. The act of GIVING = needing NOTHING, or at a minimum, it is convincing the mind that we have more than enough. These are all forms of abundance thinking. The act of giving something away is very powerful. It is a statement and demonstration to the mind that in our current reality, there is more than enough to go around. We believe it so much that we need to give some away. The act speaks *"Here, take some of mine...I have too much"*! These all promote a mindset that believes it has ENOUGH, appreciates it, and what we are goes far. The world is a mirror, but it doesn't reflect back to us what we are on the OUTSIDE, it reflects back to us what we are on the INSIDE. We are the magnet. That's the whole basis for "Be what you wish to see in the world!" We attract what we ARE! The world reflects it right back to us. We need to BE IT TO SEE IT! It's an inside job! We must BELIEVE, it starts with belief! Once we believe, THEN...what we are goes far, but not until that is true for us! The belief in it and amplifying that belief by visualizing in the correct contextual TIMEFRAME matters. So, if you are going to take the time to really focus with the intent to manifest something, make sure you have the timeframe right. YOU ALREADY HAVE IT, and the belief factor is proven by the emotional anchors you tie to it in the mindscape such as heartfelt appreciation. These emotions are TIME RELATED, meaning these emotions only happen once something has already happened. It exists NOW! That's why the time aspect of the visualization is so important! If we are projecting "LACK" with a wanting attitude, then what reflects back to us? More "want"!

To summarize:

GRATITUDE in advance is the most powerful form of prayer. That means we have put it in the past, in our mind, and BELIEVED IT. What is that? A POWERFUL VISUALIZATION! That's not a "projection" it is a REALITY, NOW! As far as the mind goes, it is true already...and so it is. That's BELIEF! That's what the man was talking about. Tell the mountain to move, and it moves.

FAITH can be a challenge, and context matters. Getting our mind right about how we relate to it can cause a little indigestion though because of the intricacies and internal gearing. It takes some contemplation to really "GET IT". It is almost as if the "wanting" aspect of our experience is sort of compartmentalized with faith being used as the buffer to maintain PRESENCE, KNOWING that all of our efforts will produce what we need. Ultimately, since that is true and we believe it, that ultimately gets us what we "want", but in the meantime, we can LET the "wanting" aspect of it GO! In the release of all that self-created pressure and the dialed up want / NEED, the universe sort of just ALLOWS it to come through...and it comes through abundantly with the release! It's like a dam break of sorts, and once that seal is broken, it just comes gushing through. The difference is that we aren't pushing, pushing, pushing and wanting, wanting, wanting...we are ALLOWING! It is soooooo much easier, and life just flows peacefully, abundantly! Once seen, this can't be unseen. Once we see it relative to one thing, we realize it applies to EVERYTHING. The implications are staggering, and so we see. We must implement it in our lives in other ways as well, which means a mega focus on THOUGHT and watching them. We must be aware of what they are doing and what they are producing. So, we are right back to the beginning. We must watch our thoughts with a ton of energy, massive awareness, and FOCUS. Faith matters, this is why. With observation, we can see how that impacts our lives, quite literally by the microsecond. Everything affects everything. Belief and trust play right into this in a BIG WAY! Faith, belief and trust are the mental tools we use to tend to our garden. We cultivate with heartfelt emotion, focus, attention, and PRESENCE. Awareness oversees this immaculate perception! We are the garden, and so we GROW!

The biggest challenge relative to faithing is not generating the "futures" that are compelling, that's easy to fix! We all want what we want. Once we THINK BIG and create that amazing future, it can be positively invigorating to make it real! Picturing it is FUN, we get all kinds of excited about it. The mind loves to do this, which is the problem and the answer. The answer, in some measure, is that it provides a major spark, and energy. The problem, or challenge is that it must be available for use! Timing wise, that energy can get lost in the transition back to now since we are basically playing with time! When we come back to reality the mind can bog down because of the dissonance. The realization that the whole thing was an illusion, that we were kidding ourselves, can be truly deflationary, mindset wise! We didn't succeed in making it believable. Oversight reveals this as the key element within the process because we were all pumped up, and in that hot second the air just came out! Once we are deflated, the energy level is no longer giving us the push we need to go make it happen! Therefore, it can be seen that the "excited" energy needs to be captured and preserved somewhere within that process. That's where faith comes to the rescue. The answer is faith, because that's the buffer between "presence" and the future. Faith is used to LOCK IN the energy within the methodology and transition. With presence solidified, it takes that newfound energy, magnifies it and then that dialed up energy is used to purposefully become it NOW! The moment becomes supercharged and "BECOMING" is quite naturally enhanced and directed by the overseeing higher "SELF" faithfully! This can be "SELF" serving, so that's where it can get tricky. CHOICE is always available with presence. Choose wisely! Selfishness is not the goal...so this is truly where we see if and when we are in alignment. AWARENESS SEES ALL!

The "GOAL" was just the goal, and then with awareness and oversight, we can see where and when we may have been misguided... At the end of the day, LOVE is truly the answer! Some "times", that's not what we become in our ambitious efforts to "ACHIEVE", succeed, accomplish, and WIN! The realization will present itself that while we may visualize some amazing things, we can't serve two masters. This is yet another form of dissonance when this realization comes! It can be a real eye opener as well. The "will", willpower, and all that energy we just captured is AMAZING! It can be used to produce and BECOME anything. But was it "aimed" right? With great power comes great responsibility. DO GOOD!

So, to have some fun with this, and as an example, I have explained this unique perspective as if we are a bus driver and all of our passengers are the ego selves /

baggage that we tend to carry with us. It is fairly extensive, and kind of funny too, so let yourself play with this conceptually a little bit and expand on the thought process visually in the mind. Relate this to your life and substitute in some of your passengers / baggage as you see fit. It will make it more powerful for you if you can identify some of the more influential characters and "drivers" within your "bus". Please use your imagination here, it will help you to really take in the story and its meaning. Your bus is the mind, and the passengers are the "hackers" who are attempting to have you go their way / get you to turn / do this or that. They invite / trigger you into their alluring stories with all kinds of captivating theatrics...depending on their <u>wants</u> and needs!

This is an enhanced and expanded version of the original BUS DRIVER analogy in the book: "Be The Instrument". Play along mentally, as I compare and exemplify it as the MINDSCAPE. Stay with the idea that YOU are supposed to be the bus driver...and by all means, please have some fun with this.

14

THE FAITH BUS DRIVER

Picture this. YOU, acting as the higher "SELF" are driving the faith bus. There is a BIG rolling sign on the front and it says **"FAITH BUS"** in BOLD letters. This hypothetical bus is fully loaded with passengers that all have different ideas of what faith means, and of course all kinds of destinations in mind. In fact, some of these passengers WANT to go backwards, and some WANT to go forwards. Some WANT to go left and some right. Below is a description of what is going on in the bus, and what these passengers are doing <u>TO YOU</u> vs FOR YOU as the driver: You may want to read this both ways as follows.

First: you can read this as if these passengers are doing and saying things at you or TO YOU, and then read it again in a different way #2.

The second time: read it as if the passengers are doing and saying things FOR YOU, so that you can see something new, and interpret it from a different stance more receptively. This is a different way of experiencing life. Life happens for us, not to us and perceiving life in this way is a major difference maker. Consider this story, and the stories in your life from these different vantage points. The vantage point, or attitude is that I am being a student of my "selves" constantly looking for the lessons they will teach me. That is a different way of receiving life...RECEPTIVELY vs resisting life every time it pushes on us. The "selves" are delivering us "messages" all the time. We just don't see them as messages, so they are not perceived or received. It is as if they were meant for someone else, so we IGNORE them, but in fact, they were FOR US all along the way. The road, the journey, every detour, every pothole, every storm, and even the signs that are posted are FOR US. We need to be paying attention. "Ignore" ance is NOT a solution, it is a recipe for a lesson not learned and some level of unconsciousness.

KEY NOTE: Each one of these passengers has the capability to "trigger you", by pulling the bus string. I'll explain this in a minute, just make a mental note that this is a potential "bleepage". YOU need to keep your eyes on the prize, THE ROAD! That requires PRESENCE!

This bus example is primarily an A / B scenario...with a potential wild card C scenario as well. The essence of it though is that the passengers are either from the past, or the future. This represents places you have been, and places that you INTEND to go. The passengers think you are going to take them where they want to go. In fact, they consistently and persistently try to steer, sway, or influence / persuade you to go their way. They have lots of conniving and even deceitful ways of doing this. Their philosophy, to be sure, is: "My way or the highway". The end justifies the means in ego land, and we have a whole busload of egos telling & selling all kinds of ideas / stories with their various attachments, drives, wants, needs, fears and desires. These are all pushing and pulling them in different directions.

On the left and right side of the bus is a string that the passengers can pull to get your attention as the bus driver. The passengers from the past are all on the left side of the bus, and the passengers of the future are on the right side of the bus. Conceptually, you might call the center aisle "the moment" because that is where / when these past & future selves tend to meet and switch "gears". Mentally the "selves" are constantly flip-flopping back-n-forth through the moment, but they never stay IN IT. As the FAITH bus driver, with focus and awareness, we do our best to keep the aisle clear and OFF LIMITS to the selves "WITHIN" If we are to maintain our presence in the now moment then the center aisle MUST remain clear, yet these passengers often try to get in there and work their way to the front so that they can drive the bus. So, keep this in mind as the bus driver, that with awareness and a full onboard "consciousness" monitoring system, they are locked on their respective side of the momentary aisle but constantly fighting to get in there. It is a barrier that cannot be entered or crossed and because of this the selves tend to bicker across the aisle in order to be heard, voice their opinions, make their point, and go their way. Once in a while, they actually do bleep their way into the aisle and start to make their way to the front of the bus. They do try to take us over from TIME to TIME. Please note that their way is not <u>THE</u> way. But their way is going to teach us something, so pay attention. Let's assess this scenario. By the way, awareness sees ALL this happening. It is the aisle monitor.

1. **The PAST passengers** keep pulling the string wanting you to turn around and make a U-Turn or simply refer to what they "know". They think about and see the imagery in their windows, and it reminds them

of something in the past and they want to go there. They keep pulling
their string wanting you to THINK of and FROM that very worthy past
and the perspectives that past generated. It might be from a moment
ago, a few days ago or a few decades ago. There was a destination that
really made an impact on them one way or another and in an instant,
they THINK that they are still there, and that the mind strategies /
directions that were created THEN still work today. The problem with
these folks is they have no discretion, and it doesn't matter if that strategy
/ experience / impact was good or bad, they still want to go there because
it's the only thing they know. They have old paper handwritten notes
and map printouts that are so worn they have holes in them. Some didn't
even print right from the early internet days or have water wear from
spilling drinks, rainy weather, and miscellaneous food stains as well.
Some of these maps are from many years ago and are drawn/printed
with varying degrees of "updates" too. That said, from different print
years, they each have different roads and places of interest which may or
may not still be there, in reality, NOW. They don't even SEE the new
roads that were built since that map was created because they are still
looking at these old maps. They tend to want to go revisit places that
made an impression on them, good or bad, and many of these places
are no longer on the newer maps, they've been torn down and don't
even exist anymore. In some cases, there's nothing there, and in other
places something else was built in its place. Unfortunately, none of this is
shown on their map, so they keep doing a double take wondering what's
wrong with their map. They are very confused, and a little bewildered,
sometimes even overwhelmed. They can't figure out where we are, quite
honestly. It seems to be "unknown" all the time. When they consult with
their friends from the past it can create some conflict because they are
basically looking at the same thing with "different eyes" (a different map
of reality...that's not reality!). Neither of their maps match reality 100%.
Nothing ever looks the same. That's why it is unknown to begin with,
it is unmapped territory, we are always blazing new trails. The problem
is that they are still on the bus and have 1 or more fingers on the string.
Each time there is a fork in the road, they see the different scenery and
relate to it in different but familiar ways and so they are pulling on their
string to get your attention. Depending on the weight and "impact" of
the imagery that brings up from their past, they are seeing it through
their imaginary lenses. (what used to be.) Their "relative" attachment
to it, and the WEIGHT of it in their eyes will determine how hard
that past passenger is pulling on the string and the harder they pull the

louder the sound is amplified in your ears as the bus driver. Quite simply, it is distracting as they converse amongst themselves and banter about who's map is right / wrong. It's really an entertaining show and some of the stories that these people tell are absolutely fascinating. Drama at its BEST! In fact, some of these passengers are just as captivating as the road we are on, it's almost as if they are actually driving. Quite convincing sometimes, and the stories...OMG! The stories they tell are UN-faithing believable. They truly put on an amazing show as they butt themselves into the aisle to tell them. Sometimes they can really grab our attention as we are looking in the rear-view mirror and this can take our eyes off the road. (Captivated by time, in the past.) That is, after all where / when these passengers live, in the past...and so they never truly see the amazing scenery for what it is in REALITY...NOW. They are missing out. Meanwhile, they capture our attention from "TIME" to time as they jump into the aisle, and we see them in the rear-view mirror telling their dramatic stories. BLEEEEEEP: We interrupt this program to introduce the future "selves". While we are unconscious, the future "selves" can very easily hop into the aisle and play their games too. So, pardon me while I steal this "presence" moment (joking around here) to tell you about these characters.

2. **The FUTURE passengers** on the right side of the bus all have different ideals, and they are a pretty vocal group. Many of their ideals are conflicting because these passengers' range in maturity from your current age to when you were much younger. From a consciousness perspective, this may be even past lifetimes if you subscribe to that "belief" system. So, from a dreamy storyline perspective we see all kinds of things being broadcast "for sale" in the seats and aisle ways of the bus (MIND). Each future passenger sees different futures and different imagery. Some are really good, and others can be extremely bad. We hear, see and feel these drama-infused storylines as glorious, or horrific scenes. As their stories are told, we see the sights and hear the sounds associated with these ideals, goals & dreams. Like it or not, they are streamed for everyone as they are blatantly broadcast on the in-bus theatre screen. Their "alter ego" future self is telling a much different story though, it is filled with fear, shock and awe, just as captivating, but in a bad way. Bleep by bleep, and sometimes quite abruptly, one interrupts another, and it can be a chore to stay focused. It is quite a show and the tone can change in a flash creating an entirely different atmosphere inside this bus. (the mind). These jokers are all interjecting them "selves" into the aisle ALL THE

TIME! Of course, this comes along with their associated "PROJEC-
TIONS". Based on these projections, these future passengers all have
GPS coordinates sort of plugged in and are watching to make sure you
are on track and headed their way, towards their desired destination.
BTW, some of their GPS coordinates are flat out WRONG! While they
THINK they know where they are and where they are going, they are
essentially clueless. The epitome of the "back seat driver" but not even
aware of where we are to begin with, no less WHEN. Each time a fork
in the road comes up they are pulling on the bus string and trying to
get your attention to make you turn one way or another, so you stay
on track. They have a schedule to meet, they NEED to be there at
a certain time too, so they are a little edgy. Because of their timeline,
they are under pressure, and in order to get to their place in time, they
need you to listen to them and do what they ask of you. TURN, or
go straight, step on the gas, or hit the brakes as they yell directions,
all while pulling the string at the same time. The other problem with
these passengers is that they are NEVER SATISFIED. There are a wide
variety of these future passengers, to be sure...all with varying pitches
and tones, some voices are deep and loud, and others are a little softer and
even some squeaky ones. You know what happens to the squeaky wheel
right? LOL Some are feminine, others masculine, some dominating and
others not so much. They are all just trying to spin the situation, grab
your attention so that you listen to them. They <u>WANT</u>, this is their
specialty and how they operate. "WANTING" is a way of life for these
"wanna bees". Depending on what they want and where they need to
be to get it, that will determine which way they want you to steer as
well as how fast you need to accelerate to get there. Want, want, want...
that's all they do. Once they "get", if that actually happens, they go
right back to wanting something else. They're never satisfied, never
happy. Some of them have very specific destinations in mind and they
are committed to it... These folks are so excited to get there that they
are literally pulling your strings at every turn BEGGING for you to
turn left or right to stay on track and on time. By all means, HIT THE
GAS, because as soon as we get "THERE" well then, they'll be happy.
Yeah right, I'll believe that when I see it. LOL. These jokers are never
happy. The opposite is also true. We see the extremists and their negative
projections too, so their friend is telling you to hit the brakes or flat
out STOP. They see nothing but scary fearful "stuff" coming down the
road and certainly want you to AVOID THAT. You must slow down
or steer clear of that if not pull over and stop all together. That would

be devastating and ruin their life for sure...DRAMA! Then of course, some of your favorite future passengers on the bus are so sweet and nice, super courteous and respectful, but they have no idea where they are going. They keep tugging on the string when there aren't even any turns coming up, asking "Are we there yet"? Can you say CLUELESS? Yep, some of these future selves pull your strings for no reason. Adventures in LA-LA Land. Ha-ha. These future characters are an opinionated group, that's for sure, and the conflict amongst these folks is REAL. It's easy to see the real issue with a little elevation from above it, but they can't see it because they are all in their imaginary worlds "WANTING" different things. One bleep to the next, bleeps over bleeps even, our "TIME" is almost completely bleeped out. One way or another, depending on who is acting out or speaking the loudest, you have to try to make sense of this madness. This one wants this, that one wants that, and the other one a few seats up wants something completely different. Someone ultimately is going to be disappointed because you can't turn left AND right. LOL In fact, hitting the gas and slamming the brakes, as these conflicted passengers have us doing, is using valuable fuel which is churning and burning energy, our most valuable resource, not to mention stressing our transmission and internal gears as the driver. Obviously, we need to get where we are going but this stop-n-go action makes for a herky-jerky ride for everyone. That alone can make some unhappy passengers. It is a recipe for griping and groaning, and these passengers tend to complain amongst them "selves" until they get really frustrated. They end up leaving some unfiltered "reviews" in a highlighted and often "TIMES" that ends up being in a very LOUD manner because it has built up for so long. They complain quite a bit because no matter where we go, they look around and say "*This is not what I asked for*" or "*This is not where I wanna bee*". Funny thing is, that's true even if it IS what they asked for, or where they wanted to be a few minutes ago. It's like the rules all of a sudden just changed. Never good enough, never satisfied...at least, not for long anyway, if at all. Never-the-less, we keep going and as we do these pranksters tend to trick us into taking many unproductive detours. Then, as if that wasn't bad enough, they point the finger at each other as to who's idea it was to do that, go there, etc. That's when their friends on the left side of the bus get involved again...so the "C" scenario comes into play quite a bit too. The bickering and "I" told you so's come out to play, but they sure don't play very nicely. It's getting ugly in here and the stress level is surely escalating. These fools don't know what to do, what to believe in. Faith? What's that? (sarcasm)

3. **The CROSSFIRE:** Scenario #3. In reality, there are way more than 3...
   but let's keep this simple!   This is when / where it gets really interesting
   and quite honestly, the stress factor WITHIN the bus gets to be a little
   bit more of an issue. You, as the bus driver, are watching the road. Eyes
   front, right? So, you can't see the passengers because you don't have
   eyes in the back of your head with the exception of glances from time
   to time in the "rear view mirror". These future and past passengers are
   talking amongst themselves in their past or future imaginary worlds,
   and some are talking back and forth across the aisle as well. Some are
   pretty friendly, and cordial. For the most part, these future and past
   passengers agree on how things were and how things "should be". That
   is why they sat next to each other to begin with. The whole concept is
   well known. You hear it all the time. Birds of a feather flock together...
   "Kindred spirits". This idea is so true and completely validated when it
   comes to our "bus" (the mind). Similar folks (thoughts) tend to group
   together. So, they are having normal conversations, in a normal tone of
   voice, at normal volumes because they like to surround themselves with
   like-minded people. Mostly, this is not seen or heard consciously, or even
   felt in a substantial way as the passengers are not really moving around
   much. In reality that is because they are unconscious. At times, the road
   is seemingly peaceful and quiet, until something "ON THE ROAD"
   causes an uproar. It stirs up some emotions and the passengers all seem
   to jump out of their seats at the same time. They all RE-act, but they
   each see things with DIFFERENT EYES so the re-actions are all over
   the map, so we are not quite sure which way to turn, internally or externally. Something is SEEN outside their windows that doesn't match
   their reality, the one in their imagination. Everything changes when the
   scenery in reality doesn't match the imagery in their remembrances or
   visualizations. The dissonance can be a real problem. It's like the deer
   in the headlights. Keep in mind that some passengers got seated next to
   someone they despise, and they absolutely cannot agree on where they
   are going anyway. These folks are bickering amongst themselves mostly,
   but every now and then they are yelling at someone across the aisle too.
   These folks are creating a commotion because not only do they need to
   talk over and above the "normal" people having normal conversations,
   but they are also fired up, and NEED to be heard so they are talking
   louder to make sure their adversary hears them and their point. The
   problem is that the bus has not gone "their way" in quite a while and
   their patience is waning. As they are getting more frustrated, they can
   get pretty vocal, and sometimes that can be pretty intimidating because

they really want to get where they are going. Of course, they want to get there sooner than later, and it seems like we haven't made any progress at all. Heck, some are even complaining that we went backwards. What one "self" wants is certainly more important than another "self" (sarcasm) NOTE: The level of "WANTING" is really getting heated up. This is when the crossfire amongst these passengers (thoughts) can really escalate. Remember, these are not patient people, they have an agenda, and a timeline. On top of all that "NOISE", these future passengers are tracking their GPS and if you missed their turn, they are telling their friends on the left side of the bus to pull their string too. If their friend on the left isn't paying attention, they start screaming across the aisle at whomever will listen, to tell them to pull their string. They can't agree on where we just were, or where we are going. We have to go back. We missed a turn. HEEEYYYYYYYYYY!!!!!! Louder and louder, they get pretty ridiculous, obnoxious even. This is NOT where we are supposed to be...when the ego passengers NEED to be somewhere, have something, do something, well...you had better get them what they want or where they want to be. Tricksters, pranksters, salespeople, and even some deceitful manipulators are all on the bus. Oh JOY...we get to drive this bus with them and all their friends and all they want to do is blame each other for why we are where we are and were where we were. We are here, pointing to their fictional map of reality, and we are supposed to be OVER THERE. (wanting) Ha-Ha What a charade.

So, that's the scenario. This is what I refer to as the MINDSCAPE! Just wanted to point that out. With a FULL BUS LOAD of these egoic passengers, and all that going on, we have a variety of GPS coordinates and directions, some of which are wrong, and others that may have worked years ago but the road has changed or doesn't even exist anymore, what do we do? Also, I forgot to mention that as their bus driver, this is a long journey, and you need to periodically stop for gas and / or to just rest for a bit. These passengers are from all different walks of life and each of them has different priorities as well as "triggers". Those triggers result in them pulling YOUR strings. During the day, as the road goes up and down and around the bends, they are seeing the scenery pass by and this is generating imagery that is tugging on these internal "triggers" because they THINK they know where they are (memories), or where they are going(projections). That makes these folks pull YOUR bus strings over and over again, for different reasons, because they are all looking at DIFFERENT things through their personalized "windows". Some passengers just create noise, and /or grumble and groan measuring and comparing every turn of the steering wheel, acceleration being too slow, too fast, and even griping about how fast or slow you are braking to slow down. That's not to mention the guy, girl, bus, truck in front of us. The passengers (the "selves") criticize and blame them a lot, oh and they also JUDGE you under their breath. Sometimes, they just blurt out random insults, seemingly from nowhere because you are not listening and not going their way, or you are just doing it wrong. "POOR ME", no one listens to me. Whaaaaaaah, wailing and crying all pouty and mad. There is a generalized NON–acceptance of reality. If they aren't mad at you, they are griping about someone or something else...that's just their nature. COMPLAIN! Why do they complain? Because their internal core state is "wanting", that's all they do. Once we get to where they wanted to be they want to be someplace else. Ridiculous, all this "wanting". No one ever appreciates "having" anything. Oh, and BTW, you have to listen to all this crap. It's your JOB, you are the bus driver and are at the mercy of all this EGOIC noise! I mean, you can't just IGNORE them, or AVOID them... they are on the bus pulling your strings. To say the least, this is a treacherous road with all this going on behind you...distracting, at best.

BTW, as a quick interjection here, if you really break down and dissect the "egoic" word to understand the way to transcend the ego in the name of growth, it will look something like this. As these little ego "selves" show up in the mindscape, we realize that they are trying to show us something. It is FOR US, so that we can learn. So, I dissected the word, EGOIC to conceptualize it a little bit better.

E-GO-I-C: As little mE GOes, I "C" = see... with awareness.

Broken down that goes like this.

E = Eyes SEE. It is Extremely important that as "I" go...

GO = through things, take action with massive self-awareness so that "I"

I = "I" as the higher SELF can see...

C = SEE the truth, vs just seeing these lower "selves" and all that they do, think, feel, say, visualize, WANT and "need".

Summarized that means "I", as the higher "SELF"...EXPERIENCE GOING, with awareness, so that "I" can SEE reality. Again, life happens FOR ME, not to me. The key is seeing the progressions of these experiences with awareness. This EGOIC vantage point equates to a new level of awareness and IN-sight. When broken down, relative to the bus driver example, this translates to eyes in the back of your head as you <u>watch</u> all these passengers WITHIN the bus. (This is within the mind, our thoughts and "internals" with oversight.) Highly simplified, that means that as the little "me" goes down the road, the higher "I" sees. Little mEGO, "I" SEE! Higher / lower. Silly, I know but that's an easy way to look at awareness from the higher SELF perspective as we watch the little selves and all they do and say for the lessons they provide. Simplified, that means that as the higher SELF, I must take action with massive awareness so that I can see what happens as a result, not only externally, but WITHIN ME as I am driving this BUS called ME. I am the BUS. ME GO; "I" see. That's the intricacies of a powerful vantage point personified: when life is truly happening "FOR ME" and not "TO ME". That's also the OVER-seer perspective. What that translates to is that these little ego selves and their elemental disparities are the "teachers" and it takes us on many egoic bus rides, some of which are quite an adventure. Thank GOD for shock absorbers. LOL. In reality, though, your shock absorbers are your F-words. Used properly, Forgiveness and Faith have much power and truly do add balance, peace, poise and grace under pressure. They enhance just about every ride we go on, and every experience we go through. With this level of freedom, life is like a walk in the park, it is actually quite entertaining!

OK, back to the story, driving the bus. Imagine this scenario, you are tired, it's getting DARK, and you have a whole host of back seat drivers, but you can't see where you are going because one of your headlights is out, maybe BOTH. (Not in the moment, blinded by the past or future, or BOTH!) A lot of these passengers are getting frustrated, lots of people are in the aisle and throwing things at you clamoring for your attention. They are annoyed with your driving, lack of attentiveness to their "needs" and want to just take over the wheel. Remember their core "MOTTO" is WANT. They want what they want, and they want it NOW, or at a minimum, very soon. They are no longer content to just sit back and watch as the bus goes the wrong way, so they keep getting louder and louder telling you instructions or jockeying to take over the driving. Meanwhile they are imagining this place down the road even further. Multiple destinations all bleeping in and bleeping out of their "windows". No one agrees on who should drive, but they all want to because you are just not getting it done. You are no good, and no matter how amazing the scenery is, you have failed to get them where they want to be. Some are excited, some are scared, some are obnoxious, and others are just throwing their hands up in the air. It's a real variety of characters in here "WITHIN" this bus.

Somehow, some way, you manage to maintain the driver seat, despite all the battles going on amongst the passengers wanting to drive... It's been a long day, and you are just plain tired. You can't really SEE all that well because not only is the sky now pitch black, but the weather has also taken a turn for the worse.

Your energy level is extremely low, and yet the passengers keep pulling your strings and / or grabbing for your bleeping attention, spinning you around and so you can't keep your eyes on the road, even though you can't see it anyway, as much as you would like to. You can't HEAR effectively either because of all the noise and chatter bleeping in and out, some more prominent than others. This is a recipe for disaster. All of these passengers are still on the bus clamoring, no one ever gets off. You can hear all this murmuring & bickering going on, some folks are louder than others, but because it has become so loud you can't really make out what any of them are actually saying. It's a BLUR of NOISE! Bleeeeeeeeeeeeeeeeeep, and nothing is heard. There is that one passenger that keeps blurting out random directions super loud. It is amplified in your ears over and above the rest of the noise, like one massive bleep, and it is so intense that it scares the crap out of you. So, you are completely on edge and basically FEARFUL because you don't know who to listen to, what they are saying, or if you are going to go off the road and hit a tree. It's also possible that someone else in the back is going to get scared, scream and / or just jolt you out of your seat for whatever reason they feel. The fact is you don't know what's coming. Your head is basically on a swivel TRYING to take it all in but it's impossible. This is one of those moments where you pretty much just take both your hands OFF THE WHEEL, throw your hands in the air, and then as a stubborn little child you plug your ears too. Here is a novel idea, let's close our eyes and hope for the best, but that's not a solution, is it? HOPE is not a strategy. Needless to say, it is a very unstable and erratic environment with a lot of uncertainty from moment to moment. Who the heck are you supposed to listen to? It seems like no one is ever happy. No one knows where to go to get some relief from all this STRESS! When we are here, they WANT to be there, when we are there, they WANT to be here, either way they WANT to be someplace else. All we WANT to do is make someone happy, even for a moment, to be appreciated. So, now look what has happened. We have succumbed to the "WANTING"! Funny thing is that all we wanted was a little peace and quiet. Maybe a stretch here, but how about a little LOVE and appreciation. (SELF-LOVE) Sheesh, would it kill you to throw a compliment up to your tireless driver from TIME to TIME? Dang! How about a little appreciation over here?!?!! I mean, look where I have gotten you to

Anyway, sorry for the RANT. These passengers obviously don't care about "ME" or what I WANT. Haha Each passenger from the past has a full set of images and emotions tied to destinations from the past they are seeing through their imaginary windows, and they are wanting, but can't "have" because it's in the past. These intermittent visions from the past are brought up by all kinds of things, like successes, failures, good moments and bad. They are triggered by the things they see out their "windows" as we are driving. Likewise, each passenger from the future has future agendas, ideals and wants they are seeing through a much different set of windows. Depending on what they see, that indicates whether we are headed in the right direction, or NOT. But they are not even truly seeing the present landscape, which is really beautiful. They are missing virtually the whole thing because they are so busy visualizing where they are going to be, someday, some "time" for the most part. They are so enthralled and captivated by their WANTING that it truly consumes them. Sometimes they settle down for a while, but in general, they are not very patient. They don't care where they are, they want to get to where they are going. Quite honestly, these folks WANT to drive but they have blinders on, and they can't even see where they are most of the time...so when the bus passes a cop with the flashing lights, it scares them and they yell out, scaring everyone, mainly because it spooked them. They didn't see that coming and then everyone got freaked out simply because they had tunnel vision, essentially BLIND!! Want, want, want...they don't even see the road we are on.

So, in this situation, what kinds of things happen to us as we are the bus driver driving down our own personalized road / journey? ...hypothetically of course. Do we see the signs, learn our lessons, and take the turns, or do we let someone else drive? Do we get all caught up in this chaos, get all stressed out, bleeped out, or are we able to make some sense of it all? Here are just a few scenarios that could present themselves:

1. You get fed up, stressed out, so willingly you just give up and let someone else drive because they convinced you to. The ego can be very convincing too and that's just easier. Easy is appealing to the EGO. (**"SELF" sacrificing**! The higher "SELF" was the sacrifice. So the lower self takes the low "easy" road when we go unconscious. The easy road doesn't usually get us where we "wanna be", or where we had envisioned as a goal. Wanna be's don't make the tough choices)

2. One of the passengers "takes over" the wheel because you get tired, sidetracked, and / or distracted so you let your guards down. The ego can be cunning, manipulative, and very deceptive. (**"SELF" deception**! The higher "SELF" was deceived. So, we take many detours, make many wrong turns, mistakes. We fail to be present to our MIND in order to make important, and effective / timely choices)

3. One of the passengers scares you out of, or physically pulls you out of the seat and grabs the wheel; a hostile "take over". The ego can be very

compelling w/ fear and / or desire. So, we RUN to the back of the bus, afraid to look out and see through the front facing windshield at all (TO SEE REALITY.) We are essentially shielding our "selves" from it, closing our eyes to it. (This is a manner of **"SELF" protection**, succumbing to FEAR. Alternatively, we are throwing our hands up in the air closing our eyes and ears while taking some "HOPE-IUM". Once again, hope is not a strategy. If I am in the back of the bus with my eyes closed (i.e. unconscious) then I have no control, NO CHOICE as to where my bus goes.)

4. You are forced to stop to refuel. This whole operation called life takes a ton of energy...babysitting all these jokers. The ego has a way of tiring us out with all its shenanigans. (**"SELF" depletion**, we used up our resources churning and burning energy. So, we get tired out, burnt out. Stopping is really the only, and safest option when we are so tired out that we can hardly keep our eyes open.)

5. You get bogged down by all the noise and don't know which way to turn, so you are idling and overwhelmed, going nowhere... STUCK! This is where we PASS TIME with endless scrolling, TV, and / or wasting time / energy on other useless tasks OCCUPYING the mind with "side-tracks" and games. (**"SELF" stagnation**. The higher SELF makes no progress because it is dazed and confused, unable to FOCUS and / or hibernating, not willing to engage, take on anything new. Basically, maxed out, stressed out, and probably crashed out somewhere in "Vedge" mode)

6. Several people are pushing and pulling on the wheel, and you end up hitting the curb and damaging the tire. This causes some "turbulence" in the bus and people are all blaming each other for the chaos. Everyone gets a "TIME OUT" for bad behavior. The ego causes inner conflict which causes mistakes. **"SELF" torture**, and **"SELF" absorption** equate to overwhelm, internal & external bruising, damage from life & the "selves" beating us up unconsciously, blaming this or that or each other internally and externally, ranting and raving with various emotional flare ups. When we internalize these errors and failures, they become **"SELF" absorbed** and that can wreak havoc creating all kinds of internal issues, health problems, dis-comfort, DIS-ease, UN-ease, and UN-REST. None of these are good for the body and certainly don't add to peace of MIND or balance. Mental, emotional, and physical pain increase unconsciousness.)

7. The passengers get so loud and obnoxious, and you get so sidetracked that you get in a more substantial accident. **"SELF" harm**, whether purposeful, or not, can be a real issue. **"SELF" punishment** can take things to even more extreme levels once we have the opportunity to "think things over". As we look back in agony of what just happened when we were unconscious. The accidents cause delays and then EVERYONE gets in an uproar. This ends up being a major delay of game penalty box scenario. The ego causes wrong turns, backing up or going backwards, and costs us TIME & delays. Overwhelm: this causes an inability to focus. Unconsciousness and unawareness tend to yield "BAD" stuff, bad situations, and bring us to undesirable destinations and often we need a do over because we went backwards, or simply lost TIME because we had to fix something. Fixing things costs us more energy, adds frustration, and probably costs us some $$$, no less TIME! Sometimes, that thing is US, we broke. That's where the statement "Haste makes waste" comes from. It is the mind trying to get where it is GOING. It is envisioning a particular outcome and time blocked in that future time-slot vs being PRESENT to do what is necessary to get there. As a result of this momentary unconsciousness, errors happen, so we waste time fixing them and / or fixing ourselves because we have health issues or broke something

8. Exhaustion: You get so tired from all of these accumulated burdens weighing on your shoulders, and confused due to the overwhelm, that you pull off to the side of the road to rest for a minute. You've been carrying this "stuff" for so long that your shoulders are weary, and your body is hunched over from the weight of the world that it is even hard to walk. Crack, rattle, and roll used to be a cool song on the radio, now it is your body making noises. LOL. Anyway, you have to try to rationalize, gain a consensus or some clarity to make some sense of it all because NO ONE CAN BE PLEASED! It is laborious and time consuming, because everything hurts, and no one agrees on anything, on top of depleting even more of your energy chasing down random thoughts (brain "storming".) You end up giving up, **"SELF" sacrifice**, and allowing a group decision, by voting on where they want to go. No one can agree, so this is somewhat of a confused MESS. You end up being the tie breaker or flip a coin. This is a GIVE UP stage in which we throw up our hands in the air and just take our chances...maybe LUCK with help? **"SELF" sacrifice** doesn't feel good and only adds to that deep core "WANTING" state. The alternative is writing down the pluses and

minuses as each passenger weighs in on life's various situations because you have so many things that are pushing and pulling you in different directions that it is impossible to consider and weigh them all at the same time. This requires considerable time in contemplation which means that for safety's sake, you need to pull onto a rest stop and work it out. (Lack of "SELF" direction, stalling patterns, inability to move forward. Too many captains.) This is where you just hand the keys to someone and let them drive.

9. You are convinced that something went wrong, and you make a u turn and start going backwards. The GRIND. Spinning our wheels, doing things 2 and 3 times in order to get it right. This adds to frustration, confusion, time loss, feelings of stagnation, uselessness, finger pointing, and all kinds of external / internal charades & blame games. **"SELF" Blame**, and bad aim feed more issues. Negative self-talk, being **"SELF" critical**, succumbing to **"SELF" judgement**, and more **"SELF" torture** only serve to prolong the agony or make it worse.

10. Add any other scenario relevant to your life.

Obviously, we have a lot of lower "self" issues going on. Needless to say, that's the EGO. We thought that we were acting as the HIGHER SELF, when in fact, one of the lower "selves" interjected again and took us over. These lower ego "selves" step in all the "TIME" and cause all kinds of havoc, it's a real trail of tears when we succumb to the time thief.

The solution: Oversight, with a higher level of **"SELF" AWARENESS**, and **"SELF" MASTERY**!

Call it "time management" but from a completely different perspective: overseeing time as a progression in order to maintain PRESENCE! So, back to "bus" iness. Just realize, in our hypothetical world, lots of things can happen while you are the bus driver taking care of business. Keep in mind that when you are stopped to get fuel other stupid stuff happens. Many of the passengers hop in YOUR seat and imagine where they were or where they are going, even full well knowing they can't drive. They are plotting their agendas and trying to come up with a way to get you to go their way, one way or another. So, they play their games, and plot their strategies, taking their turns "mapping" and playing things out as they see them, or as they should be...showing them off to everyone on the in-bus theatre system. (On the mind screens. They hacked in and took it over). This is essentially EGO tricks via unconsciousness. The funny thing is, there's no gas in the tank, you are going NOWHERE because you have no gas (energy) to get there. Even in this "down time" these imposters are demanding your attention so you can't even get a bit of rest or a good night of sleep. They are so busy "projecting" or remembering (or both) that the mind just RACES, doesn't sleep well and there is no rest for the weary. Sleepless nights equate to more unconsciousness during the day because we are all tired out from a lack of sleep.

To the point: As the bus driver, YOU need to take and MAINTAIN CONTROL. However, that is typically answered by responding to life with a big ole BUT. But this, or but that...excuses, delays, procrastination, detours, avoidance, and resistance. But, but, but...it's never the right time.

But the passengers are unruly, misguided, and quite honestly out of hand. That's the "selves", so they come up with TONS of excuses, justifications, and reasons WHY! Why this, why that...BEWARE! "Why" typically GETS ANSWERED and JUSTIFIED! We don't want those answers, we need to ask better questions. "WHY" answers equate to going down one-way streets the wrong way. It means delays, wrong answers, and a good chance that something bad happens. You get penalized, a ticket, and / or more PAIN ahead. So, instead of asking that question, in a generic fashion, to all of them or the air, like why, why, why with a blank stare...or generalizing a useless question to all of them at the same time, we need to realize where we are directing the question, and try to figure out a better question to ask. #1 To whom or what is the question directed? Is it inward, or is it directed outwardly, towards LIFE, the world outside. STOP here. Re-focus, Re-frame, Re-balance, and reign them ALL in. Tell them all to QUIET DOWN, stay out of the aisle, and SHUT THE FAITH UP so you can deal with this ONE THING, as an ISOLATED learning opportunity. Via the loudspeaker or whatever means possible you must help them to understand that ONE VOICE is all we can hear at a "TIME" and go right ahead and deal with that voice. After all, this is the FAITH bus...why the heck did they even get in my bus anyway if they weren't going to have a little faith? They must begin to consider the possibility and hopefully grasp the concept that they are just shitty drivers, or at a minimum, start to TRUST that you might be better! Otherwise, they could have driven their own bus down the wrong roads at the wrong times! When FINALLY, these folks ALL UNDERSTAND that you have it all under control (with faith and trust), THEY ACTUALLY DO IT! They quiet down, and even better, they quit PULLING YOUR STRINGS with TRUST and FAITH that you will "GET IT DONE"! Of course, you have to be able to imagine a scenario like this for it to happen. LOL

So, with all this QUIET, you can now HEAR the slightest little murmur from the passengers (the "selves"), and you JUST got done fueling up, cleaned your windshield, and can SEE very clearly ahead FOR MILES. YOU have just installed the latest software to the bus and now it is telling you ahead of time where the detours and speed traps are REAL TIME. CLARITY! (Heightened awareness / PRESENCE)

To summarize, if you haven't fully made the connection, the passengers are the ego "selves" in the MIND, and these selves all have different "voices", each of which "pulls your strings" or "triggers you", in one way or another. These are geared towards their attachments, wants, needs... some good, some bad. On top of the voices that are coming from our past and future "projector" selves, we have other "voices" that are generated from previous instructions, beliefs, teachers, parents, grandparents, siblings and all kinds of people and stuff that we have "bought into" over the years. They are all trying to get your attention, one way or another. They tell all kinds of stories & present all kinds of imagery...good and bad. These are sale pitches, propaganda to OBSERVE but not necessarily buy into. It is your bus; you can take it where you wish. Just because you are driving past some really enticing restaurants, or "tourist" attractions, does NOT mean that you need to take the detour, stop, or turn in every time. Don't take the ego bait. STAY FOCUSED, PRESENTLY!

You have to HUSH the crowd so to speak, QUIET the NOISE to make sense of it at all. The other problem is that you really like some of these passengers and some of their stories are very compelling. (The more formidable attachments / commitments). After all, some of these "ideas" / stories represent authority figures and their views / instructions and they are supposed to KNOW. Certainly, you don't want to let them down. Someone somewhere along the line made an impact on you for whatever reason, and each has their SPIN and "voice". That has to be lived up to. We must at least do that, if not a little MORE. There are bare minimums that must be met. If we are going down that road, well...we can't stop here. The EGO and its various friends combine to make up a very cunning machine / SPIN doctor. The gearing of this machine, (your mind) is quite incredulous, and it is constantly swirling up lots of medicine in the form of stories to make you FEEL SOMETHING, good or bad. Again, it is a machine, and it has very little to no discretion, it just keeps spitting out thoughts, words, stories and agendas repeatedly...all generated from the scenery. The problem is that the scenery is taking these passengers backwards or forwards to a place in time that doesn't exist NOW, and they are responding to that "ILLUSION", going in to the "TIME-LOCK" and PULLING YOUR STRINGS! These "selves" try to SELL their story and their agenda TO YOU, to get you to BUY INTO IT, to go their way, yet they all have different destinations in mind, and again, they are seeing an ILLUSION! Not only is what they see FALSE, and their agenda (beliefs) based on it, they are so conflicted that you literally cannot and will not please everyone, if you can please anyone. As you can see now, this is a real shit show. As a result of all these shenanigans, the present moment and the higher "ME" that's supposed to be in it keeps getting bleeped out and is NOT PRESENT. Sometimes, as the murmur level begins to elevate in volume again, with the same old people raising their voices, you just want to throw your hands up in the air and just yell SHUT UUUUUUP, SIT DOWN!

What's the answer? Well, it isn't a simple one, but it is effective. It takes a strategic approach though, which can take some time to implement. Once again, this can be problematic because people always want the quick fix and true growth doesn't happen that way. It is a process because there is not one universal answer. Each of these folks is different, looks at things in unique ways, and that requires perspective, context, and a much higher level of understanding. While there isn't just one answer that will solve all of this madness, there is ONE universal THEME that will help address and "CURE" all of this "craziness" though. That can actually happen quite quickly once implemented and RE-enforced w/ TRAINING and practice. The answer is LOVE, more specifically "self"-LOVE.

It's actually demonstrating LOVE internally and externally. When directed inwardly towards the "selves" and their foolishness /shenanigans, it is the HIGHER "SELF" that is providing the lower "self" the love and understanding it needs to GUIDE: self-love. That's the tool that is used to TEACH! It is how we grow, and these lower ego "selves" learn their lessons. Each individual passenger has their own attachments, drives, motives and they all come from different times, places, and various "understandings" as well. They've all made their mistakes, bad calls, bad turns, bad ideas, etc. So, in reality, there is only one possible TOOL that can truly understand, with empathy and compassion, ALL of these little "selves" and their vantage points. Isn't love the answer? Not just any type of love though, a "motherly" type love. (Unconditional!) Motherly love provides that love with empathy, understanding, and TEACHES with warmth and TLC. That's why love is the ultimate relational tool that truly heals from WITHIN. It is the absolute best thing that we can provide, to our "selves". SELF-LOVE with a mother's touch and finesse. LOVE THEM ALL, with empathy, consideration, and UNDERSTANDING... HEAR THEM! By hearing them, and caring for them, we can have a heartfelt understanding...and move forward. After all, these elements of our "selves" are just wanting to be heard, understood, and LOVED. That's all they really want. So, we have to empathize, understand them and give them what they need: LOVE! That means "self" love, to be sure. With it, the bus moves forward. People are satisfied because they understand. They truly thought that they were providing value, but at the end of the day, we grew out of them.

We know it, see it and even feel it. So, they start getting off the bus. As a result, it is easier to "MOVE ON" without them weighing us down. On top of that we don't have to listen to all their distractions and shenanigans, they aren't on the bus anymore pulling our strings. After a moment of reflection, maybe reminiscing for a hot second, we are understandably letting them go. Bottom line, that's just NOT ME anymore. I AM NEW NOW. We let the little "selves" go, one at a time.

LET THEM GO

That's the strategy, and it works. The problem is that you can't hear and understand them all at the same time, and on top of that, it is a moving target. As we move forward, life moves forward, things change, the moments change along with what is needed in each moment. As things change different characters within the bus pop up to meet the moment, and sometimes each other. As these "voices" WITHIN the bus take their moment in the sunlight to speak up and be heard, we address their concerns, needs, wants with "self-love". That takes TIME, to do this one by one...and that is why this is a process. More specifically, it's a JOURNEY, that's for sure. It is supposed to be FUN! Just think of all the people you'll be helping along the way. This is the epitome of "self" help. In a lot of cases, we need to UN-learn some stuff we have learned that's just bad "intel". One by one, over time and a lot of miles, through the ups and downs and curves in the road, in all the different types of weather and varying degrees of light and dark, LISTEN...as they try to grab your attention (pull your strings: triggers) and take over the steering wheel. JUST PRIOR to the moment, on the cutting edge of now, JUST BEFORE THEY GRAB THE WHEEL, hear their story and understand their agenda / sales pitch with massive real time awareness. CONSIDERATION: Tone the conversation down if you have to and deal with some of these unruly passengers first. The goal here is to BE THE BUS DRIVER, not the BUST driver. If you don't gain control of this bus and its passengers, you are going to go bust. By hearing their messages, and GETTING THEIR LESSON, true or false...you can steer the bus WISELY. That is, you have a say, a choice, and with a timely focus, you can move forward with the appropriate "ACTION" vs RE-acting without thought, without "CHOICE", unaware and unconscious. If you are "asleep at the wheel" (NOT IN THE MOMENT) there's no telling what your bus might run into, or who might grab the wheel and choose for you. The re-action will be from their agenda/programming that just came out of the "darkness" in the middle of the night and that RE-action may not be appropriate to the CURRENT road and its turns which we can't see because we are asleep at the wheel anyway. For all intents and purposes, we have taken a back seat, and they are driving. That means they are CHOOSING our life and our path...the road ahead is somewhat "PRE-destined" in a manner of speaking. With wisdom, we can do better.

We can have a voice and a choice.

HAVE A VOICE AND A CHOICE!

With experiential WISDOM, these realizations really hit home, and our IN-sights are dialed in. As within, so without makes perfect sense. There is a new comprehensive understanding that is totally internalized and appreciated. These IN-sights are happening FOR ME, not TO ME as I am experiencing life and so we look at life much differently. This experiential knowing and experiencing from this new perspective is a huge shift and it allows us to wake up to a new reality in which we are much more receptive, so lessons unfold quite naturally all the TIME. By WAKING UP, fully aware with PRESENCE, we have the capability to quite literally shine the light in the darkness, on THAT belief system that was just activated WITHIN (a passenger, one of the "selves" pulled our string). FULLY AWAKE AND AWARE, NOW the higher "SELF" can elevate and evaluate whether that is a valid "pull" or not, and either we still want to subscribe to that belief or make a NEW CHOICE to go in a NEW direction. As the bus driver, in the bus drivers' seat, with a clear windshield and a quiet bus, we have the power of CHOICE! We can take this bus wherever we want to. We have the steering wheel and can hear the REAL TIME GUIDANCE that is fully updated presently. If we are asleep at the wheel, any one of these passengers can take over the steering wheel and take us anywhere they want, at any time and we will automatically be going their way. It is as if we literally got up out of our seat and went to sit down next to them, on that side of the bus. At that moment, there is no telling who might hop in the driver's seat to drive but it is typically the one that got us out of our seat, so we need to BE WATCHFUL. Sometimes, it is as much of a surprise to one of the little "Me's" as the other little Me's. Not funny, really, but the higher fact is: WE had no choice; we were not in the driver's seat anymore.

Higher "SELF" control is warranted, NEEDED. We may need to hit that virtual rewind / replay feature periodically too...so we can see what REALLY happened in those lost moments in "time". That is where understanding comes in. We can see the "triggered self" in the light of awareness only nanoseconds later.

Please remember that when these passengers RE-act, they are RE-acting from and to an ILLUSION. Over time, how successful can this truly be? Talk about a fried transmission, these passengers would be changing gears so fast our vehicle would be SHOT. The moral of that story is: don't let them drive the bus. We need to MAINTAIN OUR SEAT. NOW! <u>Our presence is required here</u> to attain the Higher "SELF" awareness necessary to receive the guidance and master the "selves". Stay PRESENT "NOW" with CONTROL in the moment. The alternative, of course, is seeing the same stretch of road over and over again or something that looks strikingly similar because we refuse to change, turn, adjust our internal climate control or hit the gas petal for that matter because we were not in the moment. If we are not PRESENT then we cannot even steer, brake, accelerate, etc. We have no control. Some "times" we might have "LIMITED" control depending on the extent to which the "selves" have taken us over. These ego selves can be quite disguised and / or hide in the shadows of the mind until the very last millisecond before they take us over in a FLASH. That is why we need to be alert as the flash happens. That is the "flash of IN-sight", we see it as the lightning strikes. As we are looking WITHIN, the flash truly lights everything up, shining brightly even into the dark corners of the mind, there is no place for the little ego selves to hide. Awareness SEES these "selves" as well as all that they think, see, hear and feel. This is how we achieve a higher state of "SELF" MASTERY.

PRESENCE IS REQUIRED!

At the end of a long road, we have STOPPED TIME to SEE, periodically in a massive amount of previous present moments. This is enough to get a fine education from all of these IN-sights gained OVER time as the overseer of the "selves" within. "OVER" meaning high above TIME, the lower ego "selves", as well as sequentially in accumulated time slots as these lessons are learned and they compound. This is certainly a different manner of putting in our "overtime" and way more productive. Looking down on time from above can be extremely INsightful. LOOK WITHIN, as these ego selves' step in and make decisions based on their attachments, drives and fears, it is seen, processed, understood and "corrected" if necessary. Each "VOICE" is heard, each feeling is processed. All thoughts are watched, digested and addressed in the moment and as a result we begin to know and understand our "selves" better than we ever have before. We see their individualized LIMITS as they "choose" for us, and we see the result.

WE must attain and maintain FREEDOM!

HIGHER SELF-CONTROL

As a result of seeing this as it happens with presence, that life experience / lesson is absorbed into who we are going forward. It becomes experiential as we see through awareness and observe the "internals" that are driving it REAL-TIME.

It is amazing to watch the selves from this higher perspective, as they relate to time, and then watching and seeing life as a real time unfoldment. By being better at observing as the director of traffic WITHIN like this, we can see "from above" what their internals are having faith in. As the "selves" change their focus, and their attention wavers, or shifts, we see it. As we see these "shifty" selves shift, there is a momentary opportunity to "catch the thought" as it is shifting and just about to CHOOSE...but before it is choosing, as decisions are about to be made. Sometimes we'll be quick enough and maintain our consciousness firmly planted in the NOW, (Our bus seat). Other times, it'll happen too fast, and we will have missed it and although that particular moment we get diverted and were unconscious for just a millisecond, we know it and we see it just after the fact. This reveals more opportunities to "self" correct. This further increases our awareness and as we digest life experientially in this manner, these "corrected" selves quietly and peacefully exit the BUS (our mindscape). They are taught their lessons and quite efficiently, without much of a fuss at all, they are "LET GO". They are understood, processed, and forgiven if needed, since they may have made some mistakes. As a result, they quit pulling our strings because the fact is, they are no longer on the bus to pull them. Since they are not on the bus, neither are their attachments. Psychologically speaking, we let them go...along with all of their wants and emotionally based needs, comforts, attachments, storylines, regrets, sorrows and / or their persuasion tactics / self-deception and whatever else these ego selves are into. So, having LET THEM GO, we no longer need to listen to their endless sales pitches and propaganda. What a relief. Wouldn't that be wonderful if these relentless ego-tele-marketers in the mind lost our number? All of a sudden it gets really quiet in here. HA-HA. Peace at last. That means my virtual phone stops ringing, so I don't have to answer that call...I am not "TRIGGERED" so my focus is more stable. I am not constantly "on the other line" dealing with one of the "selves" in the past / future having to call my "SELF" back to the PRESENT. That DIS-tractor factor is a detriment to our ATTRACTOR factor. That's fixable with more consistent and unwavering presence.

YOU now have a true understanding of what FAITH is, how it works, when it works and BELIEVE because you have seen it happen real-time, with presence repeatedly. The journey has revealed many lessons along the way which has built a massive amount of TRUST in this F-word. The understanding is that faith is actively generating MY LIFE, every moment, and it is seen as it does it. The selves that had been using it incorrectly, have been dealt with, understood, educated, forgiven and LET GO. They peacefully, and willingly got off the bus and completely understood why. They must do so because they were standing in the way of freedom and becoming. With this new wisdom and presence, free from the "selves", YOU can take NEW ACTIONS and BE NEW consistently with PRESENCE. Without the "selves", their attachments, false thoughts & stories, your vision, and hearing are pure. FREEDOM, and CLARITY at last! It is from this space that change is possible.

With FOCUS, TRUST, FAITH, and PRESENCE you can take that step into the next moment. This is where and when TRUE CHOICE is available. Freedom meets the UNKNOWN...and GOD is there, in the eternal NOW, YOU MERGE! LOVE is one of the available choices. With God & pure guidance in the NOW moment, Love is unconditional, and this is when LOVE can call the shots and because you merged LOVE is the answer. Our "empty cup" is filled with exactly what is needed in the moment, and we accept it / become it. We see the choice and BE the choice. The moment, with presence, is where and when ALL CHANGE HAPPENS because we are FREE to CHOOSE. That is "BECOMING". That's why faith and forgiveness matter, because they provide and protect that freedom. Love is FAST, it happens NOW!

ALL CHANGE HAPPENS NOW!
We must get there and STAY THERE!
We do that with the F-WORDS: Forgiveness & Faith!

With presence and freedom, YOU are THE INSTRUMENT, by CHOICE. YOU ARE LOVE and LOVE RESPONDS, that is when love truly is the answer. As we become love, repeatedly, we BECOME our highest and BEST SELF. That starts WITHIN. We give the world what we are. If all we give our "selves" is LOVE, over and over again...that's the habit. We become it.

SELF-LOVE via forgiveness and letting go offers us a new beginning by releasing the past every moment in which we enable it. We use it to excuse & forgive the lower "self" that erred, didn't hear something, didn't see something, misunderstood, lacked presence, got sidetracked, made a wrong turn, etc. Self-love is the absolute best alternative. Enabling and embracing it as a skill is necessary when self-correct mode is needed. When we "F" up we need to Forgive first, and then FAITH up for the next moment, this is the SKILL that makes that possible. We, as the lower "selves" offer up a lot of opportunities to be FAITHOMIZED!

FAITH UP!

Faith up so that we don't have to FESS UP to the aftermath of the mistakes and missed opportunities. We get faithomized moment by moment. As we do, we attain and maintain our presence. We attain it with the skill of letting go, with forgiveness, our First F-word. We maintain it with our second F-word, Faith by letting go of the future, and our attachments to it full well knowing that our presence is required to GET US THERE!

Once we are there, presence allows!

15

USING FAITH AND IN-SIGHT
BEING AN INSTRUMENT OF CHANGE

I F YOU ARE STILL asking how? You have the answer, NOW! Now is always how...with presence, and preferably with LOVE! Love is obviously only one of many choices that are available once we are FREE to CHOOSE! We see an array of options, but there is likely only one that is the highest and BEST choice available in that moment.

We need to concentrate, and / maybe even spend some time in contemplation mode sometimes. Particularly around moments of mistakes or one of life's many detours...we need to take our TIME! Seriously, give our "selves" a time out to ponder and recollect for a moment in order to see more clearly going forward. As a matter of fact, we do re-collect our "selves" to assess what the heck they are doing. As we approach these moments, or see them in retrospect, we can see opportunities where we can be new and we either seize the moment, or we see that we could have been "NEW" and yet we were not. It is these lessons that allow us to front run thoughts and make it happen / BE better the next time around the ole block. One way or another we need to strategize and maximize each moment and in the times that we don't, we grab a quick lesson because we failed to do so. We need to figure out a way to ISOLATE that moment where a decision is being made so that we have JUUUUUUST a little bit longer in that moment to CHOOSE. It may very well be the same time slot and the same length, but because we are so much more prepared for it, and open...the new moment feels like it is longer, and we have more time to ACT. Obviously a second is a second, so in my conceptual world I break it down into milliseconds, or fractions of a second, and assess accordingly. Stuff happens fast in life, so breaking it down into segments of time is super helpful in the way that I look at things. To drill down and isolate the actual time slot that I missed something and then go back to see what it was that grabbed my attention is transformational. This repeat / rewind function is what ALLOWS the IN-sight, and the lesson to be captured / implemented for future moments. That lesson is absorbed and as a result, it is used to transmute the ego and neutralize the "selves" going forward. This empowers the higher "SELF" as it is growing through the lower nature / lower selves / ego. It sees the attachments that bleeped us out of the moment...and the ego "selves" that were "attached" are taught their lessons and let go.

As a result, we DE-tach, and ELEVATE. This constant state of becoming is like growth mode digitally enhanced and sped up. Ego transcendence mode is extraordinary and FUN. I make it somewhat of a game, or a personal challenge to catch my "selves". I define that as a state of being WITHIN from ABOVE, which I am ever vigilant and observant, literally ON THE PROWL for lessons. I am like a submarine on the HUNT for ANYTHING resembling a force to be reckoned with. This is a RECKONING, and it does need to be dealt with because it is underneath the surface of the mind, SUB-conscious. When it becomes CONSCIOUS, that's when it needs to be dealt with. That is what we want. That's what present awareness does, it highlights and enhances consciousness. It is completely 100% dialed in with massive awareness. We ultimately can see and observe the slightest ripple on the water (the surface of the mind, thought waves). That is the clue to look underneath, WITHIN. We become the submarine in the sub-conscious to ROOT OUT the ego elemental disturbance AT THE CAUSE. It's not at the surface, it is underneath those surface level emotions. Yes, the surface ripple was detected, the internal ALERT was triggered. As a result, all of our senses and input receptors are sent to their battle stations, alert and ready for their instructions, ready and willing to ENGAGE! Our RADAR is now on high alert, all systems GO, alert level jacked up to red or orange. This is an ever ready and UNWAVERING PRESENCE whereby we are consciously awaiting a lesson, ready to pounce on it to learn, and ACT NEW! It's like a virtual war game, however, when we ENGAGE it is not to KILL the enemy...it is to MAKE PEACE with it and LEARN! LOVE not WAR! Understand and transcend INTERNALLY!

This is a much more receptive and peaceful way to live life vs pushing against it all the time. Another way to look at this modality is that it is the alternative to the philosophy that the EGO must DIE, I must kill the ego. That strategy is always alternating between "offensive" and "defensive" mindsets, neither of which works. This equates to the pushing and pulling we feel and see if we are paying attention. Offense, defense, offense, defense...and neither gets the lessons due to this fight or flight mode and a lack of presence. That equates to unconsciousness. Offense mode gets over excited and jacked up to "KILL", to "GET", to "ATTAIN", "ACCOMPLISH", "WIN", so it overdoes it. It is too aggressive to see anything. Defense mode is the exact opposite, it doesn't go forward, it retreats, or just stands still with its guard up. Defense as a mindset or "mode" pulls back from the experiences in life all together so it "won't" take the next steps that are needed to learn. Once we are in defense mode, it can become tough to get going again, we go quiet, stall out, hide out. We will not engage, try, we are too afraid to fail, or anticipate pain. Resistance mode has turned into avoidance mode. Fight or flight...that's not receptive, is it? It's also not peaceful. It uses up a ton of energy starting, stopping, getting scolded, and retreating into our temporary shells again. Not only does it use up our precious energy, but it also puts a lot of STRESS on us mentally and physically. Up, down, and all around...but never present.

UNCONSCIOUSNESS BURNS FUEL!

Another problem with "The ego must die" strategy is that when we tell these unruly passengers (the ego "selves") to SHUTTTTT UP, or "go to war", which means resist, push against or fight with them. They can get angry, emotional, or whatever else, and often times that means that they fight back. We push, and they push back. It's like an internal tug of war, and then we see resentment, anger, frustrations, snide remarks, animosity, blame, etc. That means a lot of chatter, cross currents, negative "self" talk, pushing against everything, forcing things. When that doesn't work, the ego "pulls back" or goes into avoidance mode. These are both unproductive modalities, because the underlying problem WITHIN is not addressed or seen. It is resisted or avoided. Offense mode takes the aggressor attitude, and defense just goes quiet, retreats, or puts its head in the sand afraid to take action for fear of yet another mistake...and then getting bopped over the head again by the alter ego. That's where pain and suffering come in, we anticipate it, and it can be a vicious cycle. The main reason is that we are turning too soon, stopping too soon, going around things, avoiding, not confronting the "issues". The issues are the "selves", their modalities and attachments as well as TIME, and how they relate to it.

One of the key differences with these attitudes is that when we go into an offensive stance, in particular, it is basically the opposite of slowing things down so that we can see things more clearly. As emotions get involved, life's situations get more heated and then effectively speed up. As a result, in essence, we see LESS clearly, less detail because things move too fast for us to take it all in and on top of that, the "selves" have muted out our ability to process ALL of the information because we are seeing through a biased / weighted set of eyes. (partial data set) These "selves" can start showing out, acting out and they can really get BALIGERANT as they get more and more emotionally attached to their perspectives, wants & needs. Go to war mode = fight or flight. Remember too that when these "wants" get super important, they become DEMANDS, or heavily weighted NEEDS and then what the "selves" don't want comes into play more heavily because then we are inviting FEAR to the emotional party. Uh oh, we think: **what if I don't get what I want or NEED?!**" I might DIE or not get my way. The emotional extremes, and fear can create all kinds of mental & psychological havoc, and when it is heightened it results in an avalanche of emotion that can strike in a heartbeat and really disrupt the minds' ability to process information. In some cases, it can literally shut it down out of sheer terror...and we are frozen, useless or make hasty / bad decisions. The body even shows signs of this "stress" in many ways. Note how you feel after demanding situations and tough days vs the easy situations and easy days.

Fear has many names and depending on the severity, it can show up in the mind / body in many ways. Mild worry, angst, dread, distress, stress, panic, phobias, nervousness, anxiety, butterflies, sweat, jitters, stomach upsets, etc. etc. The ego has many faces, and they are like that mole in the mole game; they just keep popping up randomly and we have to keep bopping their heads over and over again trying to keep them down. That's called RESISTANCE, the approach is flawed...it doesn't work! It is also a recipe for "ignore" ance (IGNORANCE). When we ignore stuff and try to go around it, we become IGNORANT of the lesson that was supposed to provide understanding FOR US! But, we were busy, occupied, in fight or flight mode rather than being RECEPTIVE to it. We had our GUARD UP, and so we were basically "self" immunized from growth. YIKES! That's not good...It's like a growth inhibitor, but we did it to ourselves. The basic reason is because we see the result, not the cause, so it is never really seen for what it is at that deeper level. When we are unconscious or unaware, we see life as happening to us, not FOR US...yet. So, we RE-act to life rather than hearing, seeing, feeling and intuiting the lessons that are available. They slip right on by due to our unconsciousness. They go unnoticed, because we are ignorant or unaware, unawake, LOST IN THOUGHT! We don't dig underneath the surface emotions to address the actual PROBLEM. The "selves" are the problem. They can't SEE what needs to be seen because they are attached TO IT. We must DE-tach to SEE. With separation, presence, and oversight, it can all be seen presently, with consideration, empathy, LOVE and now understanding. We are gradually explaining to these "selves" that their shit doesn't work, NICELY. This opens their eyes to a new way of looking at things / LIFE. This is that more elevated perspective. It is balanced, peaceful, and RECEPTIVE. With this incredibly stable and acutely aware state, we can show them how to get out of their own way, a way THROUGH, not around the obstacles. This is an understand and overcome vs an overwhelm, avoid, resist or retreat scenario. Seeing with new eyes. Where formerly we saw roadblocks, and obstacles, now we show the solutions to our "selves". We get that the selves want what they want and that they can be a little selfish or even demanding some "times". They may even want to go to war over it, fight mode. With UNDERSTANDING and a newfound respect for this higher education they are "getting it" (The lessons) and are "delivered" as a result. That is what "IN-sight" does, it delivers us from our "selves" and their limitations as we look WITHIN from ABOVE! As a result, we arrive to the moment, we are delivered in and stay IN the moment, and we are also delivered what we need IN the moment.

As we detach and elevate from our normal perspectives and the internal turmoil, we are delivered, slooooowwwwly, over time, from these former / future "selves". As a result, they ALL either get off the bus or quietly and respectfully sit down in their seat and don't pop up much anymore, if at all...with the exception of a situation with a more powerful "trigger". The mind is a much quieter place! In addition, there is a "new sheriff in town", a super powerful one, and this higher "SELF" with the big star on their hat has really earned some respect with the selves as they are taught their lessons with a mind for playful education vs punishment. It's truly a new angle on things, showing where we can improve, but making it more of a game, FUN, with a sense of awe and amazement. Cheerfully optimistic. That's a different stance vs one that is approaching life with hesitancy because we are afraid of getting scolded or punished all the time. What a concept, acceptance of minor imperfections and learning lessons peacefully and productively vs getting thrown into "SOLITARY" or subjected to more pain and "suffering" of some kind. Cool. This has earned this new sheriff a new and much higher level "SELF" RESPECT! This new Sheriff is not a bully, and having been treated with empathy, compassion, and LOVE, it is turning some heads on the "inside". This is quite new, and as a result, the lower "selves" really do shut up and start listening, but not because the higher "SELF" demanded it, it is because they finally "see the light" and understand. They are really starting to get the full picture. Sometimes they get their lesson, and are appeased momentarily, and they sit back down only to pop back up again later. Other times, they truly do get it, 100% and then they just exit the bus. Hopefully they don't get on someone else's bus, LOL. What this truly means is that once a lower "self" and its associated pattern or behavior is seen consciously, acknowledged, and "dealt with", it is no longer SUB-conscious. It is in the light of day via awareness, and so it no longer blindsides us, or triggers us going forward!

The sheriff (higher "SELF") is here with awareness to help and the guidance it receives is actually HELPFUL. Not only that, but it was also delivered with compassion and LOVE. Kid gloves...NICE! We should listen more attentively, and we know it, so we do. This can be a real "AHA moment" at times when something is seen and understood so vividly. The effect is a further empowering of the higher SELF. So, when the more powerful triggers happen, the little lower selves are looking UP to the higher SELF awareness for solutions vs the many detours the ego selves would have previously exposed us to. That "SAVES US" from our "selves" and what would equate to lost time, frustration, mistakes, missed moments and missed opportunities. Avoidance and resistance are seen and processed, so we effectively avoid the avoiding, and resist the resisting. LOL. Actually, by being aware of it as it is starting to happen, it just doesn't happen, Higher "SELF" awareness doesn't allow it. What would be resistance and / or avoidance becomes acceptance, understanding, and progressively NEW ACTIONS...new CHOICES, which enables even more NEW CHOICES. It's progressive and builds on itself. Receiving, perceiving, and growing...becoming NEW, over and over again.

We end up with peace of mind, more time, and a better overall "UNDER-STANDING" is evolving that defaults to growth mode with the experiential KNOWING that follows. Ignorance and resistance don't work. As a result, we do our best to WAKE UP, become 100% conscious with PRESENCE and maintain that state so that we can get the lessons in the moment, NOW. We are seeing with new eyes and listening with new ears. Growth becomes constant, with awareness, because the higher SELF sees the whole data set, not just part. Since the WHOLE is now revealed, limits are seen and UN-limited, we have more opportunities to become whole, NEW and UN-limited. ALL is understood, processed and we BECOME available in the moment to take the appropriate and NEW ACTIONS accordingly with PRESENCE and guidance. One after the next, these ego elements are isolated, understood, and transcended. Class is dismissed and the freedom bell rings.

Just because one of these characters gets up out of their seat yelling and screaming, and / or consistently demands our attention by pulling our strings, that doesn't mean we have to "cave" to their demands. We do need to listen and understand though, as these bull-headed aggressive personalities show their ugly faces. The difference is an acknowledgement that we are not ignorantly and immediately dismissing them, or resisting their slanted views. We are not "internalizing" them, burying them, fighting against them, or pushing them down inside only to see them BOP right back up later either. We are taking that fraction of a second to listen, pausing ever so slightly for a millisecond to provide a HIGHER level of

"SELF" LOVE, guidance and understanding in each and every life situation that is provided for us. Each lower "self" is dealt with, understood, loved and LET GO with compassion and empathy (or whatever it takes). And then, with RADICAL PRESENCE, we make ALL NEW decisions, take all new ACTIONS when and where they are needed.

Unwavering presence in the moment = FREEDOM from the "selves" and all their shenanigans. The MIND is QUIET! It is at peace, balanced, and stable but also attentive and energized. In this state, the mind is FREE and available for optimal usage. FREEDOM is powerful and life changing as we see life's situational dynamics with precision and focus. Time seems to slow down as our processor is NOW 100% available to PROCESS. The moment seems to unfold in slower motion allowing us fractions of seconds longer to take in more data and then make more effective decisions (CHOICE). This makes choices seem more readily available to us. The moment expands...and as it does, WE EXPAND because our choices are augmented, and we are seeing them sooner in the thought wave progression. Growth mode means that more and more opportunities are seized...BECOMING NEW is NOW an option in each and every evolving moment. We are FREE to become and become and become...more and more as we UN-LIMIT the selves and become FREE! FREEDOM offers CHOICE!

You are <u>NOW</u> FREE to CHOOSE,
YOU have a CHOICE!
Maintain your seat, peacefully driving the bus.
(KEEP THE AISLE CLEAR with PRESENCE.)
UNWAVERING "SELF" control, with a full serving of FAITH!
CHOOSE WISELY, NOW!

The WISDOM to know the difference is very real and attainable. So, now that we know that conceptually, we need to arrive to the moment with faith, empathy, and consideration so that we can respond IN the moment with PRESENCE / LOVE...how do we do that consistently and <u>wisely</u> with all the little "selves" running around in our heads trying to distract us and go their own way. Life "stuff" always seems to be getting in the way...well of course it is, as you can see, we bring it with us...a BUSLOAD. That's the baggage, we need to lighten the load. LOL.

The short answer is as instructed above, it is done with a lot of energy, patience, empathy and persistence. It is a laborious process and can seem slow at times. Each time we learn a lesson, we release our former "selves" and let them go. Use the F-word, Forgiveness if needed and move on with the other F-word, FAITH! The key here is that we get the lesson FIRST, and then we gently and lovingly guide that former self that provided the lesson FOR US to the doorway. With appreciation for having received the lesson, we "give thanks" and let it off the bus. That means letting go AFTER THE LESSON, not before. Appreciating lessons is a whole new way of living vs getting angry, frustrated, or emotional in any way over mistakes and / or missed opportunities. As a result of this true and NEW guidance, we learn our lessons well, peacefully, with acceptance, right now, we do NOT postpone them. Kindness is the rule as we see these opportunities internally and externally. So, we BE KIND to our "selves" and others. These are real time growth opportunities that are constantly being provided and ampli-fied by life FOR US. They are further highlighted by the dramatic & "needy" emotional "selves" WITHIN. It's almost like they are raising their hands saying, "*Pick me...pick me*" and so we do, and we gladly and enthusiastically enjoy their "IN-sights" and then we happily let them off the bus. (Meaning: that level of self has been transcended). We are truly thankful for the lesson whether given to us internally or via life externally. By the way, that's learning a lesson with a SMILE and sometimes even a nice laugh vs the many other alternatives. This makes a BIG difference relative to our peace of mind. We see these lower selves as the teachers they are, "angel's" vs what might be perceived as "devils" when we get angry with our "selves". They really can be a form of angel, or guide / "deliverers" and we should appreciate the in-sight they provide with amazement and ongoing THANKFULNESS. This is true spirited and welcomed growth, with acceptance. Very impactful and life changing. Being receptive to life and its many lessons just changes the way we look at things, how they impact our lives, how we receive them, and most importantly, how we implement and use it towards our own personal "evolution". We can even laugh at our "selves" with loving compassion and make life FUN vs taking things so seriously all the time.

As we grow through each moment becoming NEW, learning our lessons as we go, and moving on, it develops into this constant state of "becoming". The delay fac-tor is minimized and quickened, so progress ramps up. Our stream / river flows faster. We are not losing time taking steps backwards, wasting time, emotionaliz-ing, complaining, internalizing, looking back and carrying that baggage forward dragging it through the moment. We are also not regretting, and by NO means are we SUFFERING because of mistakes or errors. Makes sense, right? These are all time wasters. Not only that but they are also eating up precious resources: ENERGY! Therefore, we don't allow the TIME thief access to the moment. (That's the ego.) As a result, we are not CHURNING energy. Frustration, anger, and the other less productive states are "stressful" to the body, and MIND... they are now seen as a complete waste of energy. So, they are more easily overridden in favor of more peaceful, productive & beneficial mindsets and attitudes. The internal change happens much faster. In fact, as we pay closer attention, this is seen earlier in the process and we know that we NEED this energy, so we just don't go there anymore. If we do, we get out of these states much more readily, sooner. KNOWING how much energy is available for use by NOT staying in these states is a motivating factor to NOT stay in them longer than it takes to see and understand what brought it on. As we see it show up inside of us, the internals that drive it are awoken, the gears start to grind a little bit, or we feel a twinge of emotion, or maybe a "different" bodily reaction to life. This alert system is highly tuned, and it clues us in with these internal signals to pay closer attention. As these "programs" are just about to be engaged within, we stop them in their tracks, awake and aware, educated and processed...we let them go and move on. Call it an internal "cleanse" or a lubrification of one's internal gears. The result is that the "bad program" never engaged, potential crisis averted, the mistakes never had an opportunity to happen.

For the purpose of EASE, the "LUBE" is called "peace of mind" which equates to presence and balance regained. AKA: FREEDOM! This elemental internal oil sinks into everything, every gear and internal component within. It moves through us and transforms everything we do, what we are, who and what we become as a result. What's interesting is that it becomes VALUED and PRO-TECTED. You might even say that it is sought after. What we are is our magnet, so the result of that lightning-fast internal lube job, is that the bad program never ran, so the bad result never happened. Peace of mind is maintained, and presence is NOT lost, which leaves the door open to NEWNESS. We literally closed one door, purposefully, and opened a new one. With awareness, we saw the whole progression. Even during adversity, presence is maintained by this overarching awareness that constantly provides lubrification and light where and when needed. You could also call it "midnight oil"[1] and it is used in the darkest corners of the mind to spread the light of awareness. Shining that light brightly on these internal gears that are binding and grinding lubricates them and gets them going again. All "FREED UP"! It is the light in the dark, that virtual wakeup call that oils the machine. Progress continues, growth grows forever expanding on itself in an exponential fashion, growth on growth.

I guess in movie land that would be the miss "take" never happened so take two was not required. We got it right the first time. Think about how much time we could save, and how much more we can get done by not having to go through take 3, 4, 5, 10, ...1001... etc. because we are awake and aware enough to do things "right" the first time!

How much energy might we save by saving our "selves" all that effort and frustration...not to mention how much more efficiently the machine runs when the gears are not grinding. Without oil, engines run pretty hot, they may even seize up. We are no different. We must mind our internal gears and watch what they are rubbing up against to see what is causing that heat. Awareness sees this and provides the lubrification needed, so that we don't get emotionally "HOT"! **"Cool the engines"**[2] It's **"More than a feeling"**[3]! These are a few fun Boston songs to use as reminders, so we don't get too fired up and / or sleep-walk through life. Use the midnight oil, turn the light of awareness on.

We know and completely understand that we can't stay in growth mode "becoming" if we are constantly deterred / sidetracked by the ego selves and their shenanigans out of "TIME" and in the "DARK". At the same time, we MUST get the lessons they provide, with awareness. So, there is a balance here and understanding it strategically is beneficial so that we can dial it in. An internal roadmap is enabled, and it acts as an ever-present GUIDE so we know immediately when we have gone off course and then we can gently & efficiently guide our highest and BEST SELF back into the game...IN THE ZONE, NOW. PRESENCE is re-established peacefully and efficiently. The primary necessity to do this consistently is ENERGY which fuels awareness & focus allowing us to stay PRESENT!! That's why preserving it is so essential

Awareness is our lifeblood. It helps us to maintain our PRESENCE. Having said that, we need to keep the machine fueled up and ever ready with the energy necessary to power it up to STAY AWAKE and AWARE!

I know that all sounds really easy when said in that way and it is, conceptually, but to really internalize this process and make it experiential requires a ton of energy, as detailed previously. It is surprisingly demanding and this is especially true in the beginning. It does get easier over time, with practice though, so keep at it. It can't hurt to have some additional instructions, like a cheat sheet or a model. So, where can we get some additional guidance from some insightful angles? I mean, even **Jesus** said:

"The spirit is willing, but the flesh is WEAK!"[4]

What did He mean by this? How do we get stronger "flesh"? Well, first...it's not so much the flesh, or the body at all for that matter, it is the mind / the processor and its ability to stay present long enough to receive the guidance needed in the moment. This is a processor efficiency issue which can be optimized with more of an internal roadmap, oversight, outlining & implementation exercises. We just need to change where we are processing FROM, and how we do it so that we can do it more efficiently and effectively. The mind actually needs some training in order to show it how / when to get out of its own way. It may even take some tough love, in some cases. So, let's hear some new inspiring words of wisdom and coaching from a new angle. Unless we have some new "AI" installed in the brain, we are going to have to work at it. The higher "SELF" with awareness IS the "AI". There is a caveat though, this new software needs to be installed and integrated. That requires our involvement and EFFORT. It must be powered up and enabled.

For further guidance, let's take a look at the Poem at the beginning of **Emerson**'s Essay on **Self Reliance**, with John **Fletchers**' help, it tells exactly what to do, in a different way.

This is really cool:

> **"Ne te quaesiveris extra.**
> **Man is his own star; and the soul that can**
> **Render an honest and a perfect man,**
> **Commands all light, all influence, all fate;**
> **Nothing to him falls early or too late.**
> **Our acts our angels are, or good or ill,**
> **Our fatal shadows that walk by us still."**
> *Epilogue to Beaumont and Fletcher's Honest Man's Fortune*
> **Cast the bantling on the rocks,**
> **Suckle him with the she-wolf's teat;**
> **Wintered with the hawk and fox,**
> **Power and speed be hands and feet."[5]**

Emerson Self-Reliance is downloadable here:

https://emersoncentral.com/ebook/Self-Reliance.pdf

See my comments line by line. Of course, this is my own interpretation/translation. I think this provides us excellent recommendations and a solid overall framework relative to teaching, learning, and methodologies geared towards a higher level of self-awareness and SELF-MASTERY! Assuming a progressive and persistent application, these are very powerful suggestions and techniques that CAN and should help take us up another notch leading into transcendence:

"Ne te quaesiveris extra."[6] (Latin; Stretch your arm no farther than your sleeve will reach. Translation: Do not look / seek outside yourself. Look WITH-IN!)

"Man is his own star; and the soul that can Render an honest and a perfect man,"[7] (Consider the "SOUL" the highest and best OVER-SEER version of "SELF" which is constantly in teaching mode, seeking out lessons FOR US to GUIDE US! This is what provides the opportunities FOR US to receive the IN-sights we need for growth. Once we are conscious enough to receive the lessons we are literally DELIVERED from our "selves". So, when the soul delivers the man and teaches it the "lessons" which cause it to BECOME perfect = live from SOUL or SPIRIT higher "SELF" vs. from the lower versions of the "selves". This NEW man is FREE & balanced, the empty cup..."delivered", open & ready to be GUIDED, "NOW", in the PRESENT MOMENT!! FREE TO CHOOSE! This is the quiet, lubricated, balanced, and peaceful mind scenario. Innocence, like the dove, or child at play, wide awake, unbiased, aware and present. Picture a joyful and open approach to life, willing and smiling, laughing even. We can see, hear, and even feel life flowing in this state of joy, at peace, unafraid and willingly trying life on moment by moment completely open to ALL the information that the moment is providing. All that we need is at our fingertips, 100% awake, aware, and PRESENT, life changes, because we change. We are in COMMAND, at PEACE, in a flow state. This is what it meant by rendering an honest and perfect man. We are balanced, FREE and capable of CHOOSING with dominion, and from a mighty powerful stance)

"Commands all light, all influence, all fate;"[8] (IN THIS STATE, "man" is open to, and can receive perfect instruction, and as a result he is the master of him "SELF" and his circumstances. Life is EASY, or at least it feels easy when life is flowing like this. Everything just kind of falls in place, quite naturally. That's one reason why they call it a flow state. All the information we need is at our fingertips AND because we are present in the moment, we have commanding CHOICE, NOW!)

"Nothing to him falls early or too late."[9] (With PRESENCE: "NOW" is always how with patience, peacefulness, calm understanding, balance, and impeccable timing. He is always in the "NOW", so how could it be early or late? Early=past, late=future. We are constantly in an optimized and maximized state of becoming, NOW. NOW is HOW. We don't succumb to the "TIME" thieves. Namely: the past and future ego "selves". We are FREE to CHOOSE, NOW!)

"Our acts our angels are, or good or ill,"[10] "Our acts" means our <u>RE</u>-actions as the lower "selves". They literally do speak louder than words...good or bad, they deliver our results and "IN-sights". They are our Angels because they teach us about our "selves" and what they did, as well as what they thought to get the results that they got. We can optimize LEARNING and GROWTH by paying closer attention to our results; seeing when, why and how we got them. This gives new meaning to failure because it is seen in a different light...as an OPPORTUNITY and a requirement so we can appreciate them which is a different LENS with which we look at life and the lesson itself. Failure is viewed and SEEN as a necessary "evil" so to speak because it is how we LEARN and GROW and let it go. So, if we are going to learn and grow, and NOT HOLD ONTO THE PAIN and suffer as a result of mistakes, then what is there to be afraid of? If there is NO FEAR, there is no resistance or avoidance. Consider the challenge ON with a heightened focus. That adds real time CLARITY. Life takes on new meaning. We see it differently, RECEIVE it differently. These results getters, the "selves" or former "Me's" are also the passengers on the bus, our angels TEACHING us. We see them with awareness, experientially w/ oversight and they are CONSTANTLY giving us what we need, lessons. The lessons they provide are very specifically FOR US with every last detail highlighted so that we can SEE, HEAR, and even FEEL them as well as intuit / learn the "why" of it all. To be clear, and relative to these ongoing lessons: the "why" question is not a "whoa is me" type question. It is a re-framed and targeted revelation seeking modus operandi within which we gain MEANING and IN-SIGHT. This is true SELF knowledge, a "HIGHER" education that is immediately useful and so it is implemented in our lives.

With massive awareness, we see what these "selves" ARE within us, their internals, and then we observe what they "deliver" FOR US in the moment, as well as why, so we have an opportunity to be delivered from them in fractions of seconds. We also see in hindsight sometimes that we were NOT delivered, so we can "SELF correct". This is how and why we GROW and are more ready for the next moment. We got educated for the next "time" slot. Angels teach with kindness, empathy & LOVE! Our reactions are our angels as long as we use them wisely and TEACH with self-love. Lessons are accepted more readily, and they are more easily "digested" and implemented when delivered with kid gloves. That means a heavy does of CARE and LOVE! Self-love is an amazing and empowering tool, ANGELIC!

RE-actions = ANGELS!

"Our fatal shadows that walk by us still."[11] (We see via these lessons the "selves" that are still lurking around WITHIN. They are still on the bus. Now that the bus is a little more empty (quiet mind), we can see and hear these jokers a little more readily and clearly. It is like when someone enunciates something very deliberately, it is a little more prominent, observable, hearable and understandable as a result. We know that we can't skip the lessons, else the ego selves stay on the bus, and keep pulling our strings which brings us to the same lessons repeatedly. That is the meaning of "walk by us still". They are teaching us about our "selves" because they are the selves, which points out our own issues that are problematic. LOL. Seriously, we have to understand the shadows that still lurk WITHIN us, so we pay closer attention. These are often referred to as shadow "selves", and they operate in the shadows of the unconscious mind, so we work on our consciousness, trying to observe the "bleepers". These shadow selves are unseen and unheard and can run around in the dark corners of the mind unbeknownst to us until we wake up and shine the light of awareness on them. This is when and where we need that midnight oil...to break the gears loose that are stuck or grinding and holding us back. They are LIMITING our higher life that could be happening with oversight, IN-sight and a little more LIGHT! (The light of awareness) We need to shine it on the shadows which means "darkness", these are our lower EGO personalities we are either unconscious of, or we ignore / resist. If we are unconscious to them, well...we need to GET conscious, WAKE UP! We need to learn the lessons they bring us, and they constantly put in front of us until we get it. Angels guide, right? We need to LISTEN to the guidance and lighten up. If our "acts" are our angels, then the guidance is coming from our own re-ACTIONS as the lower "selves" and the things they bring to us as experiences. They are <u>FOR US</u> and with awareness we see it that way. Then the net of that is that as the higher "SELF", with this heightened awareness, we are teaching our lower "selves" the lessons as we receive the guidance in the moment, or arguably just before the moment in milliseconds when we are super tuned in and completely in the ZONE. As we grow, the speed of learning grows and as such, the speed of SELF-LOVE must also grow. We get faster at learning, or the angels (our re-actions) get faster at educating us. Timing is HUGE, milliseconds matter when it comes to getting the lessons and then having the presence of mind, resolve, and intestinal fortitude to make BOLD, stand up, impactful and some-times courageous new choices / decisions. We don't get hung up in self-blame, self-torture and other self-defeating behaviors. We are now FREE! As a result, rapidly escalating good decisions can create major turning points very quickly and the pace blazes forward in rapid succession, step by step, faster and faster. Timing is not "off" anymore, it's ONNNN! This is why lessons can build on each other so quickly. It equates to a fine education, progress, and evolution at the **"Speed of LOVE"**[12]...**"FASTER"**[13])

Epilogue to Beaumont and Fletcher's Honest Man's Fortune

"Cast the bantling on the rocks,"[14] (When we are ignorant, arrogant, avoiding, resisting, dismissing or just plain missing lessons in one way or another, we may need to be "scolded", but not in the traditional way of thinking, like as in punishment. It is really just a way of saying that that we need to be shaken up a little bit to AWAKEN, become conscious, alert, and aware...get back to NOW and presence. Because we are obviously not paying attention and missing things, a jolt, or a snap of the fingers is necessary to wake us up out of our temporary slumber. Once we re-optimize our state, come back to "NOW" in the land of REALITY, mindset wise, we can get the lessons we are missing and be more "disciplined" with our mindset going forward. Sometimes we bog down because we are plateauing or digesting gains. Other times we are just not getting it (the lessons). We are sometimes blind to our "selves" and don't see where, when, or how we need to "self" correct. Presence and awareness are being lost for some reason, our attention to detail, focus and perception has wavered. So, the recommendation is that we throw the young child (lower "selves') to some tough love on the rocks so that we become more receptive again. The student had been missing lessons, skipping class. These are the passengers on the bus (the lower "selves" in the mind) that need our empathy, love, consideration, guidance and understanding. Sometimes this will require a more serious intervention. We must be harsh with our "selves". Tough love stings a little bit, and it might hurt to cast the "self" on the rocks like that. Giving it an education. Being honest with oneself. That means a wakeup call sometimes. If sugar, hand holding, and / or empathy / love is not working, then maybe a harsher intervention will do it? Sometimes we need more of a red flag type alert to be "SELF" disciplined w/ some tough love in order to snap our "selves" out of a poor state and wake the heck up.

As the higher SELF, we need to know what works for us individually and use these internal tools to TEACH with whatever methodologies work. Sometimes that may be more of a drill sergeant type of command, demanding attention so that these lower versions of self can learn the lessons they need to learn. Growth requires incremental stepping-stones at times and this helps us to manage our state of mind as well. Remaining receptive and open to the guidance in the moment is KEY. Because we know the methodologies that work for us personally, we can teach with skill, motivationally with persistence without offending our "selves" or putting us into poor, less receptive / less productive states. That puts us into stall patterns or the penalty box where we lose more time, or worse, we make untimely poor decisions and go backwards. Bottom line, some "times" we need to see what we don't want to see. We need to be alert and aware. So, take a cold shower, do something active to get some blood flowing again. Maybe run around the block, do 50 push-ups, ride the bike for a bit, shake your own shoulders. Jump up and down, do some jumping jacks, pushups, run in place, get on the treadmill for a few minutes. Do something to grab some energy. Alternatively, drink a tall glass of ice water, take a big deep breath, or do some rapid breathing to send some extra Oxygen to the brain. One way or another, send your "self" an alert of some kind. Whatever it takes for you to WAKE-UP and regain your focus and PRESENCE.)

"Suckle him with the she-wolf's teat;"[15] (Have you ever heard a mother wolf growl at her young pups when she is wanting their attention, or they are misbehaving? It is a deep rumble of a growl that shakes your chest and turns your head. I have heard this up close and personal, thankfully from a safe place. It is quite intimidating. So, that is the attention grabber that was used to grab the young child's attention in the previous step. The "kid" is NOW awake, aware, present and receptive again with their eyes and ears wide open. This is a state of mind where we are ready to be taught and can actually LEARN in a highly alert state. That is when the mother wolf comes in to coddle, train, and prepare her children for LIFE. Wolves represent: Teaching skill, perseverance, endurance, strength, loyalty, success, thought, intelligence, pathfinders, intuition, learning. Wolves take every care to educate their young and are devoted. Who better teach? Mothers teach with empathy and compassion, LOVE. What is more representative of love in this earthly realm than a mother's love? Love truly is the answer, and the best way to learn. We must give it to our "selves". Then, the selves must be receptive to the advice. They must LISTEN to and HEED the guidance; it is available NOW. Are you going to refuse or deny mother wolf? NOT ME, ha-ha. We are teaching our "selves", every moment of every day, with an overarching awareness, presence and AUTHORITY! Just do it with LOVE, the ultimate guide. Add a little patience too because children don't always get the lesson the first time it is shown to them. They are distracted by all manner of things, so it may need to be taught in different ways, at different "times" in various contexts as well. That's why Mothers are so forgiving. They LOVE with all their heart and truly understand. Their lessons are given with tenderness, patience, care, empathy, kindness, and because the lessons are given with this ultra-soft delivery if / when needed, the child remains receptive and open to the guidance. That's us, the highest "SELF", teaching the lower "selves"!)

"Wintered with the hawk and fox,"[16] (Hawk=Nobility, clarity, awareness, observer, the soul, truth, foresight, discrimination. Fox = Cleverness, protection, intelligence, diplomacy, feminine magic, adaptability, discretion, integration and playfulness. This is combining AWARENESS as the observer and exceptional VISION, clever LOGIC to the Heart and LOVE, the soul side of the equation and integrating them all for a complete person. The FOX is cunning, cerebral, and fast, we need that mental agility to out fox... the fox, the EGO. First, with the eyesight of the HAWK, we SEE IT, then with the mental agility of the FOX, we BEAT IT TO THE MOMENT, mental training at its best. "SELF" vs "self", higher vs lower. The wolf, hawk & fox are teaching us new life skills. We must practice these skills to get better at it, <u>FASTER</u> with agility and the abilities we need to be more nimble and efficient at it.)

"Power and speed be hands and feet."[17] (We NEED to be charged up with energy to be our highest and best SELF. Our source power MUST be available and ready for distribution. We must use it to be nimble and decisive mentally, and this training must translate to empowered ACTIONS moment by moment, FAST! Strength & GOD SPEED, we need the SPEED of unconditional LOVE in order to get us there. Conditions DELAY, and there is not enough "TIME" for that when decisions are needed NOW! That's why we must arrive and STAY in the moment to ACT, NOW vs experiencing that momentary delay because we have to get back to the moment! PRESENCE means SPEED! We must be fast, focused and decisive with the power of CHOICE! Everything happens NOW, or it doesn't happen at all, it is as simple as that. Once we are prepared, awake, aware, and 100% focused in the moment with presence, we must be willing and able to ACT! We are the proverbial tiger waiting to pounce when the moment is right. That's the AHA moment, we either get the "prey" and we "WIN" a victory, accomplish something, or we get a lesson. That means that with this overarching awareness, from the overseer perspective, the higher "I" caught the lower "me" red handed. LOL When we miss opportunities, or make mistakes, that is when we get these lessons. With power & speed though, we get them IMMEDIATELY...that's fast. With power, speed, and agility, we can learn very quickly. As an example, we can catch the ego in its wanting "state" and it is GAME OVER, for that ego self. It is seen by the hawk & fox internally, educated by the She wolf teacher within, processed with power and speed by the higher "SELF", and LET GO instantly. That's super-FAST!! The "Speed of LOVE"[18]. This lightning-fast progression is a description and recipe for FAITHOMIZING the "selves", one at a time, with LOVE! Look within, there are endless opportunities).

FAITHOMIZE THE "selves"!

GOOD STUFF, RIGHT? Understanding is powerful, and we MUST do it. We must enable this state of becoming and with this newfound freedom, we must TAKE ACTION, faithfully. UN-attached, and UN-limited, the possibilities...

Readiness is no longer a question!

I want to reference **John Fletcher's "An Honest Man's Fortune"**[19] because to me this is a very powerful statement, and for some reason it was left out in some cases, or not acknowledged. Check this out:

> **"Doth not experience teach us all we can**
> **To work ourselves into a glorious man**
> **Love's but an exhalation to best eyes**
> **The matters spent and then the fools fire dyes**
> **Were I LOVE, and could that bright star bring**
> **Increase to wealth, honor, and every thing."**

In simpler terms, what this is saying is that internally, with observation / awareness, we can see and acknowledge that "If I was / am LOVE", then the lesson is learned, and I can become it. With presence, if we SEE love (as the choice) IN THE MOMENT (via our guidance.), we can become it...and breathe it out in our experience, our RESULTS. And furthermore, WHEN WE SEE IT, **"That matters SPENT"**[20] and that old foolish "self" that was not love, that little "self" that I was in previous moments is GONE, SPENT, no longer ME. The inspiration and fire that was formerly me just died as I GREW out of it, with UNDERSTANDING, and "I" LET IT GO. The lower ego "self" was guided, in the moment, it got "taught its lesson", it learned, and we let it off the bus. Since it no longer serves me... I have RISEN UP and BECOME NEW. It no longer "walks by us", as Emerson stated. That FOOL is no longer in the shadows and can no longer affect me, "trigger me", and as a result, it can no longer LIMIT this new ME. I am wise to it, and as it is seen, I am UN-limiting the self that I was a moment ago. Each moment of becoming, I am NEW, born again out of what I was...I AM NEW...I AM...I AM...new and new and new...dying to my former selves and growing out of them over and over and over and over again, faster and faster and faster and faster. You GET IT?!?! This is a constant state of becoming and actions speak louder than words. When we see anything less than this as we look within, as we experience life, we can see it immediately. As seen, we step into the moment and self-correct as needed. Growth on growth, forever expanding. We are constantly showing up to life as our HIGHEST and BEST "SELF" to date.

Are YOU PUMPED? Excited to get this going?

OK, BREEEEAAAATHE!!! I know, it's FUN! So exciting! SIT DOWN, SHUT UP! LOL :)

I am joking of course. (referring to the bus driver's example) This is just a quick & hopefully funny reminder that we can also be blinded by excitement. The future can be really enticing, and those grandiose images and scenes the future "selves" paint can certainly start us off and running too quickly. This is where we can unfortunately get a little too far ahead of ourselves (the mind is in the future time-slot), which is enough for us to get blindsided because we are not present, AGAIN! LOL

BE CONSCIOUS, AWAKE, AWARE... PRESENT, NOW...not later! HAVE FAITH!

As much as we can generate the energy for it, and at every possible opportunity, with as much empathy, consideration, and all the LOVE we can muster up within, we need to let go and let LOVE answer. LOVE IS FAST! Let it be the Instrument of change WITHIN! Once we master this "habit" with the lower "selves" then our nature is to reflect that "SELF-LOVE" out into the world as well. So, basically that means when we don't, we either see it, hear it, or feel it because we are out of "alignment". When situations present themselves and something less than that responds to life, we SEE IT and KNOW! We get the lesson the lower "selves" needed to learn and CHANGE our MIND! Knowing that as the higher "SELF", we could have done better, we immediately do some retrospectives super quickly to understand what, or whom it was that took us over so that the next time, it can't do that. We must be wise to it. In this way, we are increasingly more ready to BE THE INSTRUMENT by becoming what is needed in the next moment. Better and better, "Faster"[21] and faster and faster...with LOVE & WISDOM.

Looking at this broken down, it is being an instrument of constant change, WITHIN. Sometimes that is a tough pill to swallow, particularly if we are somewhat comfortable. Yet, life demands growth. Complacency is not a recipe for expansion and who wants to stand still anyway. So, in this state of becoming we are constantly GROWING. That means making mistakes, understanding, letting go, and trying again. We learn a lot of lessons, assuming we are paying attention. Let go and let GOD is essentially the same philosophy, assuming GOD = Unconditional LOVE! That means an unconditional acceptance of our own mistakes as we grow into better and better versions of SELF.

Forever expanding, **GROWING and becoming NEW**! I wrote this out for myself as follows to remind me of what that looks like in my mind:

GROWING:

G aining

R equired

O perational

W isdom

I nternally

N ow, with

G OD, as my guide!

****Letting love answer is an actual skill, and it requires training. The good news is that LOVE IS FAST once it is fully implemented.

If GOD is unconditional love, and I am using that as a model to the best of my ability, then I am doing the best I can to show up each and every moment inspired and ready to BE THAT in the world. As humans, that's not always what happens is it? The cool thing is that with this philosophy of growing and BECOMING, we see when we are NOT LOVE. We see when we did not accomplish that and we respond to life in less-than-optimal ways as our lower "self" vs higher "SELF". In storm land, it is after the lightning strikes that we see the damage it caused. That can be true in our lives as well. So, after seeing some of these moments after the fact, we start to see it sooner in the progression or thought wave. In similar situations, we start to see it AS IT HAPPENS, but we are still too slow to catch the wave. We are technically getting really close, but we are still on the back side of the thought wave. Eventually we see it AS the lightning strikes, which essentially shines the light on it in ultra bright fashion. Once thoughts and patterns of thoughts are seen in this way, that FLASH of IN-sight is truly used, internalized and it becomes experiential at that point. This is the moment when the lesson has been learned and the unconscious becomes CON-SCIOUS! We were aware enough to see it and out of this growth mode our highest and best version of SELF emerges and we become NEW. Once it is experiential like this, the very next time that this situation pops up in our life we can see the thought waves as they are building but BEFORE they clash, and BEFORE the storm. This is how an internal storm can just dissipate and never even happen. It's like the wave just disappears, vanishes into thin air. POOF! It is the peace of ALL UNDERSTANDING! There is some satisfaction in this too: Calm, serene, imperturbable PEACEFULNESS as an essence. Imagine responding to life from this state with a smile on your face that is virtually immovable. That is a reliable foundation, mindset wise, and it's ROCK SOLID! That means presence, wide awake, aware and completely 100% dialed in. Receptive, balanced, and READY with unwavering faith to TRUST the guidance, and BE what is needed in the moment. Growing means ever readying this higher "SELF" to maintain this foundational steadfast-ness. Being immovable or unshakable mentally requires practice, confidence, FAITH and TRUST. This is how that is achieved, moment by moment by moment with freedom and presence. Faster and Faster we become love which is the instrument of change for our "selves" WITHIN, and each time we get better at it. It builds on itself each time we flex and use this muscle as we show up to represent as our highest "SELF" with presence. This is a process though, and please take a moment to really understand this progression.

First, we see things after they happen, we fail, and then we get the lesson. Then we see things as they happen, we fail and then we learn the lesson faster. Then, finally we are fast enough to get the lesson before something happens because we literally saw it coming. Once the lesson is received and internalized, it isn't needed anymore from that point on. That equates to the "WISDOM TO KNOW THE DIFFERENCE!" Reinhold Niebuhr "The serenity Prayer". This requires presence in order to represent as our highest and best SELF, in the moment of NOW completely 100% available, balanced, ready & receptive to what the moment needs. That is when we can:

Re-**PRESENT!** Not to sound cocky or arrogant, but we are the GIFT we give to the world. We must BE PRESENT and available mentally (FREE) to deliver the best PRESENT that is possible in the moment. Each moment is a new opportunity, so when we present a bad present (the lower "self"), we can grab a lesson and give a new one, a higher and better "SELF", in the next moment. We can get better. The gift that keeps on giving doesn't need to be a bad one when we mess up...we just learn and grow and let it go. NEXT! That's what it takes, be NEW! NO REGRETS, just do the best we can. Each time it's a little better.

Admitting failure doesn't make us small, it allows us to get the lessons and be bigger. That means for others as well as for our "selves".

We can't do this if we are not present, NOW. We need to wake up and SHOW UP with massive awareness and focus, energetically... and consciousness is required. We can learn to do this in ALL situations with unwavering presence. NOW! That is how we can LIVE this prayer:

"God, grant me the serenity to accept the things I cannot change; Courage to change the things I can; And wisdom to know the difference"[22]

In order for this to become a reality in our lives, we must be listening and watching with the ears that can hear, and the eyes that can see. Presence with this overarching awareness and a focused state of RECEPTIVITY is what opens us up to the guidance that is available in the moment. With extraordinary perception, the eyes, ears, and feelings / heart, are totally dialed in and responsive at the SPEED OF LOVE! That is LIGHT SPEED, because we are using the light of awareness and PRESENT already to provide the answer by becoming it. I like to say that it is always the right time to do the right thing. In life, we are presented with many opportunities to give our highest and best "SELF", one that is optimized, maximized and READY, in that moment. That means a STATE of mind and body that is 100% prepared for this moment, NOW, to be what is needed both INTERNALLY and EXTERNALLY. We can only represent in that fashion when we meet the moment with presence in the right state of mind & body. Our state is dependent on us, our perception of reality, who we bring into the moment as our best SELF, as well as the beliefs we hold true deep in our hearts. Faith is generated from deep within this CORE. We build this foundation with strength, patience, energy, persistence, commitment and tools in order to be able and balanced, with a peaceful heart as we enter each moment with FREEDOM TO ACT. God willing, hopefully one of those tools is LOVE. Love is a powerful tool, probably the MOST powerful one and extremely FAST. Now we have the mental stamina, presence and the skills needed to use them consistently and productively. This energizes, optimizes and maximizes the mind and body to SHOW UP and LIVE UP to our BEST LIFE, as our BEST SELF!

BE THAT—FAITH enables this capacity WITHIN. It means to truly re-**PRESENT**! After all a present is a gift, right? Faith presents us to the moment with FREEDOM to become LOVE.

Love is a GIFT...GIVE IT!
You are the GIFT, share it!
Share your highest and best "SELF"!

It's actually a pretty simple formula for success. It goes like this:

Be LOVE, Give LOVE, GET LOVE!

By following the guidance, we are delivered, IN THE MOMENT and we can give our best "SELF". In essence, we are delivered to and from our "selves" from this higher SELF perspective. As we see it happen, we make it happen. Share YOU, in all your glory...the highest and best version of you is AMAZING! Go BE IT and have some FUN with it too!

Every now and then the universe likes to TEST US. Did you notice? We are given a kind of gut check to assess our intestinal fortitude, so to speak. These are the times when we really need to STEP UP and into our highest and best SELF. Energize and optimize so we can MAXIMIZE! This is an opportunity to further our growth experientially and KNOW ourselves even better. Maybe this is to perform under pressure, there is a little more at stake, or the environment is not ideal...passing the test is a moment of glory, and should be cherished and celebrated. These internal victories are STAND UP and CHEER moments that we can truly feel good and internalize some true satisfaction and acknowledge our "SELVES" for the progress / growth. It is all right to express some quality LOVE for our SELF for these triumphs. Even if they are small successes, they build on the last one and grow into massive accomplishments over time. REWARDS are motivational and these are good opportunities to treasure, maybe even give your "SELF" a pat on the back for a job well done, and some kind of award / reward. This encourages further growth on the path. There are many challenges, so please do take a moment here and there to breathe it all in. Appreciate the JOURNEY, the milestones, and the victories periodically.

It feels as if these internal accomplishments should be recognized in a more substantial way, and they really SHOULD! However, individually they are not necessarily singled out and seen / celebrated with the exception of our own internal acknowledgement of a powerful and very personal understanding. The silent satisfaction in these moments is AMAZING. What we must realize is that every day forward from here on out, "I" bring the world a better ME. That should be an internal celebration and fully acknowledged. We should feel good KNOWING that in every moment we are doing our absolute BEST! So don't forget to pat your "SELF" on the back from time to time.

Quick tidbit: The outside world is NOT always going to recognize these internal victories...but YOU KNOW! Let that be enough. YOU ARE ENOUGH! These are huge milestones, major steps forward, and each step builds on the next. Keep on steppin up. A silent conquest of oneself builds up our foundational CORE! That gives us the strength we need to step up again. It provides the intestinal fortitude that is necessary to GO FOR IT, and MAKE IT HAPPEN. This is an absolute requirement to STEP UP IN LIFE! So, go ahead and put that arrow back in your quiver. You may very well need it in the next moment.

When life smacks you in the face and says, "*You are not enough*" or just a moment ago it says, "You were not enough", NOW you have an extra arrow and the tools / skill to answer that call. Step into and up to the challenge. The answer is: I may not have been then, but I AM NOW. That's steppin up. That could be relative to a failure a moment ago, ten years ago, or as a child... "I AM" is a powerful statement. Take another BOLD shot with better aim, better tools, and a better mindset.

Whatever the challenge is, keep your F-word tools at your disposal. Forgiveness & Faith MATTER because they provide us with FREEDOM, peace of mind, clarity, focus and the unwavering SELF control called PRESENCE. With this masterful skill we have UN-limited the "selves" and we have become UNLIMITED! Some "tests" are more difficult than others, and if we are low on energy, or we get caught off guard, so to speak, we still make mistakes. We are human, and we still mess up from "TIME" to "TIME" if you get my drift. If we get caught up in the "TIME-LOCK" we are NOT FREE! Don't get caught up in time...grow NOW instead. Growth requires failure, so that we can get more lessons. Mistakes are OK, expected even. Maybe not wanted, but since we are human, they are expected to some degree. Just take a moment, shake it off, get balanced and ready, absorb / understand & get the lesson. Then, rebalanced and re-optimized, 100% present, take another step forward. NO REGRETS and NO baggage. If apologies are in order, then by all means hand them out genuinely, whole heartedly. Use that internally and externally to whomever, or whatever, and whenever needed, don't wait. Sincerely, forgive & have faith, say "NEXT", all the better for the lesson, NOW! That applies externally as well as internally.

This process frees us up to ACT, in the moment faster and faster, better and better. Freedom allows a higher degree of focus, and less mistakes too because there are no distractions. We are mentally & physically faster, more nimble and ready to TAKE ACTION as our highest and best SELF.

Forgiveness frees us from the past "selves", and faith frees us from the future "selves". That means FREEDOM from an endless array of thoughts and attachments these "selves" would be "projecting" on the mind screens. These are released and let go in favor of presence and guidance in the moment when we can TAKE ACTION, at the SPEED OF LOVE!

They both work essentially the same way in that they are a protective mechanism WITHIN! The present moment is where it all happens, the zone, so we must BE THERE (NOW!). Faith matters because not only does it provide good reason for eternal optimism as a general attitude, but it frees us up and allows us to maintain our PRESENCE untethered to the futures we like to imagine or are fearful of. Faith is the tool that protects us from the future "selves" and all their illusory distractions allowing us 100% availability NOW to go make that preferred future happen. The difference is that NOW the "outcomes" we might have been attached to are no longer weighing on us as that is LET GO in favor of FAITH that it will work out exactly as needed. FAITH allows presence. Presence is basically unchained, or disconnected in a good way, untethered from the "OUTCOMES" we picture in our mind...good and bad. So, PRESENCE stands high above FEAR and DESIRE. THE PRESENCE IS FREE! Presence allows us the freedom to take action with 100% focus and availability to use all of our internals efficiently, completely optimized and maximized.

Faith provides and protects presence.

PRESENCE = FREEDOM

Have FAITH, and remember that FAITH IS A SKILL!

FAITH:

Forever free

Acting

Increasing

Thresholds of MIND, with TRUST. PRESENCE &

Happiness, IN THE MOMENT!

Another way to look at this is that faith builds on itself within itself as follows:

Free

Action

"I"

Take

Having FAITH!

FAITH IS FREE!

Without all that projecting and remembering, presence is a whole lot more peaceful as a BONUS too. The whole thing is quite incredible. It looks something like this as a progression, relative to TIME. The idea is to STAY PRESENT, NOW using all the tools provided here in. This is a summary of sorts:

TIME: The PAST.........GATE.........PRESENT.........GATE.........the FUTURE

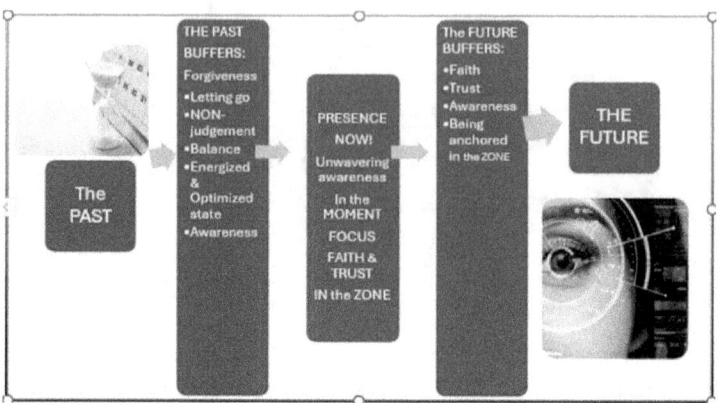

As a "TIME" progression, presence is sandwiched between two virtual gates, one behind and one in front of us. This is conceptual, mentally speaking, relative to the evolution of time. Forgiveness and Faith deliver and protect that PRESENCE / FREEDOM in the moment. This gives us access via awareness in a state of receptivity to the context & content of the moment, IN the moment as it happens. Forgiveness DELIVERS us to the moment and Faith helps us to STAY IN THE MOMENT! It keeps us FREE, focused & balanced with MASSIVE TRUST to take action, in the ZONE...NOW! That's the way I see it, I sincerely hope it helps. Let me know about your successes.

****** For more on this and other related topics, please see the book called "Be The Instrument". By Doug Giesler. Watch out for the next book in the series too. There are more F-words to consider. The first was forgiveness, then this one on faith, and the next is:

"The **F**-word, No not that one...FEAR and why it matters!"

This one will be a deeper dive into the mental dynamics and physical barriers related to the conquest of fear and it will get into detail. All of the various challenges and hurdles that arrive on our doorstep, and seemingly get slammed IN OUR FACE will be addressed and caressed. The fact is, the barrage only speeds up and becomes more confrontational, so we need a way through, not AROUND it. Methodologies and modalities for overcoming the various mind obstacles that involve fear, worry, and future negative oriented mindsets that tend to get in our way will be provided. TRUST experience, and believe me, I have the battle scars to prove it. Thinking back, and looking back through 25 years or so of journaling so that it serves you too.

BEST TO YOU and YOURS!

Regards,

Doug Giesler

https://www.betheinstrument.com/
https://www.whatthefwords.com/
https://www.unlimityourlimit.com/

Be The Instrument is on Facebook:
https://www.facebook.com/BeTheInstrument

Be The Instrument is on YouTube:
https://www.youtube.com/@DougGiesler-BeTheInstrument

If you have an F-word you would like to see a future book about, please let me know. I am considering the next one and want to help. How about Failure or Fortitude, maybe a more in depth analysis of FEELINGS / emotions? Let me know your thoughts.

"We'd Love To Hear From You!"

Joelle and I know how much the information in this book has impacted our life and it would be a pleasure to hear about how it has positively impacted yours as well. Please take a few moments and write down YOUR story below. Then you have your choice in how you want to get it to us.

1. Go to this web link **TheFWordFaith.com/yourstory** and sumbit the story for consideration to be published in the next printing of this book or to be featured on our websites.

2. Scan or take a screenshot and upload it to our Facebook Community Page.
        Facebook.com/groups/WhatTheFWords
        *Make sure you tag me so I get notified.

3. Tear out these 2 pages and send it to me by snail mail:
Office Address:
C/O Doug Giesler
316 Koons Street
Leesville, SC, 29070

_____

_____

_____

_____

_____

ALSO BY
Doug Giesler

BOOKS

- **Author:** Be The Instrument

- **Author:** The F-WORD, NO not that one... Forgiveness, why it matters

- **Co-Author:** "*Cracking the Rich Code*" Vol 16. by Jim Britt. Endorsed by Tony Robbins. See Chapter entitled "Unlimit your limit", by Doug Giesler

- **Co-Author:** "*The Art of Connection*" Vol 5. by Robert Jones, Doug wrote 2 pages for the year 2025. One is geared towards Self-Actualization, the other is about Unlimiting mind "sets"!

BE THE INSTRUMENT

HOW YOU CAN MASTER THE ART OF FLOW FOR PERSONAL & PROFESSIONAL SUCCESS!

DOUG GIESLER

SHATTER CEILINGS, NOT DREAMS
& EXPLORE THE HORIZONS!

UNlimitYourLimit.com

Accomplish goals, find your flow, make a meaningful impact, all while cultivating a profound sense of peace and tranquility.

Achieve peak performance, attuned, aligned, and spiritually connected.

Discover an array of techniques, mindsets, and practical life skills designed to evoke an astounding sense of well-being, comprehend the requirements for reaching that state, and effectively maintain it.

Imagine being FREE! Free from FEAR,, overwhelming emotions, and free from limited / disturbing mindsets! This toolbox presents an opportunity for growth and a new sense of freedom in every moment. Produce an UN-LIMITED state of mind, massive self-awareness and astounding situational awareness on command.

Wisdom, expertly explained, step by step, how to mindfully get in the zone for optimal performance. Secure understanding and balance with EASE! Confidently attain success with extraordinary peace of mind!

Doug Giesler is a transformative coach and thought leader dedicated to helping individuals achieve optimal performance and inner peace. In "Be The Instrument," he shares practical strategies for overcoming limiting beliefs and unlocking true potential. Drawing from his experiences of generating top performance while uplifting others, Doug equips readers with actionable insights to foster success without sacrificing tranquility in today's fast-paced world.

Through proven mind hacks and spiritual practices, Doug invites readers to explore beliefs and cultivate self-awareness. With a positive outlook, he embodies a transformative philosophy that inspires change. "Be The Instrument" guides readers to become catalysts for personal and collective growth.

BE THE INSTRUMENT

BE THE INSTRUMENT

Power is available for use...this book is designed to show just how that can be captured and maximized without overloading your circuits!

Peel back the layers of the unconscious mind and expose the many faces of the ego that tend to limit us, blind us. Neutralize them and empower the higher "SELF".

See opportunities where time stands in our way, gaining access to the moment; enhance that elevated perspective, neutralizing our "demons" and overcoming our limitations.

...with the innocence of a child (Dove) and a balanced perspective, we can step into the moment, empowered and connected with higher vision.

On the cutting edge of NOW, consciously create in the MOMENT!

Learn more:

https://www.betheinstrument.com/

Follow Doug on Amazon for updates and new releases!

a

amazon.com/author/douggiesler

in

linkedin.com/in/doug-giesler/

Praise for
'Be The Instrument'

"*Doug Giesler's Be the Instrument stands on its own as a book designed to help the reader "convert fear to faith". It's a journey written about by countless authors, in a myriad of ways. This book manages to help the reader travel side by side with Doug, intimately connected with him as he insightfully explores the mental processes awakened in a reader dedicated to self exploration and growth. The format is powerful. One can have a conversation with him by reading simply a paragraph, a page, or a chapter. On these merits, I would highly recommend this book!*"

Patricia G. Simmons, M.D.
Board Certified in Psychiatry & Neurology

"*A thought provoking and motivational work. 'Be The Instrument' breaks down in easily digestible steps how to get you out of your own way and achieve the goals you set for yourself. The everyday practical knowledge and real life stories of the author helps shift the mindset towards action right now! It's an exceptional motivational work!*"

Jaie Hart
Author: *Changing Perspectives, So It's Over, Now What?, Understanding Forgiveness,* and *Expanding Horizons.*

"I've just finished my first reading of 'Be the Instrument' by Doug Giesler, and let me tell you, it's been a wild ride of self-discovery! I've been an avid nerd/geek/zealot for Personal Development, Self Help, Enhanced Human Potential, and Spiritual Growth content for the last 42 years and this was refreshing. This book isn't your typical self-help fluff—it's a heartfelt journey that'll make you laugh, cry, and probably do a happy dance or two.

Doug's writing style? It's like having a chat with your wisest friend over a cup of coffee. He's got this knack for breaking down complex ideas into bite-sized nuggets of wisdom that'll stick with you long after you've turned the last page.

What I absolutely adore about this book is how Doug weaves together practical tips with soulful insights and personal stories. It's not about becoming a productivity machine—it's about finding that sweet spot where your ambitions dance in harmony with your inner peace. Trust me, it's magical!

I found myself nodding along, scribbling notes, and even getting teary eyed in a few spots (don't tell anyone!) as I worked through the exercises. Doug's approach is like a gentle nudge that helps you uncover layers of yourself you didn't even know existed.

If you're feeling stuck, overwhelmed, or just in need of a perspective shift, 'Be the Instrument' is your new best friend. It's not about following a rigid set of rules—it's about tuning into your own unique melody and letting it guide you towards a life that feels authentically YOU.

So, grab a copy, find a cozy spot, and prepare to uncover new possibilities that'll leave you feeling inspired, empowered, and ready to rock your world. Doug Giesler, you've created something truly special here. Thank you for this gift!"

Garry Johnson
Infinite Mastery Consultant, Retired Master Hypnotherapist

"In today's fast-paced world, filled with noise and distractions, finding a path to fulfillment can seem daunting. However, "Be the Instrument" by Doug Giesler offers readers a transformative journey toward achieving peak performance while maintaining inner peace.

At its core, "Be the Instrument" serves as a beacon of hope, guiding readers through personal growth and spiritual alignment. Doug Giesler provides a roadmap for reaching goals and discovering a deeper connection to oneself and the world.

This book redefines success on individual terms, exploring the nuances of overcoming limitations and transcending the ego. Through practical techniques, spiritual practices, and heartfelt wisdom, readers are empowered to navigate life's challenges with resilience.

A central theme of "Be the Instrument" is the importance of finding one's flow—a state of being where everything falls into place effortlessly. Doug shares insights on cultivating this state, guiding readers toward self-discovery and understanding.

Presence, the art of being fully immersed in the present moment, is another key concept explored in the book. Through mindfulness practices and practical exercises, readers learn to tap into clarity and awareness.

"Be the Instrument" takes a holistic approach to success, emphasizing the alignment with one's true purpose and fostering a positive mindset. The book promotes a win-win philosophy that uplifts not only oneself but also those around them.

As readers embark on this journey of self-discovery and personal growth, they are reminded that true success is measured by inner fulfillment rather than external accolades. Whether striving for peak performance in career, relationships, or personal endeavors, "Be the Instrument" offers invaluable wisdom and practical tools for thriving in every aspect of life.

Are you ready to unlock your potential, find your flow, and become the instrument of your own success? The journey awaits."

EINPresswire
SAN FRANCISCO, UNITED STATES
May 10, 2024

"Be The Instrument is masterfully written to challenge your inner genius. Doug delightfully guides you on an educational tour of your hidden beliefs. He then expertly leads you on a journey of personal empowerment that will touch every area of your life. If you are seeking a more fulfilling life this book is a must read. I would pick up 10 copies to share with your friends and family. They will thank you for it!"

Jim Britt
15X international best-selling author and world's top 20 Success coach and top 50 most influential speaker.
www.JimBritt.com

"Doug Giesler's "Be The Instrument" is a standout in the self-help genre, offering a fresh perspective on personal growth and transformation. Giesler candidly shares his journey of overcoming self-imposed limitations, pro_viding readers with practical wisdom and actionable steps to turn fear into faith and realize their full potential. What sets this book apart is its unique "overseer" concept, a framework that empowers readers to observe and guide their mental processes more consciously, helping them manage emotions and resistance effectively.

The author's engaging and relatable writing style makes complex ideas accessible, using vivid stories and analogies like the "faith bus" and "beach ball" to illustrate key points. Giesler's incorporation of music, quotes, and exercises enriches the experience, offering a multi-dimensional approach to personal development. More than just motivational, "Be The Instrument" serves as a practical guide to mindfulness and self-discovery, encouraging readers to actively engage with their minds for significant growth.

I highly recommend "Be The Instrument" to anyone yearning for a creative and insightful approach to self-improvement! It's not only inspiring but also a transformative resource that fosters personal growth and a deeper understanding of oneself, making it an invaluable read."

Robin Nemesszeghy
Author, Relationship Intelligence Coach

THE "F" WORD

NO... NOT THAT ONE

FORGIVENESS

WHY IT MATTERS

DOUG GIESLER

SHATTER CEILINGS, NOT DREAMS
& EXPLORE THE HORIZONS!

TheFWordForgiveness.com

When unconsciousness prevails in the shadows, the "F-bomb" often comes out, temporarily relieving the tension, but postponing the cure. Solution; Grow through the experience with the other "F" word: Forgiveness.

FORGIVENESS: F-orgiveness is an understanding of the human condition. It is an overarching acceptance of this imperfect thing called the mind / ego inside us and others. It gives us the opportunity to let go of the past and everything that might draw us there, eliminating our "attachment" to it and allowing us access to a skill called PRESENCE, in the moment! FREEDOM from the past is incredibly liberating!

Doug Giesler a transformative coach and thought leader, explores the profound power of forgiveness in 'The F Word - Forgiveness." Drawing from personal experiences and spiritual insights, Doug guides readers through the challenging yet liberating journey of forgiving oneself and others.

His warm, positive approach offers practical strategies for overcoming resentment, healing emotional wounds, and unlocking inner peace. Through this book, Doug invites you to embrace forgiveness as a catalyst for personal growth and positive change, empowering you to live a more fulfilling and harmonious life.

Praise for

'Forgiveness'

"Doug Giesler has done it again! In "The F Word—Forgiveness," he delivers a mind-blowing exploration of personal liberation that will revolutionize how you think about your own consciousness.

Immediately get your hands on this powerful roadmap to mental freedom. Doug brilliantly unpacks one of the most critical challenges we face in our own lives. His insights into how our minds unconsciously drift between past and future are both profound and practical. What sets this book apart is Doug's unique ability to break down complex psychological concepts into digestible, actionable wisdom. He doesn't just tell you—he shows you exactly how your mind plays tricks on you, and provides a clear pathway to reclaim your power of choice.

The book's core message is transformative: forgiveness isn't just about letting go of past hurts, it's about liberating yourself from the mental prison of unconscious reactions. Doug's writing is like having a wise friend who sees right through your mental patterns and offers a compassionate hand to guide you toward true freedom.

Whether you're struggling with past resentments, feeling stuck in life, or simply want to become more aware of your inner landscape, "The F Word—Forgiveness" is your ultimate guide. Doug doesn't just teach forgiveness—he reveals it as the ultimate act of personal empowerment.

A must-read for anyone serious about personal growth, conscious evolution, and living a life of genuine choice and freedom. Highly recommended!"

Garry Johnson
Infinite Mastery Consultant, Retired Master Hypnotherapist

"Doug Giesler offers a fresh and insightful approach to understanding and utilizing forgiveness. His writing style is both engaging and easy to understand, making even the more complex concepts accessible and relatable. I particularly appreciated how he connected the idea of forgiveness to our mental processes and the power of presence in the moment.

This isn't just a self-help book; it's a practical guide to cultivating self-awareness and unlocking personal growth. I highly recommend it to anyone seeking a deeper understanding of themselves and a more fulfilling life. It's a book that will stay with me, and I'll likely reread it again in the future."

Robin Nemesszeghy
Author, Relationship Intelligence Coach

ABOUT THE AUTHOR
Doug Giesler

How to Unlimit your limit, attain massive success in your personal and professional life while enjoying extraordinary PEACE of MIND, which is often elusive in this fast-paced world!

Doug's real-life experience in consistently generating top performance while helping others has inspired several books. His proven mind hacks, spiritual techniques and attitudes provide real life skills geared towards making limits a thing of the past and creating idealized futures where our world is a better place to live and play! Every day, every moment is an opportunity to understand and UNlimit a limit.

Doug provides a virtual tool chest for heightened self and situational awareness allowing you to overcome obstacles, break through barriers, overachieve and Self-actualize! He teaches a win-win philosophy with a big smile, and a positive attitude. Grab this opportunity, study this philosophy and WIN!

Follow Doug on Amazon for updates and new releases!

a

amazon.com/author/douggiesler

in

linkedin.com/in/doug-giesler/

WHERE TO FIND DOUG

WEBSITE:
www.UNlimityourlimit.com

LINKEDIN:
https://www.linkedin.com/in/doug-giesler/

AMAZON:
https://www.amazon.com/author/douggiesler

DOUG'S OTHER WEBSITES:

www.BeTheInstrument.com

www.SCLakehomes.com

www.RealEstateLakeMurray.com

www.RealEstateLakeMonticello.com

www.RealEstateLakeCarolina.com

www.RealEstateLakeWateree.com

1. Dottie Giesler. Doug's childhood. Mom quote, from when I was a kid: THANKS MOM!

2. William Shakespeare, English poet & playwright, As you like it, Act 5, Scene 1. Also notable: widely quoted online. Here is one source, 3,2023: https://www.folger.edu/explore/shakespeares-works/as-y ou-like-it/read/5/1/ And another: https://www.goodreads.com/quotes/71-the-fool-doth-think-he-i s-wise-but-the-wise

3. The Bible, English Standard Version: Luke 23:34

4. Esther & Jerry Hicks, book, "Ask and it is given", Hay House Inc. Oct 1, 2004 https://www.abraha m-hicks.com/

5. The Bible, American Standard Version, Exodus 14: 21-22 Note: Moses. This is something He did on the TV show as well, I was just acknowledging the action as symbolism. This is simply my opinion!

6. The Scorpions, Band. Song: "The Winds of Change" VIDEO LINK: https://youtu.be/n4RjJKxsa mQ?si=7Hi-48S4tNteCgNp

7. The Scorpions, Band. Song: "The Winds of Change" VIDEO LINK: https://youtu.be/n4RjJKxsa mQ?si=7Hi-48S4tNteCgNp

8. Sri Nisargadatta Maharaj, I AM THAT, book: Chetana Private LTD. Dec 5, 1999, https://www.m aharajnisargadatta.com/, https://www.amazon.com/Am-That-Talks-Nisargadatta-Maharaj-dp-8185 300534/dp/8185300534/ref=dp_ob_image_bk

9. Sri Nisargadatta Maharaj, I AM THAT, book: Chetana Private LTD. Dec 5, 1999, https://www.m aharajnisargadatta.com/, https://www.amazon.com/Am-That-Talks-Nisargadatta-Maharaj-dp-8185 300534/dp/8185300534/ref=dp_ob_image_bk

10. Sri Nisargadatta Maharaj, I AM THAT, book: Chetana Private LTD. Dec 5, 1999, https://www.m aharajnisargadatta.com/, https://www.amazon.com/Am-That-Talks-Nisargadatta-Maharaj-dp-8185 300534/dp/8185300534/ref=dp_ob_image_bk

11. Sri Nisargadatta Maharaj, I AM THAT, book: Chetana Private LTD. Dec 5, 1999, https://www.m aharajnisargadatta.com/, https://www.amazon.com/Am-That-Talks-Nisargadatta-Maharaj-dp-8185 300534/dp/8185300534/ref=dp_ob_image_bk

12. Ernest Holmes, The Science of MIND, book, TarcherPerigree, August 24, 1998. quote, Note: This is also the magazine my wife and I read daily: Science of Mind Magazine, monthly publication: https://scienceofmind.com/

13. Ernest Holmes, The Science of MIND, book, TarcherPerigree, August 24, 1998. quote, Note: This is also the magazine my wife and I read daily: Science of Mind Magazine, monthly publication: https://scienceofmind.com/

14. Emerson, Essays: The Oversoul, Ralph Waldo Emerson, www.EmersonCentral.com Web Marketing Now. Accessed 3/13/2023 https://emersoncentral.com/texts/essays-first-series/the-over-soul/

15. Marshall Sylver, Passion, Profit & Power. Audio Cassettes, January 1, 1993. 6 cassettes and a workbook. https://sylver.com/ This was a course I bought years ago. Passion, Profit, and POWER was the name of the course. In the video presentation he demonstrated this principle. It was very cool; the man is talented! He also has a book by the same name, Passion Profit Power, January 21, 1997. Simon & Schuster Paperbacks.

16. Peace prayer: France 1912, often credited to St. Francis of Assisi. The author is actually unknown but may have been Father Esther Bouquerel as it first appeared in La Clochette magazine in 1912.

17. Johnny Nash, song, released 1972, I can see clearly Now. VIDEO LINK: https://youtu.be/b0cAWg TPiwM

18. The Bible, King James version, Mathew 13:12

19. Credit to AI-Eli Art / Facebook profile for the image, with approval

20. Louise Hay, book: You Can Heal your Life. Hay House. 1984, Website: https://www.louisehay.com/

21. The Bible, Legacy Standard Bible, Mathew 8:13

22. Ralph Waldo Emerson, 1803-1882 Peter Pauper Press, White Plains, NY. Essays, The Oversoul, Accessed Online 3/13/2023 via https://emersoncentral.com/texts/essays-first-series/the-over-soul/ and downloadable here: https://emersoncentral.com/ebook/The-Over-Soul.pdf

23. Ralph Waldo Emerson, 1803-1882 Peter Pauper Press, White Plains, NY. Essays, The Oversoul, Accessed Online 3/13/2023 via https://emersoncentral.com/texts/essays-first-series/the-over-soul/ and downloadable here: https://emersoncentral.com/ebook/The-Over-Soul.pdf

24. Ralph Waldo Emerson, 1803-1882 Peter Pauper Press, White Plains, NY. Essays, The Oversoul, Accessed Online 3/13/2023 via https://emersoncentral.com/texts/essays-first-series/the-over-soul/ and downloadable here: https://emersoncentral.com/ebook/The-Over-Soul.pdf

25. Ralph Waldo Emerson, 1803-1882 Peter Pauper Press, White Plains, NY. Essays, The Oversoul, Accessed Online 3/13/2023 via https://emersoncentral.com/texts/essays-first-series/the-over-soul/ and downloadable here: https://emersoncentral.com/ebook/The-Over-Soul.pdf

26. Ralph Waldo Emerson, 1803-1882 Peter Pauper Press, White Plains, NY. Essays, The Oversoul, Accessed Online 3/13/2023 via https://emersoncentral.com/texts/essays-first-series/the-over-soul/ and downloadable here: https://emersoncentral.com/ebook/The-Over-Soul.pdf

27. Ralph Waldo Emerson, 1803-1882 Peter Pauper Press, White Plains, NY. Essays, Spiritual Laws https://emersoncentral.com/texts/essays-first-series/spiritual-laws/

28. Ralph Waldo Emerson, 1803-1882 Peter Pauper Press, White Plains, NY. Essays, Spiritual Laws https://emersoncentral.com/texts/essays-first-series/spiritual-laws/

29. Ralph Waldo Emerson, 1803-1882 Peter Pauper Press, White Plains, NY. Essays, Spiritual Laws https://emersoncentral.com/texts/essays-first-series/spiritual-laws/

30. Ralph Waldo Emerson, 1803-1882 Peter Pauper Press, White Plains, NY. Essays, Spiritual Laws https://emersoncentral.com/texts/essays-first-series/spiritual-laws/

31. Ralph Waldo Emerson, 1803-1882 Peter Pauper Press, White Plains, NY. Essays, Spiritual Laws https://emersoncentral.com/texts/essays-first-series/spiritual-laws/

32. Within Temptation, Band, SONG: "Ritual", VIDEO LINK: https://youtu.be/a_LDPcRjMs4?si=m-rxB7tdyg7OSE92

33. Boston, Band, SONG: Cool the engines. VIDEO LINK: https://youtu.be/jw0YNvlFOrI?si=h3_g PCj3EXa-752Y

34. Boston, Band, SONG: More than a feeling. VIDEO LINK: https://youtu.be/t4QK8RxCAwo?si=U9NuYmldoFIbXTtq

35. The Bible, Legacy Standard Version, Mathew, 26:41

36. Ralph Waldo Emerson, 1803-1882 Peter Pauper Press, White Plains, NY. Essays,: Self Reliance h ttps://emersoncentral.com/ebook/Self-Reliance.pdf Credit to John Fletcher as well as this is from a quote from "An Honest Mans Fortune" John Fletcher,1579-1625, edited by Ralph Waldo Emerson, 1803-1882, An Honest Mans Fortune, Parnassus, An Anthology of Poetry, Boston, Houghton, Osgood and Company 1880; Bartleby.com 2013. Accessed 3/13/2023 here: https://www.bartleby.com /371/266.html

37. Ralph Waldo Emerson, 1803-1882 Peter Pauper Press, White Plains, NY. Essays: Self Reliance https ://emersoncentral.com/ebook/Self-Reliance.pdf

38. Ralph Waldo Emerson, 1803-1882 Peter Pauper Press, White Plains, NY. Essays: Self Reliance https ://emersoncentral.com/ebook/Self-Reliance.pdf

39. Ralph Waldo Emerson, 1803-1882 Peter Pauper Press, White Plains, NY. Essays: Self Reliance https ://emersoncentral.com/ebook/Self-Reliance.pdf

40. Ralph Waldo Emerson, 1803-1882 Peter Pauper Press, White Plains, NY. Essays: Self Reliance https ://emersoncentral.com/ebook/Self-Reliance.pdf

41. Ralph Waldo Emerson, 1803-1882 Peter Pauper Press, White Plains, NY. Essays: Self Reliance https ://emersoncentral.com/ebook/Self-Reliance.pdf

42. Ralph Waldo Emerson, 1803-1882 Peter Pauper Press, White Plains, NY. Essays: Self Reliance https ://emersoncentral.com/ebook/Self-Reliance.pdf

43. RUSH, band, SONG "Speed of Love", VIDEO LINK: https://music.youtube.com/watch?v=ax_U nydwcig&si=7DcClgupKNsRKY39

44. Within Temptation, Band, SONG: FASTER. VIDEO LINK: https://youtu.be/iQVei5C2N4E?si= oodBfzr3TudFLKxp

45. Ralph Waldo Emerson, 1803-1882 Peter Pauper Press, White Plains, NY. Essays: Self Reliance https ://emersoncentral.com/ebook/Self-Reliance.pdf

46. Ralph Waldo Emerson, 1803-1882 Peter Pauper Press, White Plains, NY. Essays: Self Reliance https ://emersoncentral.com/ebook/Self-Reliance.pdf

47. Ralph Waldo Emerson, 1803-1882 Peter Pauper Press, White Plains, NY. Essays: Self Reliance https ://emersoncentral.com/ebook/Self-Reliance.pdf

48. Ralph Waldo Emerson, 1803-1882 Peter Pauper Press, White Plains, NY. Essays: Self Reliance https ://emersoncentral.com/ebook/Self-Reliance.pdf

49. RUSH, band, SONG "Speed of Love", VIDEO LINK: https://music.youtube.com/watch?v=ax_U nydwcig&si=7DcClgupKNsRKY39

50. John Fletcher,1579-1625, edited by Ralph Waldo Emerson, 1803-1882, An Honest Mans Fortune, Parnassus, An Anthology of Poetry, Boston, Houghton, Osgood and Company 1880; Bartleby.com 2013. Accessed 3/13/2023 here: https://www.bartleby.com/371/266.html

51. John Fletcher,1579-1625, edited by Ralph Waldo Emerson, 1803-1882, An Honest Mans Fortune, Parnassus, An Anthology of Poetry, Boston, Houghton, Osgood and Company 1880; Bartleby.com 2013. Accessed 3/13/2023 here: https://www.bartleby.com/371/266.html

52. Within Temptation, Band, SONG: "Faster" VIDEO LINK: https://music.youtube.com/watch?v= h-Ak041nWos&si=V7eg-SaFWmHi-nce

53. Reinhold Niebuhr, 1892 – 1971, prayer: "The Serenity Prayer"

www.ingramcontent.com/pod-product-compliance
Lightning Source LLC
Chambersburg PA
CBHW071713120626
46550CB00001B/206